AUSTRIA IN
THE NEW EUROPE

 ontemporary  ustrian  tudies

Sponsored by the University of New Orleans and Universität Innsbruck

Executive Editors
Erich Thöni, University of Innsbruck
Gordon H. Mueller, University of New Orleans

Editors
Anton Pelinka, University of Innsbruck
Günter Bischof, University of New Orleans

Production Editors
Robert L. Dupont
Gloria Alvarez

Copy Editor
Melanie McKay

Editorial Assistants
Ellen Palli
Marissa Ahmed
Rainer Fadinger
Allison Duvernay

Advisory Board

Felix Butschek
  Institute of Economic Research,
  Vienna
Wolfgang Danspeckgruber
  Princeton University
Peter Gerlich
  University of Vienna
David F. Good
  Director, Institute of Austrian Studies,
  University of Minnesota
Robert Jordan
  University of New Orleans
Robert H. Keyerslingk
  University of Ottawa
Radomir Luza
  Tulane University
Diemut Majer
  University of Berne
Andrei S. Markovits
  Harvard University and Boston
  University

Sybil Milton
  United States Holocaust Memorial
  Council, Washington, D.C.
Hanspeter Neuhold
  University of Vienna and Director,
  Austrian Institute for International
  Politics, Laxenburg
Helga Nowotny
  University of Vienna
Michael Pollak
  Institute of Contemporary History,
  National Center for Scientific Re-
  search, Paris
Peter Pulzer
  All Souls College, Oxford University
Rolf Steininger
  Director, Institute of Contemporary
  History, University of Innsbruck
Gerald Stourzh
  University of Vienna

Publication of this volume has been made possible through a generous grant from the
Austrian Ministry of Foreign Affairs via the Austrian Cultural Institute, New York.

AUSTRIA IN
THE NEW EUROPE

Contemporary Austrian Studies

Volume 1

Edited by

Günter Bischof
Anton Pelinka

Transaction Publishers
New Brunswick (U.S.A.) and London (U.K.)

Copyright © 1993 by Transaction Publishers, New Brunswick, New Jersey 08903

Library of Congress Catalog Number: 92-14730
ISBN: 1-56000-597-1
Printed in the United States of America

Library of Congress Cataloging-in-Publication Data

Austria in the new Europe / edited by Gunter Bischof, Anton Pelinka.
    p.   cm.—(Contemporary Austrian studies ; v. 1)
  ISBN 1-56000-597-1 (paper)
  1. Austria—Politics and government—1945- 2. Austria—Foreign relations—1955- 3. Austria—Foreign relations—Europe. 4. Europe—Foreign relations—Austria. 5. Europe—Politics and government—1989- I. Bischof, Gunter, 1953- . II. Pelinka, Anton, 1941- . III. Series
DB99.2.A826 1992
327.43604—dc20

                                    92-14730
                                        CIP

Table of Contents

EC

Ireland

the Netherlands

Belgium

Luxembourg

Portugal

Denmark

Sweden

UK

Germany

Poland

France

Czechoslovakia
Hungary

Spain

Italy

Austria

Greece

Malta

Turkey

Cyprus

▨ Associate Members

▨ Applicants

Introduction

Contemporary Austrian Studies (*CAS*) is a new publication on modern Austrian studies dedicated to an international and comprehensive interdisciplinary approach. We stress a broad, inclusive social science approach to the study of twentieth century Austria. *CAS* aims at combining all social science disciplines within its different academic traditions:

✦ Contemporary History, broadly defined as post-1918 Austrian history;

✦ Sociology, the comprehensive social scientists' approach to Austrian society;

✦ Political science, the study of domestic Austrian politics and its international relations;

✦ Economics, especially the analysis of Austrian political economy;

✦ Law, particularly its international and constitutional aspects.

All specialists on modern Austria in the global scholarly community are invited to participate in internationalizing the study of contemporary Austria in its Central European context.

The membership of our editorial board reflects this balancing of various diciplines. The balance is also a geographical one, as Austrian scholars are represented along with specialists on contemporary Austria from all over Europe and abroad.

This academic and geographic balance reveals another part of our editorial philosophy. *CAS* hopes to build a wide readership around the world. It is designed for an interested audience in academic, intellectual, political, and diplomatic circles as well as in the news media and among the interested general public. *CAS* wants to address "hot" and relevant themes in Austria's recent past as well as contemporary topics with implications for the future.

In our interdisciplinary approach we have intentionally excluded the humanities, namely Austrian literature, music and the fine arts. We realize that Austrian "society" cannot be isolated from "culture" as the flowering of *fin-de-siècle* Vienna studies so richly demonstrates. Yet given the recent flood of publications on Austrian cultural and intellectual history in the 19th and 20th centuries both outside and inside Austria, no new serial publication is needed. The British annual *Austrian Studies* edited by Edward Timms and Ritchie Robertson at Oxford University, as well as *Modern Austrian Literature* and the series "Studies in Austrian Literature, Culture, and Thought," both under the general editorship of Donald G. Daviau at the University of California-Riverside, promote Austrian cultural and intellectual studies with scholarly sophistication and in great depth.

We feel that *CAS* can fill a gap in the general field of modern Austrian studies, especially in the Anglo-American world. *Austriaca*, founded by Felix Kreissler and published at the University of Rouen, does not reach a wide Anglo-American audience. The *Austrian History Yearbook*, published by the Center of Austrian Studies at the University of Minnesota, concentrates on the history of the lands of the Habsburg Monarchy and more recently has started to increase its coverage of Austrian contemporary history. *Politics and Society in Germany, Austria and Switzerland* edited by David Childs at the University of Nottingham regularly features essays on Austria. The *Journal of Modern History*, *Central European History*, *German Politics and Society*, and the *German Studies Review* all publish articles on Austria irregularly, and occasionally even devote an entire issue to Austria. But in all of these publications, Austria remains in the shadow of Germany.

CAS is designed as a regular publication on modern Austria without a direct point of reference to Germany. As such, it is devoted to a self-confident assertion of a separate Austrian identity vis-à-vis Germany and its promotion abroad. After the unification of Germany, such a program seems even more important.

The chronological frame of reference is post-Habsburg Austria in its St. Germain borders. In time, separate issues will be devoted to the First Republic, the "authoritarian" *Ständestaat*, to the "*Ostmark*" and the "Danube and Alpine *Gaus*" under Nazi rule, and various issues of the Second Republic (occupied and neutral Austria). Our focus on modern Austria does not mean that Austria's roots in the old Habsburg Empire, or its Central European geopolitical location will be neglected. To the contrary, Austrian relations with *all* of its neighbors will get *equal* attention: Germany and Western European integration; Switzerland and Liechtenstein and small neutral power interests; Italy and Austria's traditional Mediterranean interests; Croatia-Slovenia ("Yugoslavia") and historic Balkan interests; Hungary and Czecho-Slovakia and East-Central European interests. The broadest possible agenda here is the study of modern Austrian politics, society, economics and international relations in its crucial Central European geopolitical context.

CAS is an academic publication appealing to a broad intellectual audience and fostering a multiplicity of views and perspectives. *CAS*'s typical format will feature a number of essays on a special topic such as the impact of post-Cold War geopolitical developments and European integration on Austria in this issue (volume II will feature "A First Assessment of the Kreisky Era;" volume III will deal with "Austria in the 1950s"). Usually one or two "non-topical" essays will complete the main part.

We hope to inspire a cross-fertilization of ideas through open and pluralistic debates. Perceptive analyses and critiques from abroad ought to remind Austrians that the neutralist-isolationist *mentalité*—their pose as the "island of the blessed"—is no longer commensurate with a radically changing world. Well-informed essays by Austrian scholars should inform specialists and an interested public abroad about Austrian developments and domestic political debates including broader trends in "Austro-think." For this purpose we will feature lengthy reviews of important books on modern Austria published inside and outside of the country. Austrians reviewing books written abroad and non-Austrians reviewing books published in Austria ought to bring a breath of fresh air into the often stale Austrian reviewing culture. An annual review of major political developments in Austria (elections, etc.) will be included, especially for the benefit of those who have no opportunity to follow political events in Austria on a regular basis.

CAS is academically independent and will in no way promote offical views of the Austrian government, or be given to partisan influences. The nature of Austrian politics (including the parties) and the policies of the Austrian government will rather be the objects of close scholarly scrutiny and investigation. The editors and the editorial board are united in their deep interest in modern Austria, but not partial to specific political attitudes.

CAS is the fruit of many years of cooperation by two universities—the University of New Orleans in the U.S. and the University of Innsbruck in Austria. Since 1976 student and faculty exchanges as well as international symposia and conferences have characterized this remarkable trans-Atlantic cooperation between two regional universities. In 1983 UNO and the University of Innsbruck signed a formal friendship agreement; in 1992, the year the first volume of *CAS* is published, the tenth anniversary of the Innsbruck students' program at UNO is celebrated. With *CAS* we hope to make a lasting contribution to Austro-American friendship.

When this first volume was initially planned in the summer of 1990, the timeliness of the topic "Austria in the New Europe" could hardly have been foreseen. Austria's July 1989 application to join the common European market and its repercussions on Austria's future geopolitical position in Europe was the immediate point of departure. But between 1989 and 1992 the Western European integration process was overshadowed and overtaken by the collapse of the Soviet empire in Eastern Europe and the demise of the Warsaw Pact, the fall of the wall and the unification of Germany, major Central European nuclear/conventional disarmament and the waning of Cold War superpower tensions. The disappearance of the iron curtain ended the division of Europe.

The world has seen few periods of transformation as dramatic as the years 1989 to 1992—most of it happening on Austria's frontiers. The reforms of Michael Gorbachev in the Soviet Union resulted in the "velvet revolutions" in Eastern Europe in 1989. With the "fall of the iron curtain" Austria's Eastern borders—tightly sealed by "death zones"—dramatically opened up. The 1989 collapse of the Berlin wall dividing the two Germanies and the 1990 unification of Germany was precipitated by East Germans "voting with their feet" by leaving the GDR and entering the Federal Republic from their "exiles" in Hungary via Austria. In 1991 the Soviet Union broke up after the failed coup against Gorbachev; this sped up the new politics of heated ethnic conflicts and disintegration in Eastern Europe. The declaration of Slovene independence in July 1991 led to an ominous stationing of the Austrian army on Austria's Southern frontiers, while the declaration of Croat independence led to a brutal civil war with the Serbs with the specter of spillover effects such as an exodus of refugees to Austria.

In 1992 Austria is facing unique choices in a volatile geopolitical environment. The iron curtain had cut off Austria from its traditional sphere of interests in Eastern Europe. Yet the attractions of a prosperous Austria to Eastern Europeans has produced a "mental iron curtain"—namely a xenophobic backlash among Austrians not willing to share their comfortable economic prosperity with immigrants and refugees from Eastern Europe.

In 1992 Austria finds itself strongly attracted to both West and East. While the disintegration of the Soviet Union and its former satellites in Eastern Europe is afoot on its Eastern and Southern borders, the integration movement is gathering strength in Western Europe with the creation of the European common market in 1992. Austria applied in August

1989—before the Cold War "ended"—to join the budding Western European common market. But Austria's economic and political (and potential military) integration with the West threatens its status of neutrality, which has safeguarded Austrian independence through the era of East-West tensions and which many Austrians are reluctant to shed like a skin; after all, many Austrians feel that neutrality has given them peace and prosperity; in short, neutrality has become a constituent element of the Austrian identity.

Austrian neutrality is a child of the Cold War and with the end of the Cold War will have to change its character, should it survive at all. The strict version of Austrian neutrality came under serious pressure during the Gulf War when the U.S. interpreted strict neutrality as a roadblock to Western solidarity. With the collapse of the Soviet Union, the principal outside guardian of Austrian neutrality disappeared. In Brussels, Austrian neutrality is ultimately viewed as a possible obstacle in the process of full European integration, designed to make eventually political and military allies out of economic partners.

While the attractions of Western Europe are great, Austria has ambitions to renew its traditional "bridge function" vis-à-vis Eastern Europe. At the same time, some Austrians (particularly Eastern Austrians) would like to lead the former Soviet satellites towards Vienna's nostalgic version of a "*Mitteleuropa*"—the recreation of a Danubian East-Central Europe under Viennese tutelage. This comes at a time when the new democracies in Eastern Europe are as eager as Austria to join the European common market. No matter in which direction one looks between Vienna and Lake Constance, the world is in unusual flux. *Ubi Austria*?

The authors of the following essays try to grapple with Austria's difficult and challenging new geopolitical choices in a historical context. *Charles S. Maier* takes an unconventional look at the three incarnations of *Mitteleuropa*—the mythical kingdom in the minds of Eastern European intellectuals, the nostalgic Baroque dreams of Viennese politicians, and the hard-nosed version of German bankers and businessmen. Given the capital-starved and consumer-hungry Eastern Europe, there is no doubt in *Maier's* mind that the the *DM*-rich German version will prevail over the dreamy Austrian one.

Paul Luif, Oliver Rathkolb, Felix Butschek and *Manfred Prisching* take a look at the historical, social, economic and contemporary political contexts of Austria's position vis-à-vis Western Europe. *Luif* gives a brief history of Austria and its egg dance between European integration and

Cold War neutrality. *Luif* succinctly outlines the domestic political tergiversations over Austria's application to join the EC, and the subsequent difficulties the Austrian application created for the European Commission. The procrastination in Brussels over applications from EFTA-countries has much to do with making a basic decision over the possible incompatibility of neutrality and EC-membership.

Rathkolb outlines Austria's postwar trajectory from being a "secret ally" of the West towards a carefully designed neutrality that would not allow for full-fledged Western economic integration due to a strict interpretation of the obligations of the Austrian State Treaty in Moscow. Austrian attempts at full EC-membership in the early 1960s with the attendant party political divisions create a sense of *déjà vu*. *Rathkolb* explicitly rejects the argument of a "economic necessity" for Austria to join the EC, increasingly heard again from the economic lobbies.

The economist *Felix Butschek* makes exactly this economic argument. He demonstrates the ever increasing Austrian economic orientation and integration in the Western economic system in the Cold War era. Given Austria's one-sided economic orientation to the West, the clock cannot be turned back if Austria wants to remain prosperous. The very dreams of Austrian leadership in *Mitteleuropa* that *Maier* rejects as unrealistic, *Butschek*, from his Viennese perspective, sees as a real opportunity.

Gernot Prisching outlines Austria's unique social and political structures in a historical context. He stresses the state of flux in Austria's political system. Integration into the "new Europe" threatens to steamroll over some unique Austrian social achievements—its corporate model of *Sozialpartnerschaft* and its strict environmental laws. From the perspective of the sociologist, then, seemingly economic necessity must be offset against the threats to the unique character of Austrian political economy and mentality.

Wolfgang Danspeckgruber analyzes the larger geopolitical backdrop of post-Cold War Europe against which the changes in Austria have to be seen. At a time when the entire European security structures (CSCE, WEU, NATO etc.) go through rapid and dramatic transformations and the very concept of "national security" takes on new meanings, a small state such as Austria faces particularly hard choices between the competing trends of order and disorder, and the forces of integration and disintegration in Europe. This is to show that a provincial Austrian perspective no longer will suffice to analyze Austria's geopolitical choices for the future, to prove that the "island of the blessed" is buffeted to and fro from the winds of change everywhere.

The non-topical essay is *Thomas Albrich's* article on the Jews and the Austrian State Treaty. With his extensive research in Jewish archives in the U.S., Great Britain and Israel, *Albrich* enters virgin territory in State Treaty studies and presents a challenging new thesis. He argues that the internal divisions between and within the Jewish organizations during and after World War II did not allow for a unified Jewish position in their restitution claims against Austria. They also suffered from Western support for Austria's posture as "victim" of Hitlerite Germany; the Jews, the real victims of the war, lost out to great power Cold War conflicts. As a result, Austria treated Jewish claims in a dilatory fashion and kept massive Jewish restitution demands out of the text of the State Treaty.

Brigitte Gstöhl's review essay presents some important new publications on Austria and European integration. Five other book reviews complete the review section. *Rainer Nick's* and *Sieghardt Viertler's* "Survey of Austrian Politics 1990/91" complete the volume. This succinct summary shows how the state elections of 1991 continue the major shift in Austrian party politics, especially the party realignment and turmoil in the conservative camp. With the electoral fortunes of the ÖVP in steep decline and populist *Haiderism* dramatically on the rise, the Austrian political landscape seems to be moving towards permanent change.

This volume, then, is intended to provide some parameters for the ongoing great debate about the future of Austria in international politics after the Cold War and in the new age of prospective European integration.

Günter Bischof (New Orleans) and
Anton Pelinka (Innsbruck)
February 1992

Whose Mitteleuropa? Central Europe between Memory and Obsolescence

Charles S. Maier

Great and agonising hopes stirred in Count Leinsdorf. He could not have said whether what moved him was more pain at not seeing his country occupying the place of honour due to it 'in the family of the nations', or whether it was jealousy of Prussia which had thrust Austria down from that place (in 1866, by trickery and cunning!), or whether he was simply filled with pride in the nobility of an old State and the desire to show the world that it was exemplary...It was clear to him that something must be done that would put Austria at the head of all, so that this 'magnificent demonstration of the spirit of Austria' should be a landmark for the whole world....But one thing was certain: a great idea had taken possession of him.'

[Arnheim] was a man on a grand scale. His activities extended over continents of the earth and contents of knowledge. He knew everything: the philosophers, economics, music, the world, sport...He owned a villa built in the most modern style...and a ramshackle old castle somewhere in the sandiest wastes of the aristocratic Mark Brandenburg, which looked positively like the half-crumbled cradle of the Prussian idea...He impressed [the specialists] as something utterly modern, as a man of whom there was talk in all the newspapers, a king of commerce, one whose achievements compared with the intellectual achievements of more ancient kings, were certainly outstanding...At times he had imaginative glimmerings of a kind of Weimarian or Florentine epoch of industry and commerce, an epoch under the leadership of strong personalities who would increase prosperity, who would have to be capable of combining in themselves the individual achievements of the

*technical, scientific and artistic realms and of guiding develop-
ments from an exalted standpoint. He felt in himself the capacity
to do this.[1]*

Musil evidently despised his creation Arnheim, a thinly disguised self-
important, pretentious and vulgar version of Walter Rathenau. Count
Leinsdorf he portrayed as merely feckless and antiquated like the state
and dynasty whose feeble refulgence the Count hoped to reburnish. No
book better suggests the tonalities that separated Austria from Germany.
Of course, Jewish Arnheim hardly represented all of Prussia. Nor could
the aristocratic and nostalgiac Leinsdorf, nor the attractive if bubble-
headed "Diotima" Tuzzi encompass the provincial peasants and
Mittelstände of Austria. Still the contrast illuminated a good deal.

It also illuminates two versions of Mitteleuropa. Mitteleuropa has
enjoyed a brief flurry of fashion and hope during the last years. In the eyes
of some Austrians it seems to surface as a nostalgiac diversion from the
more prosaic mission of adhering to an up-to-date Common Market; in
the eyes of others it is a potential entity in which Austria will play an
important role — once again a fulcrum on which Vienna can become a
lever for history. But Austria's Mitteleuropa is only one version of
Central Europe. There is also a German Mitteleuropa, more in the spirit
of Arnheim and less of Leinsdorf. Finally there is perhaps, most
elusively, a third Mitteleuropa, one emanating from East Central Europe,
a shadowy realm radiating outward from Prague or Budapest, or even
Warsaw, which embraces Vienna and Berlin but is not based upon them.
This brief essay will set out the imaginative contours of each Central
Europe and will ask to what degree any of them is a viable construct.

Let us start by considering the third version of Mitteleuropa, the
penumbra around Prague or Budapest. "Central Europe is back," Timothy Garton Ash wrote in October 1986, with reference to the work of
Michnik, Konrad, Havel, and Kundera.[2] As of the early 1980s, Georgi
Konrad's *Antipolitics*[3] sought the clearest differentiation from both West
and East. His Central Europe represented a revolt against Yalta, against
the supposed division of Europe by the old men who made the war:
Roosevelt, Stalin, Churchill. In Konrad's view, the West acquiesced in
the Soviet dominion in order to secure tranquility and enjoyment of their
own half of the old world—henceforth defined as Western Europe. The
other writers cited by Garton Ash were not so bipartisan. For Adam
Michnik languishing in a Polish prison or Milan Kundera in Paris exile,
oppression came from the East. For Kundera Central Europe represents

what was subjugated by the Russian juggernaut: barbaric, totalitarian, without the subtle sense of liberty that could thrive even in the hardly democratic states of interwar Europe.

The Central Europe evoked in Prague (or Paris), Poland, and Hungary in the 1980s thus tended to represent a revived claim for the autonomy of the lands between the Germans and the Soviets against the Brezhnev doctrine. It sought to establish a realm of values, geographically anchored, against the Communist imperium. In retrospect it can be understood as in effect the spiritual *maquis* under late Communism, and its very emergence suggested that the hold of Communism was decaying spiritually and intellectually, even if it had not yet lost its capacity to enforce official dogma. Timothy Garton Ash recognized that the Central Europe claimed by these intellectuals, much like the Kashubia recalled by Günter Grass, was a myth, albeit a useful one. It was " a kingdom of the spirit,"[4] but one with political characteristics. These included the idea of "antipolitics"—a revolt against the politicization of all life; "living in truth," Havel's effort to establish the individual against the corruption of power; the transcendence of a Left and Right that have no sense, the insistence on peace, the belief in civil society: all claims that miraculously came to pass in the velvet revolutions of 1989.

Ash concedes that Central Europe is a myth, but perhaps a useful one. It is "a kingdom of the spirit." Thomas Masaryk invented the concept in 1915 to differ it from the German claim for Mitteleuropa or the reality of the Austro-Hungarian Empire. Still, it was not always tolerant, and hardly unbureaucratic. In fact, Ash recognizes, the "superbureaucratic statism and formalistic legalism" that marked the old Central European empires, e.g. Austria-Hungary, also facilitated the Soviet takeover.[5] So too he recognizes that this Central Europe was hardly a region of tolerant cohabitation its apologists often claim for it. He observes that the Central Europe claimed by the intellectuals leave the role of German power outside its optic. And he understands that Central Europe encompasses several different national traditions and situations. Post-Kadar Communism, which the Konrad of the late 1980's was willing to accept, was hardly acceptable to Michnik or the Poles languishing under martial law. Nor was Havel prepared to endorse such a bargain; indeed Czech conditions did not allow him to believe that independent intellectuals might have the chance to accept it. They were too busy washing windows or stoking coal after 1968 to sign an intellectuals' social compact.

Still, Ash found the concept a congenial one in the twilight years of communism. He did not, any more than the authors he described, understand how Central Europe might find its freedom, save perhaps through the slow unremitting pressure that might erode the system and lead to oases of freedom and differentiation. "Eastern Europe *in acta*, Central Europe *in potentia*."[6] He cited the appearance of *Stredni Evropa*, the journal in Prague entitled Central Europe as a manifestation of its spirit. If the intellectuals of Hungary and Czechoslovakia saw any hope from the West it was through enforcement of the Helsinki Final Act, in specific of the human-rights "basket" of agreements that Brezhnev had accepted to get what he considered the recognition of the Soviet presence. Dismissed by Americans and many Western leaders as rather meaningless, and perhaps even just a sanctioning of the Soviet mainmise: in the East, Helsinki always held out an ideal that the Russians themselves had supposedly accepted. The Central Europe of the Hungarians or Czechs or even Poles was an entity inscribed in the CSCE, the Committee on Security and Cooperation in Europe, or propagandized by Czech intellectuals in Paris, such as Jacques Rupnik, or briefly enthusing intellectuals in the West. As Karl Schlögel took note in 1986, "A concept—Mitteleuropa, Central Europe—that had long seemed eliminated from our vocabulary, suddenly reappeared....Now 'Mitteleuropa' was back, diffuse, an aura, but not just a phantom....Mitteleuropa, so spectrally it first emerged, might yet endanger the autocratic domination of the East-West thinking in our heads."[7]

But what was to become of such a concept once the Communist Empire did cease. No longer existing merely *in potentia*, has it been able to take shape *in acta*? Havel went to the Hrad as president of his state, Michnik emerged from prison as one of the heroes of Solidarity, only to break with Walensa in 1990. Living in opposition was less ambiguous than living with power. Despite successive concessions to federalism in the Czechoslovak Federal Republic, the Slovaks still threaten secession from the Czechs. The question left by the Central Europe of the successor states, was whether their region might ever really exist except as a structure of opposition to one imperial power or another. Central Europe was a declaration of independence vis-à-svis Moscow. For an advocate such as Jacques Rupnik it must also emerge as a structure that kept the Germans at bay. "The end of the Yalta system implies the symmetrical decay of the two two alliances and leaves open the question of what is to come in its stead: a new Central Europe as a community of nations between Germany and Russia or a new version of Mitteleuropa as a German sphere of influence."[8]

Rupnik's alternative is too polarized—and indeed overstated with respect to the earlier portions of his essay. Certainly a Central Europe without some German or Austro-German presence is impossible. To be sure, 1945 brought the expulsion of Germans from Silesia, East Prussia and the Sudentenland. (Not that this ethnic category was so clear-cut. Many mixed marriages had occurred; many citizens, say, of Wroclaw or Gdynia who emphasized their Polish genes in the 1950's were happy to rediscover German chromosomes when economic advantages or rights to settle beckoned in 1990.) But Germany cannot simply be held at bay. The question is what sort of Germanic presence would be beneficial. Presumably one that is cultural without being "hegemonic."

It is with regard to this delicate balance that the spiritual heirs of Count Leinsdorf proffer the Austrian concept of Central Europe. Certainly for Minister Erhard Busek, whose conference on Mitteleuropa I attended in May 1991, the rationale for the program was largely to forge a bridge to the intellectuals emerging in Czechoslovakia, Poland, and Hungary. It provided a sanctuary for dissent. But what configuration might the emerging Austrian version of Central Europe take? Listening to the evocative prospects and memories being discussed in the Viennese Academy of Sciences, its huge baroque hall and ceiling painted with the triumph of science and art, the observer noted that Austria's Mitteleuropa was not just a congeries of Slavic lands. Austrian Central Europe emanated out of Vienna: Bohemia, Galicia, Hungary, Poland, Trento and Trieste, Croatia and Istria, all fell within its ambit. In terms of religion, it was a community of Catholic humanists and dead Jews. Repeatedly participants recalled the multiculturalism that this Central Europe had housed: all the nationalities and religions and cultures of middle Europe, cheek by jowl, occasionally getting on each other's nerves, but supposedly settling their differences under some overarching umbrella of sovereignty.

The baroque hall in which the conference was convened and the Jesuit Church next door illustrated the architectural and artistic correlative of Mitteleuropa. To be sure Vignola's Roman archetype, the Church of *Il Gesù*, with its transept dome and its volutes was to be cloned in Sicily and Mexico and New Spain as well as in Poland and Bohemia. Above all, the Baroque would testify to Austria's project for Mitteleuropa—the Catholic grace carried by the Counter-Reformation. Even the most indifferent pilasters, cliched volutes or insipid ceiling clouds and saints, lent a certain reassurance to Central Europe. (I remember driving East through Poland three decades ago and realizing at Brest Litovsk, as the reassuring baroque domes changed to onion cupolas, that I had entered a different cultural zone.) Nor was the baroque the only imperial artifact. The century after 1780 bequeathed the stolid reassurance of nineteenth century Austrian neo-classic: the sober comfortable facades looking down on pedestrians in Milan and Krakow, Vienna and Prague. Austrian Mitteleuropa included cities that Ash's Central Europe did not: Graz and Milan and Trento, Trieste and Llubjana, Zagreb and even Sarajevo. It is not surprising that in the 1990 rerun, Mitteleuropa was often a neo-Habsburg revery. Its proponents intimated that the concept, conceived and encouraged out of Vienna could bring a unity and harmony to the region Musil immortalized as Kakania. Just as once the Habsburg Empire's minorities had found protection from their dynasty against local nationalisms—hence the Jews and even the Social Democrats found the dynasty irreplacable, and certainly preferable to zealous Magyars or overbearing pan-Germans —so Vienna might today extend a sort of intellectual *Kulturschutz* over its former realms.

A roseate glow pervades this revery. "Tolerance" is a value constantly evoked. But to what extent did tolerance exist? Jews of course lived in Kakania; and historic Galicia became the memory of their elbow rubbing with Poles and other nationalities. A similar aura pervades the memories of Hungary as recalled by historians Istvan Deak or John Lukacs, who recall a certain magnate Anglophiliac liberalism. The question of anti-Semitism is a case in point. It is not that these cultures did not have Jews scaling all the cultural ramparts. But they did so in a world that was continually aware of their being different, other, alien, and Jewish. They ran the press as Jews, the banks as Jews. And in 1938 Vienna or 1944 Budapest their luck ran out as Jews. They existed on sufferance. And beyond the issue of the Jews had not the whole Vienna project ultimately depended on fire and sword as much as "tolerance". It was built on the Jesuits' and Habsburgs' reconquest of Protestant Bohemia after 1618, recatholicization, that was thorough and ruthless and which only Magyar Calvinists or Lutherans managed to resist on the borderlands with the Turks.

Despite harsh realities, Habsburg Mitteleuropa has come to claim historical truth and legitimacy. To a great extent, however, it is a literary creation. For most Western historical "tourists," it is the product of two great novelists, Musil and Josef Roth. Musil's bittersweet portrait of Kakania and Roth's *Radetzky March*: The story of the loyal servitors of the dynasty, subduing family ambitions, selfishness for the Emperor, holding together his realms, willing to die to save him as a youth at Solferino, actually dying for his ramshackle Empire in 1914, stolid, disciplined, against volatile Hungarians and god knows what other ethnic mongrels in the Galician or Croatian borderlands. Roth and Musil provide the ethnology that everyone cites as if it were anthropological research. Who knows what reality was? Cafe Central was too appealing. *Se non è vero è ben trovato.*

Gott erhalte, Gott bewahre... What the neo-Habsburg revery lacks is a material basis. It is long on culture and sentiment, short on funds. It is a strikingly non-economic vision. In good part there is no way that a state of some 8 million prosperous Europeans might adequately subsidize 50 million other far poorer Europeans. The old Mitteleuropa drew subsidies from the provinces to serve the center; there is no wherewithall to reverse the flow. The Austrian version of Central Europe is built upon cultural exchange and burnishing memories.

Here is where the third alternative comes in: as Musil intimated, German Mitteleuropa comes well-heeled. To be sure it does not depend upon money alone. As Schlögel reminds us, Berlin like Vienna used to stand at the hub of a historical entity, its spokes radiating toward Riga and Vilna and Warsaw as well as Prague and Vienna and Budapest. On the other hand, Germany's Mitteleuropa is also burdened. German served as a language for intellectuals and for commerce, but finally for soldiers. And it disappeared with the Jews who with the Germans comprised its other constitutive element:

> The territory of Central and Eastern Europe, [was] checkerboard varied and interlaced as hardly any other, not least as a consequence of the German settlements. These had only one parallel, the Jews of Central and East Europe. This was an open, but also dangerous territory.... The diaspora, that stretched from the Baltic to the Adriatic or the Black Sea like an archipelago has perished.... It required the destructive force of a thirty year war and a Blitzkrieg finale to tear apart a fabric that a whole continent had woven for centuries. In the destruction of the Central European Jews, who with the Germans served as the integrative strength of this region, the old Mitteleuropa perished.[9]

For Schlögel in 1986 Mitteleuropa seemed an impossible but necessary dream. Yes, the new German identity was rightly tied up with the West and Atlantic society, educated at Harvard or MIT, at home in Washington and Berkeley—but unfortunately neglecting its Eastern neighbors. Identity was not identification: perhaps the Germans should ask the Russians, shot down in millions, or inquire what Central European Jewery meant for German identity. "The Germans will never discover who they are from either a skewed transatlantic or trans-Elbian displacement, but only out of their placement in the center of Europe."[10]

Five years later, the Berlin whose division Schlögel took as the distinguishing trait of the postwar disappearance of Mitteleuropa is a united city. Germany's Central European vocation can begin again. Indeed it will begin again by default: no other actor is prepared to intervene in the region. The Soviet Union has ceased to exist as a unified actor; the European Community apart from the Germans remains a shadowy promise; the Americans feel no need and wish to spend no money. Where the Viennese spin a network of memories, the Germans press a policy of economic assistance and investment. No matter how many tens of billions of schillings the *Kredit-Anstalt* can invest in Hungary and Czechoslovakia and Poland, the *Deutsche Bank* will pour in many fold. So too in politics, Croatian recognition depended upon German convictions, pressed upon Germany's Western partners with new and unaccustomed vigor.

Germany's Central Europe is Protestant and Hanseatic, active and present-minded, endowed with a deep purse and for now a benevolent capitalist vision. If its protagonists indulge in memory, they recall the German elites of Posen and Riga, or if responsible writers (like Schlögel) or political leaders, perhaps the murderous violence of the Wehrmacht and SS, but in any case the 1945 expulsion and flight of twelve million refugees. Vienna's Mitteleuropa is Catholic and literary, pictorial, endeavoring to build on harmonies and cafes. The vanished Jews in Germany's Central Europe recollection are often businessmen; in Vienna's they are literati and intellectuals. The Central Europe of the Czechs and Hungarians is probably more comfortable with the Viennese myth—it threatens less, it included them once—but requires German funding. And at the moment it is beset with the travails of ethnic division. The Slovaks continue to reject the compromises of the Czechs and insist on their rights; the Yugoslavs cannot remember that their country was a brave effort to transcend petty tribalism; the Hungarians are recovering the clientelistic politics that characterized their earlier administrations. It would be a mistake to think that Mitteleuropa will provide the magic device for containing and superseding these conflicts.

Is one Mitteleuropa more valid or more promising than another? Does any version of the concept make sense, when it is no longer needed as a bridge to overcome the East-West division? Should its useful lifetime be extended? These are the policy-oriented questions that are appropriate for any current inquiry. Whether Central Europe "makes sense" or not is not for the author of this brief sketch to venture. But what seems likely is that as a guideline for Austrian policies, Central Europe will be at best a vaporous diversion. Mitteleuropa must most likely end up a German construct, because only Germany has the means to flesh it out. At best,

Vienna could play second fiddle in an Italian organized quintet, De
Michaelis's *Pentagonale*. No succession of cultural congresses in
Vienna, evocative meetings of intellectuals, programs to clean the rain
and air between the Carpathians and the Wienerwald will withstand the
influence of Siemens or the Kommerzbank in East Central Europe.
Vienna's viability as a "bridge" depends upon East and West on opposite
banks. That condition no longer pertains.

But surely it will be objected, Austria has some "mission" to bridge
East and West, to smooth the way for the intellectual and political circles
of what we used to call the "successor states" to reenter the Western orbit?
The point is that Mitteleuropa, as currently proposed, seems more an
answer to Austria's needs than to Central Europe's. Mitteleuropa, so
Anton Pelinka correctly implies, has appealed to many as a reinforcement
for Austrian national identity, less between East and West, than vis-a-vis
Germany. "Either there is a specific, national Austrian quality, or Austria
is German periphery," Pelinka has written.[11] Mitteleuropa, with all its
ambiguous and overlapping loyalties, offers Austrians a way out of this
precariousness. It beckons Austrians to participate "in no sense as
hegemon, but nonetheless as a center. Austrian identity can take on a
special allure precisely out of this community of ambiguity."[12] Pelinka
is clearly skeptical. For Austrians wanted a privileged position within
this structure. As late as 1990 they attempted to shut out Rumanians:
"Austria reinforces its frontiers—against Mitteleuropa. Austria defends
its privileges.... Mitteleuropa is quite obiously not the moving alternative
to an all-German center of gravity."[13]

My own view agrees with Pelinka's. Mitteleuropa is not a viable
enough concept to support Austria's mission; focusing attention on
German influence will ultimately undermine Austria not reinforce it. The
appropriate construct for these lands of the center must ultimately be an
enlarged European Community. Not Mitteleuropa or Central Europe,
but Europe. Pelinka cites Switzerland as the alternative model for
Austria: economically prosperous, open. But Switzerland is hardly for
export: it is a structure designed to balance Protestant and Catholic,
French, German and Italian cantons. Austria's besetting sin—now that
its Jews have disappeared—is provincial uniformity, close-minded
prejuedices: its economic equilibrium allows for a high standard of
living, but with an intense exchange with one country, not by serving as
a center for high-powered banks or multinationals. It has been the UN and
other international agencies in Vienna that have provided its main
emergence as a postwar European actor. Perhaps the Netherlands and

Belgium have a more precise lesson. The statesmen of these countries became the champions of the European Common Market and the North Atlantic Alliance in the 1950's, because they saw correctly that only such supranational structures could take them off the confined stage of hometown politics. In the larger framework they might preserve their communal values (robust in the Netherlands, precarious in Belgium) within a larger whole. Their wager, it seems to me, makes sense for the Austrians.

There is another consideration. At the very moment of emancipation from Soviet communism, the peoples of East Central Europe find any yoking together intolerable. Slovaks push the limits of federalism; the Baltic states recover their independence; Croats and Serbs indulge in a mutually destructive orgy of micronationalisms. Mitteleuropa cannot, I believe, provide a structure robust enough to contain and overcome these jealousies. Only Europe might. To be sure the European Community is not yet ready to absorb these new national contenders; nor are the countries of East Central Europe in condition to accept the discipline of the common market. Nonetheless, only the more inclusive framework can absorb their frictions in a larger whole. And only the more inclusive framework will provide points of orientation that extend beyond the banks of Frankfurt or the cultural programs of the Goethe Societies. Which is not to argue that Germany wishes to impose its preponderance in Mitteleuropa. Only that it will be increasingly pulled into roles of leadership and patronage because it alone has the vigor and resources to act in the lands to the East and South. Whose Mitteleuropa? There can be little doubt that if it is to be Mitteleuropa, it will be Arnheim's and not Count Leinsdorff's. Better that its peoples take their undoubtedly rich literary and cultural traditions—Polish philosophy or Czech avantgarde literature, Hungarian social theory and science, Austrian lyric poetry, the common capacity for irony and linguistic prowess, bittersweet neurotic love affairs and chocolate tortes—and add them to Europe's wider diversity than seek to recreate the cramped rivalries of societies that at best could balance one dominant neighbor against another. It is time to say farewell to Mitteleuropa.

NOTES

1. Robert Musil, *The Man Without Qualities,* vol. I, trans. Eithne Wilkins and Ernst Kaiser (New York: Capricorn ed., 1965), 100, 224-228.

2. Timothy Garton Ash, "Does Central Europe Exist?" *New York Review of Books,* 9 October 1986, reprinted in Ash, *The Uses of Adversity: Essays on the Fate of Central Europe* (New York: Random House, 1989), 179-213.

3. Georgi Konrad, *Antipolitics,* trans. Richard Allen (New York: Hartcourt, Brace, 1984.)

4. Ash, *Uses of Adversity,* 189.

5. Ibid., 185.

6. Ibid., 211.

7. Karl Schlögel, *Die Mitte liegt Ostwärts: Die Deutschen, der verlorene Osten und Mitteleuropa* (Berlin: Corso bei Siedler, 1986), p. 7.

8. Jacques Rupnik, "Central Europe or Mitteleuropa?" *Eastern Europe...Central Europe...Europe,* Special issue of *Daedalus* 119 (Winter 1990), 249-278, citation 275.

9. Schlögel, *Die Mitte liegt Ostwärts,* 79-81.

10. Ibid., 121.

11. Anton Pelinka, *Zur österreichen Identität. Zwischen deutscher Vereinigung und Mitteleuropa* (Vienna: Ueberreuter, 1990), 10.

12. Ibid., 135.

13. Ibid., 137-138.

Austrian Neutrality and the Europe of 1992

Paul Luif

Introduction

The "new dynamics" of the European Community (EC) has challenged the traditional foreign policy strategies of all the permanently neutral countries in Europe. In comparison to the other neutrals, Austria has often displayed a more active integration policy and has sought closer relations with the Community since the founding of the Coal and Steel Community in the early 1950s. Therefore, it came as no surprise that this Central European republic officially applied for EC membership--even before the dramatic changes in Eastern Europe had changed the security situation in Europe.

This article gives background information on Austria's foreign policy, of its integration policy, and describes in detail Austria's response to the new developments in the EC. The membership application and the reaction of the EC conclude the paper. Because Europe is in a process of political and economic transformation, any look into the future must be provisional The present article only gives an account of the current state of Austria's integration policy.[1]

The Basic Dilemma of Austria's Foreign Policy 1945-1990

Since the end of World War I, Austria's political elite and the general public have been uncertain about its place in Europe. Some have argued that Austria belonged among the small countries of the Danube basin, the *"Nachfolgestaaten"*. Others advocated an *Anschluss*, i.e. a joining with Germany because Austria was considered not to be viable. This alternative was actually the first choice of many politicians (and perhaps also of large parts of the population). But the Treaty of St. Germain from 1919 stressed Austria's independence and therefore prohibited any close political or economic cooperation with Germany. Austria was left very much alone in the international arena. In the 1930s, cooperation was initiated with Fascist Italy. This meant further isolation from Western democratic powers. In 1938, with the help of the German army, Adolf Hitler united Austria with Germany. This move, welcomed by many Austrians, improved the strategic situation of the German war machine and was an important step toward the military conflagration that destroyed most of Europe.

After the rebirth of Austria at the end of World War II, it was obvious to the Austrian political elite that the country should avoid the isolation of the interwar period. That meant active participation in the institutions that organized international political and economic relations in Western Europe. But here Austria was to face a dilemma: at the end of World War II the country was liberated, but it was also occupied by the troops of the four allied powers that soon became opponents in the Cold War. These powers did not want to let Austria integrate fully into the camp of the adversary.

Therefore, Austrian foreign policy after World War II has been marked by two opposing forces. The political imperative has pushed Austria toward cautious and prudent behavior in relation to the superpowers that dominated the Cold War. But external economic relations have made it necessary for Austria to participate in the international economy, especially in trade.

The four-power occupation after the end of World War II did not entail a political division of the country as in the case of Germany. Nevertheless it meant an increasing economic gap between its two parts. Western Austria—under occupation of the United States, the United Kingdom and France—developed in a way similar to the other West European economies. But Soviet occupation of Eastern Austria discouraged Western investments. Along with the exploitation of Austria's oil fields, the Soviets brought East European style economic planning to bear upon industry in its zone of occupation.

In spite of the Soviet Union's opposition, the Austrian government participated in the economic organizations set up after 1945. Austria took part in the Marshall Plan (1947), the European Payments Union (1950) and in the creation of the Organization for European Economic Cooperation (OEEC), which managed the distribution of U.S. aid to Western Europe. The OEEC also guided the first steps toward the liberalization of trade among the West European countries. In 1948, Austria became a member of the International Monetary Fund and the World Bank. It joined GATT in 1951.

Austria also tried to become member of the United Nations and the Council of Europe. But in contrast to the economic organizations, these more political institutions did not accept Austria as a full member. It joined the UN and the Council of Europe only after the allied forces had left the country in 1955.

The *State Treaty for the Re-establishment of an Independent and Democratic Austria*, signed by Austria and the four Allies after more than eight years of negotiations on 15 May 1955, has been the basic document of Austria's newly found postwar sovreignty and freedom. It includes several far-reaching obligations like the prohibition of the *Anschluss* (Art. 4), the protection of the rights of the Slovene and Croat minorities (Art. 7), the maintenance of democratic institutions (Art. 8), the dissolution of Nazi organizations (Art. 9), and the prohibition of special weapons (Art. 13).[2] Practically all of these duties were accepted by the Austrians without any opposition.[3]

But the Soviet Union wanted an additional guarantee that Austria would not become part of Germany again or join the Western alliance after its troops had left Eastern Austria. This further political "price" for Soviet withdrawal from Austrian soil was *permanent neutrality*. Austria and the Soviet Union agreed on the Swiss model of neutrality. It seems that both were satisfied that as an institute of international law permanent neutrality entailed a determinate amount of obligations—in contrast to Sweden's neutrality policy or the "nonaligned" foreign policy of Yugoslavia and countries in the Third World.

The Main Elements of Austrian Integration Policy
Neutrality

The Swiss model provides for distinct obligations that a permanently neutral country has to observe in peacetime as well as in war. The principles were delineated in the so-called *conception officielle suisse de la neutralité* from November 1954,[4] documents listing duties of a political, military and economic nature. The Austrian federal constitutional law on permanent neutrality (26 October 1955) is much more restricted in its list of obligations:

1. For the purpose of the lasting maintenance of her independence externally, and for the purpose of the inviolability of her territory,

Austria declares of her own free will her perpetual neutrality. Austria will maintain and defend this with all means at her disposal.

2. For the securing of this purpose in all future times Austria will not join any military alliances and will not permit the establishment of any foreign military basis on her territory.[5]

In explaining the contents of this law, the Austrian Chancellor Julius Raab said that the *military* neutrality of Austria did not include any duties and obligations in the *economic and cultural* field.[6]

This deviation from the Swiss model was also clearly revealed when Austria joined the United Nations in December 1955. Austria's specific interpretation of permanent neutrality was further displayed when it became full member the Council of Europe in April 1956. At that time, neither Switzerland nor Finland had joined the Council of Europe. In May 1956, Austria concluded a customs agreement with the European Coal and Steel Community (ECSC) and a few months later Austrian politicians started to talk about joining the ECSC.[7]

The crushing of the Hungarian uprising by Soviet tanks in October 1956 made the Austrian government more cautious. Since the Soviets started to criticize Western European integration efforts, in particular the newly founded European Economic Community (EEC), circumspection was seen to be more appropriate. Austria began to opt for more loose economic integration with Western Europe (see below).

But even in the 1960s, many politicians still talked about *military* neutrality and rejected *economic* obligations.[8] A reason for this attitude can be found in the attempt, especially from the side of the conservative People's Party (ÖVP), to obtain a close association with the EEC.[9] Only after these efforts had failed in mid-1967, and only after the invasion of Czechoslovakia by the Warsaw Pact troops (August 1968) had put renewed pressure on Austria was the expression officially renounced by the Austrian government. Foreign Minister Kurt Waldheim declared in November 1968:

> In the past, much was spoken in Austria about the so-called "military neutrality", an notion that does not exist as such in international law. It would be a too simplifying interpretation of the notion of permanent neutrality to understand by it only the obligation to remain neutral in case of war, namely not to join any military alliances and not to permit the establishment of any foreign military basis on one's own territory... The neutral state has to conduct a polity in peacetime that protects the state from entanglements in future armed conflicts or in political conflicts which can lead to such conflicts. In our century, wars are not exclusively fought by military actions, they can also take the form of an 'economic and propaganda war.'[10]

In the same speech Waldheim also stressed Austria's active participation in a worldwide policy of détente. With these ideas, Waldheim, who was Austrian ambassador to the United Nations before he became foreign minister, initiated the first steps toward a profound change of Austria's foreign policy.

Since 1970, Bruno Kreisky headed the first Socialist majority government. Kreisky pushed these concepts much further. Under his leadership, Austria's foreign policy concentrated much less on Europe and more on upgrading relations with Third World countries. The Free Trade Agreements with the European Community concluded in 1972, bolstered Kreisky's foreign policy and ended the internal discussions on Austria's integration policy for many years (see below). Austria became *guest* at the meetings of the nonaligned movement. To help to solve or limit conflicts which could lead to wars, but also to prove the usefulness of Austrian neutrality, Kreisky got Austrian foreign policy involved in areas such as the Middle East, Central America and Afghanistan.[11] In these crisis spots, Austria tried to offer meditation and proposed means for peaceful solutions. Austria's foreign policy became more or less identical with its neutrality.[12]

Appendix 1 shows these changes quantitatively. The chart illustrates official and quasi-official visits of Austrian presidents, chancellors and foreign ministers abroad as an indicator of the geographical (and also ideological) orientation of Austria's foreign policy under the different governments between 1956 and 1988.[13] It shows that until the early 1970s Europe and North America were central to Austria's external relations. In the mid-1970s, the contacts with Third World countries (especially Asia) increased markedly. Official visits to Latin America were made only between 1977 and 1982. This *globalization* of Austria's foreign policy increased Kreisky's prestige not only externally, but also internally.

Austria's status in international relations eventually became much greater than its size would have warranted. In the late 1970s, the opposition, especially the conservative ÖVP, started to criticize Kreisky's foreign policy activism because this activist foreign policy was popular and helped Kreisky win elections. The one weak point spotted by the opposition were Austria's relations with (Western) Europe in general and the European Community in particular. Since the late 1970s, the catchword of the conservatives was "one kiss less for Arafat and one trip more to Brussels."

But Kreisky's foreign policy came under pressure from the outside as well. The new Cold War reduced the maneuverability of the non-bloc countries. The Reagan administration criticized Austria's foreign policy, especially its trade policy with Eastern Europe which opened a loophole in the restrictions on transfer of Western high technology to Eastern Europe. After an initial resistance, the Austrian government had to tighten its restrictions and finally acted like a member of COCOM, the Western organization for multilateral export controls.[14]

In 1983, the Socialists lost the absolute majority and formed a coalition government with the small conservative-liberal German-national Freedom Party (FPÖ). The government slowly started to reorient its foreign policy towards Western Europe, as can be noted in Appendix 1. Relations with the European Community became the most important element of its external relations (see below).[15] The upheavals in Eastern Europe 1988/1989 did not change Austria's external orientation. The economies of the Central and Eastern European countries were not so attractive as to offer an alternative to the intensified relations with Western Europe (i.e. integration policy).

The governments of the newly democratic countries did not opt for neutrality. For them, neutrality was an "outdated concept."[16] Austria's neutrality policy also came under pressure during the Gulf crisis (1990/91). When Austria joined the United Nations, it was expected that the other members would respect its status. Should there be any obligatory sanctions or measures of collective security, the UN would make exceptions for Austria. In the Gulf crisis these expectations were not met. Even if they wanted to, Austria and the other neutrals could not eschew international solidarity (see below).

These challenges for Austria's foreign policy have led to a *reinterpretation of neutrality*. Politicians once again speak about *military neutrality* and consider neutrality to be relevant for only a small part of Austria's external relations. The obligations of UN membership have taken precedence over Austria's duties as a neutral. Although some have even suggested that Austria abandon its neutrality, most politicians favor preserving the neutral status as long as rapid changes threaten the stability of Central and Eastern Europe.[17]

The Structure of Austria's External Trade

After World War II, Austria developed close economic relations with Western Europe. Appendix 2 shows the extent of Austria's exports from the mid-1950s through the 1980s. Western Europe's large share declined from the mid-1960s up to the mid-1970s because of the increased percentage for the N+N countries[18] in the 1960s and a rise in the share of the OPEC countries (Asia and Africa).

A comparison of Appendices 1 and 2 shows how Austria's political and economic external relations developed after 1955. Europe dominates and Third World countries play only a small role in both figures. One can see that political relations were more volatile than trade. Appendix 1 indicates that Austria gradually reduced its contacts with the West, increased its relations with Third World countries and developed from the mid-1970s forward a balanced relationship with the West and the East. Appendix 2 shows the growth of the Third World countries' share during the 1970s, but on a reduced scale.

After the mid-1970s, the share of the West in Austria's external trade increased again. In the political sphere, this change took place only in the early 1980s—the economic realities had finally to be taken into account in the mid-1980s by the SPÖ-FPÖ coalition government.

The Efforts to Attain Closer Relations With the European Community (1961-1984)

When in 1951 six West European countries founded the European Coal and Steel Community, they created a new kind of international organization—a community with *supranational* elements. This new organization caused problems for Austria. On the one hand, it regulated trade of two commodities on which Austria was heavily dependent. On the other hand, the Six included Austria's most important trading partners.

As we have seen, Austria decided after some debate not to join the European Economic Community (EEC) which was founded by the six ECSC countries in 1957. The trade shares would have indicated membership in the EEC (see Appendix 3). But political factors—the Soviet attitude and Austria's neutrality[19]—proved to be obstacles. As second best solution, Austria proposed a free trade zone including all West European countries. Negotiations on this zone failed in late 1958, however, and Austria founded the European Free Trade Association (EFTA) in early 1960. It included the other neutrals[20] as well as the United Kingdom, Denmark, Norway and Portugal.

When the United Kingdom, the most important member of EFTA, applied for membership in the Common Market in July 1961, three neutrals decided to ask the EEC for association agreements. After President de Gaulle had rejected the British request for EEC membership in January 1963, Sweden and Switzerland suspended their applications for association treaties. But Austria continued its efforts to reach an agreement with the EEC. The reason for this insistence can be seen in the strengthening of the *reformist* wing in the ÖVP.   The reformist wanted more economic liberalism and a reduction of the influence of the state and the nationalized industries.   It also stressed the importance of the relations with Western Europe.   The defeat of the SPÖ in the general elections (November 1962) weakened this party's more cautious position towards going it alone *("Alleingang")*.   Representatives of the ÖVP and economists stressed the importance of Austrian participation in the *more dynamic market* of the EEC.   In June 1967, the efforts of the *Alleingang* failed when Italy rejected further talks until the conflict with Austria South Tyrol had been solved.   Factors underlying this included the continued hostility of the Soviet Union toward closer relationship of Austria with the EEC, the sudden French aversion to any special arrangement because of de Gaulle's new *Ostpolitik* and the difficulties of finding any clear-cut solutions on the institutional level for a close association resembling membership.[21]

After de Gaulle's resignation and after a compromise with Italy on South Tyrol, Austria and the other neutrals signed free trade agreements on industrial goods with the European Community (strictly speaking with the EEC and the ECSC) in July 1972.   Contrary to earlier statements, the Soviet Union did not protest these agreements.   The implementation of the treaties brought no major problems.   Since July 1977, trade in industrial goods between Austria and the EC has been free of custom duties and quantitative restrictions.   Only in the mid-1980s, when the EC decided on the completion of its internal market, new challenges appeared for Austria's relations with the Community.

The New Dynamics of the European Community and Austria's Response

In the mid 1980s, the EC countries realized that Western Europe would have to intensify its economic cooperation to reduce the lead of Japan and the United States in economic development, especially in high technology.   The proposal of the EC Commission on "Completing the Internal Market" was accepted by the EC Summit Meeting in June 1985.   To improve its decision-making capacities, the EC also amended its basic treaties through the Single European Act, in force since 1 July 1987.   This Act also introduced rules for the European Political Cooperation (EPC) of the EC countries.   It stated that the EC countries "shall endeavor jointly to formulate and implement a European foreign policy." They "are ready to coordinate their positions more closely on the political and economic aspects of security."[22]

As in other neutral countries, the first reaction to these events was that no reversal of Austria's relations with the EC was deemed necessary. SPÖ Foreign Minister Gratz saw "neither an economic nor a political reason to change our attitude."[23] But in the opposition party, the ÖVP, powerful voices called for a closer relationship with the EC (see above). In an important article, Andreas Khol, one of the younger foreign policy specialists of the ÖVP, suggested a "triple jump" towards Europe--from cooperation via association to union.[24]

A qualitative change in the integration policy of Austria's government came only in mid-1986. A group of younger politicians from the SPÖ got important positions in the government. The new Chancellor, Franz Vranitzky (SPÖ), argued that Austria should seek a "quasi-membership" in the EC. The creation of the Grand Coalition government between the Socialists and the Conservatives supported this trend. In its statement of policy (January 1987) the new government declared that intensifying Austria's relations with the EC was a "central objective" of its foreign policy.

The "Global Approach"

In spring 1987, under Vice-Chancellor and Foreign Minister Alois Mock (ÖVP), the Foreign Ministry conceived the "global approach" for participation in the internal market of the EC. In this way, Austria would aim to take part in the total substance of the internal market. This approach would also improve the internal decision-making process. Because it was feared that the large protected sectors of the economy would resist opening up and thus weaken the negotiation posture vis-à-vis the Community, it was decided that part of Austria's economy would receive special treatment. The agreements deemed necessary to assure Austrian participation in the internal market could later be compiled in a new "Europe-Treaty," which would replace the free trade agreements between Austria and the EC. By 1987, Austria had to face the impossibility of participation in the internal market without membership in the EC.[25]

Representatives of the EC made it clear that participation in EC decisions about the internal market would be reserved for full members. So at the end of 1987, the SPÖ-ÖVP government accepted participation in the internal market as merely the "next step" in Austria's integration policy. The government decided to aim at wide cooperation, which would include the solution of the transit traffic problems, the securing of Austria's agricultural exports, participation in the technology programs of the EC, enhanced cooperation in monetary matters, participation in citizens' Europe and an intensive dialogue with the European Political Cooperation. The option of membership in the EC at a later date was not excluded—provided that the EC would honor 25 Austria's neutrality.[26] After some debates in the Cabinet, Chancellor Vranitzky announced on 5 July 1988, that it would decide in 1989 on the EC question. This decision could include the possibility of an application for membership.[27]

The European Economic Area (EEA)

In his statement before the European Parliament on 17 January 1989, on the broad lines of Commission Policy, Jacques Delors, President of the EC-Commission, discussed the relations of the EC towards the "other Europeans," especially the EFTA countries. On the one hand, Delors offered a more structured partnership between the EC and the EFTA "with common decision-making and administrative institutions to make our activities more effective an to highlight the political dimension of our cooperation in the economic, social, financial and cultural spheres."[28] On the other hand, he seemed to have aimed at the Austrian ambitions for membership when he stressed that

> ...the Community is much more than a large market. It is a frontier-free economic and social area on the way to becoming a political union entailing closer cooperation on foreign policy and security. The marriage contract is, as it were, indissoluble, even though its clauses have not been applied in full. Only that *affectation societatis* which binds our twelve countries enables us to rise above the difficulties and contradictions, to advance in all areas of our collective activity. It is extremely difficult, within this all-embracing union, to provide a choice of menus.[29]

A week later Jacques Delors emphasized in an interview that the marriage contract provides for the creation of a "political Europe" with a common foreign policy and a common defense. He did not believe that the Austrians would be ready "to go the entire way with us."[30]

In response to the Delors initiative, Vice-Chancellor and Foreign Minister Mock pleaded for a continuation of the Austrian integration policy. Delors has not offered any alternative; therefore, the membership question remained.[31] According to the Socialist Party's foreign policy spokesperson, Peter Jankowitsch, the Delors initiative reflected some "nervousness" concerning Austria's EC policy. Chancellor Vranitzky was convinced that Austria should maintain its bilateral approach but also use EFTA as much as possible.[32] He believed that the EFTA countries would give a positive answer to Delors.[33] Economics Minister Robert Graf (ÖVP) wanted Delors to explain his proposal to EFTA at its annual conference in June. But he believed that the project would not work because EFTA has no common economic policy. The ÖVP wanted Austria to keep its schedule and send the letter asking for membership in mid-1989 to Brussels.[34]

Nevertheless, Austria participated in the preparatory talks that started in March 1989 between the EFTA countries and the EC Commission. The official round of negotiations to create a European Economic Area for all nineteen EC and EFTA countries began in June 1990. These negotiations have proved to be very difficult. The aim of the EFTA countries to participate in all aspects of the EC internal market (except agriculture) would require that the EFTA countries accept all regulations and directives of the EC without real participation in the decision making. For most Austrian politicians, the EEA has been seen only as an intermediate step for full EC membership. The EEA somehow resembles the Austrian "global approach"—with all the difficulties predicted by the EC side in 1987.

Membership Application

The first lobbying for EC membership came from the chambers of commerce of Austria's Western provinces, where in particular the textile industry encountered obstacles in its exports to the EC. In May 1987, the Federation of Austrian Industrialists formally demanded EC member-ship as the only possible way to fully participate in the emerging internal market. At the end of 1987, the Federal Chamber of Commerce (which represents more the small and medium-sized enterprises) changed its long-standing opposition and opted for full EC membership as well. Even representatives of the farmers' organizations now wanted Austria to join the EC. Shortly afterwards, in January 1988, the party with close links to the farmers and business groups and junior partner of the coalition government, the ÖVP, decided to request full membership in the EC.

The Socialist Party was not ready to jump the boat at such an early stage. But when the business lobbies started to push for EC membership, the labor interest groups displayed a wait-and-see attitude rather than marked opposition. In July 1988, after half a year of discussions, the Trade Union Council issued a "cautiously positive" statement on EC membership. The low growth rates of the Austrian economy during the mid-1980s account in part of this attitude. The Austrian model of deficit spending and state intervention in the economy—popular under Chan-cellor Kreisky—was not working any more.[35]

Although the most important interest groups had now opted for EC membership, the government did not reach a similar position for another year. In late 1988, public opinion polls revealed opposition growing to the membership application. Among the groups were the Greens and the (tiny) Communist Party, pacifist groups and some Socialist politicians, but also a majority of the farmers.[36] The opposition in Western Austria to the huge transit traffic by heavy trucks from EC countries and the accompanying environmental problems brought difficulties for the People's Party. In March 1989, the party lost heavily in three provincial elections; for example, it lost some 16 percentage points in the Tyrol. Foreign Minister Mock, the leader of the Party and spearhead of the faction that pushed for EC membership, had to resign. Josef Riegler— in EC questions somewhat more restrained—was elected Party Chairman at the beginning of May 1989.

In the meantime, the Socialist Party had agreed to an Austrian application for EC membership (3 April 1989). The Party specified several conditions for the talks with the EC, among them keeping the social standards in Austria and upholding the strict environmental protection laws. It stressed in particular the importance of Austria's permanent neutrality. There still existed some differences among the ruling parties on how to handle the application, particularly who should coordinate the preparations for the upcoming talks—the Socialist Chancellor or the Foreign Minister from the ÖVP—and about the financial consequences of EC membership. On 26 June 1989, SPÖ and ÖVP finally reached an agreement on how to proceed further with integration policy.

The agreement declared Austria's permanent neutrality indispensable and stressed that integration must not lead to a deterioration of social security, or to the decline of high quality of Austrian environment and consumer protection. The agreement specified that farmers should be compensated for losses incurred because of the lower prices for agricultural goods in the EC. But, against the wishes of the Conservatives, no specific amounts were laid down. The coordination of Austria's integration policy will be done in consensus by the Chancellor (SPÖ) and the Vice Chancellor (ÖVP). The Foreign Minister (ÖVP) will be in charge of the negotiations with Brussels but he will not supervise the internal Austrian coordination, as parts of the ÖVP wanted. The expected costs of EC membership will not be covered solely by cutting other budget expenditures (taxes may be raised if necessary).[37]

The contents of this agreement, which cleared the way for the "letter" to Brussels, show that the Socialists carried most of their points. The Socialists were in a strong position since any ratification of an accession treaty with the EC will need a *two thirds* majority in the Austrian Parliament *(Nationalrat)*. Therefore, the votes of both the Socialists and the Conservatives will be needed to pass such a treaty. Any other coalition of parties in the Parliament will lack that majority, (at least in the forseeable future).

On 17 July 1989, Austrian Foreign Minister Alois Mock handed the application documents to his French counterpart, Roland Dumas in Brussels. Austria applied for membership in the EEC (Art. 237 EEC Treaty), the ECSC (Art. 98 ECSC Treaty) and Euratom (Art. 205 EAEC Treaty). In these three letters, one sentence concerned Austria's permanent neutrality:

> In making this application Austria proceeds from the assumption that it will maintain its internationally recognized status of permanent neutrality, based on the Federal Constitutional Law of 26 October 1955, and that also as a member of the European Communities, on the basis of the accession treaty, it will be in a position to fulfill its legal obligations deriving from its status as a permanently neutral state and to pursue its neutrality policy as a specific contribution to the maintenance of peace and security in Europe.[38]

The Austrian membership application was not enthusiastically welcomed by the EC authorities. Jacques Delors, the President of the EC Commission, expressed on several occasions his doubts about the membership of a permanently neutral country in the EC. The Belgian Foreign Minister, Mark Eyskens, maintained that "*la neutralité est un obstacle*".[39] He even wanted Austrian neutrality to be discussed with the Soviet Union.[40]

One month after the application had been submitted, the Soviet Ambassador to Austria presented an *aide-memoire* to the Austrian government. In it the Soviet Union indicated "understanding" for Austrian activities intended to solve the problems created by the internal market program of the EC. But the Soviet government expressed its conviction that

> membership of a permanently neutral state in an organization like the European Community would lead to the loss of the real possibilities for the implementation of its policy of neutrality. Starting from this fact, it [the Soviet government] received with concern the news on Austria's intention to begin negotiations on membership with the European Community.[41]

But the Austrian authorities rejected references to the incompatibility of Austrian neutrality with EC membership. Whereas in the 1950s and 1960s most specialists in international law regarded membership in a supranational organization not possible for a neutral country (see above), in the 1970s and 1980s this position has been assailed by a growing group of authors.

An important study, commissioned by the Austrian Federation of Industrialists, regarded permanent neutrality and EC membership compatible—without any further measures.[42] The basic argument was that in the age of interdependence autarchy is not a viable solution for a small country which is highly dependent on its foreign trade. Neutrality cannot mean absolute independence. The EC treaties could be interpreted to regard Austria's neutrality as "an obligation it [Austria] has accepted for the purpose of maintaining peace and international security."[43] The Austrian government opted for an application with a neutrality clause to assure the credibility of the Austrian neutrality. According to the official Austrian position, exceptions to the EC treaties must have the force of primary Community law—that is, one must amend these treaties; a simple gentleman's agreements would not be sufficient.[44]

European Political Cooperation (EPC) and Austria

Austrian discussions leading to the membership application neglected the question of foreign policy cooperation. Austrian legal opinion maintained that the intergovernmental cooperation and the decision-making by consensus in EPC (in contrast to the supranational structure of the EC) would pose no problems for Austrian neutrality. But on developments inside the EC that culminated in launching a second Intergovernmental Conference on Political Union in December 1990 (concerning the security and defense identity of the EC) changed the minds of the Austrian politicians.

The first message came in October 1989 when Chancellor Vranitzky spoke about full participation of Austria in the Political Union.[45] The Austrian government issued in formal declaration February 1990 in an *aide memoire* to the EC Commission and all member states. This document stressed Austria's commitment to the "fundamental aims of the Community Treaties and the Single European Act" and participation as full member with "the spirit of solidarity." The government also urged a swift processing of the Austrian application.[46] In the policy statement, the new SPÖ-ÖVP coalition government declared on 18 December 1990, that it "views the Political Union project as a positive contribution to the realization of Europe's unity and [Austria] will in the framework of neutrality also participate solidarity with future European security system inside the Community and beyond it."[47]

In a comment on the European Council meeting, 14-15 December 1990, in Rome, Austrian Foreign Minister Mock (ÖVP) went even further and declared that "Austria knows that it will become member of the new and deepened Community." Austria supports the goal of political union. This includes the "readiness to actively take part in the development and construction of the future common European foreign and security policy."[48]

Other statements, especially from the Conservative side, have deemphasized the neutrality clause of the membership application. Many have come to view neutrality as only comprising military elements and being free of economic or political restraints. This shift has been justified by the changed circumstances in (Eastern) Europe. Often a distinction was made between security policy (in which Austria could participate) and defense policy (which was taboo for Austria—at least as long no new security structures have developed in Europe).

The Gulf crisis and war of 1990/91 tested not only Austria's neutrality but also its attitude towards international solidarity. When the Security Council imposed sanctions against Iraq for invading Kuwait, no exceptions were made for the neutral members of the UN. On 13 August 1990, Austria implemented the economic sanctions fully. It also allowed, in contrast to Switzerland, transit flights bound for the Gulf region. In January 1991, Austria even amended its penal code and the War Material Law. Actions performed under Chapter VII of the UN Charter concerning collective security will not be regarded as war or armed conflicts and therefore will not activate Austrian neutrality. Austria will not remain neutral in these circumstances and will support the actions authorized by the UN. This behavior was commended by EC officials.[49]

The "Avis" of the EC Commission

More than two years after Austria's application for membership, Commission presented its Opinion ("avis") to the Council.[50] The Commission's deliberations were so lengthy because the Austrian application caused a split within the Commission. Some Commissioners wanted to postpone a decision about Austria to 1996, when the treaty revisions on defense policy will be complete. Others wanted the negotiations to start at an early date.[51] The final compromise provided that no negotiations on a fresh enlargement should be initiated before the completion of the internal market (1 January 1993).

In the avis the Commission maintains that the EC will "on the whole benefit from the accession of Austria." On the basis of economic considerations, the Commission recommended "that the Community should accept Austria's application." On the political level, the Commission expresses reservations claiming that Austria's permanent neutrality "creates problems." Negotiations in the intergovernmental conference on political union "would also require the Community to seek specific assurances from the Austrian authorities with regard to their capacity to undertake obligations entailed by the future common foreign and security policy".[52]

The Austrian government has welcomed the *avis* and is preparing itself for the negotiations to go quickly and smoothly. The government expects that Austria will become a member of the EC in 1995. The opposition parties have seen less reason to rejoice, fearing that there will be problems from increased EC transit traffic and difficulties for the farmers. The Greens dread the loss of Austria's neutrality.[53]

Conclusion

The changes in Eastern and Central Europe, the end of the Cold War and the disintegration of the Soviet Union have shifted Austria's position in Europe. It is once again in the political center of the continent. With the end of the Soviet "threat" neutrality has lost its main purpose-- keeping Austria out of the superpower rivalry. Russia and the successor states surely can have no plausible justification for insisting on Austrian neutrality at a time when the former Warsaw Pact countries seek closer relations with NATO.

The Gulf crisis showed that Austria (like Switzerland) cannot maintain its permanent neutrality in a traditional, comprehensive sense. But many Austrians still favor neutrality. In fact, 80 percent opt for neutrality over EC membership, should the two be mutually exclusive.[54] Therefore, Austria's politicians sometimes send contradictory signals, stressing neutrality for interval audiences[55] but downplaying neutrality in the international arena and emphasizing future participation in European security policy.

It is not yet clear what the future security and defense policy of the EC will look like. It is clear, however, that the EC wants new members to participate fully in a future common foreign and security policy. This puts Austria in a new dilemma. Moreover, Austria would be well advised not to abandon neutrality as long as the EC defense policy is unclear. As the Yugoslav case shows, there is no guarantee that all transformation processes in Central and Eastern Europe will proceed peacefully. The Austrian government will be loath to abandon neutrality for a security policy that will be (at best) only it its infancy. In any case, it will be very difficult to convince the Austrian public to change a policy that has helped Austria to remain, in a world on the brink of nuclear war, an "island of the blessed." But this Austrian identity crisis is only a sign of the changes in Europe that have required new thinking for many actors.

NOTES

1. I have written several publications on this subject; see in particular *Neutrale in die EG? Die wirtschaftliche Integration in Westeuropa und die neutralen Staaten,* (Vienna: Braumüller, 1988), and "Austria's Application for EC Membership: Historical Background, Reasons and Possible Results," *EFTS and the EC: Implications of 1992,* ed. Fin Laursen, (Maastricht: European Institute of Public Administration, 1990), 177-206. The present contribution was written in September/October 1991.

2. On the State Treaty see Gerald Stourzh, *Geschichte des Staatsvertrages 1945-1955. Österreichs Weg zur Neutralität.* 3rd edition (Graz-Vienna-Cologne: Styria, 1985).

3. Some Articles of the State Treaty which prohibited Austria i.a. to acquire war material of German origin and aircraft of German or Japanese design were declared obsolete by the Austrian government stated that it still regarded itself legally prohibited to produce or to possess any atomic, biological or chemical weapons; see *Österreichische Außenpolitische Dokumentation. Texte und Dokumente* (December 1990), 28.

4. See the English translation in Alfred Verdross, *The Permanent Neutrality of Austria* (Vienna: Verlag für Geschichte und Politik, 1978), 36-40.

5. This official translation of the authentic German text has been taken from Gerald Stourzh (note 1), 239.

6. From Hans Mayrzedt and Waldemar Hummer, *20 Jahre österreichichische Neutralitäts- und Europapolitik (1955-1975). Dokumentation,* Teilband I (Vienna: Braumüller, 1976), 90.

7. See Florian Weiß, "Auf sanften Pfoten gehen":Die österreichische Bundeesregierund und die Anfänge der westeuropäischen Integration 1947-1957," Master Thesis, University of Munich, 147-156.

8. E.g., Josef Klaus, "Österreich und die Ost-West-Beziehungen. Rede im Institut für Internationale Politik und Wirtschaft in Belgrad am 25. März 1965," *Österreichische Zeitschrift für Außenpolitik* 5 (1965): 88-93.

9. On these attempts, see section 3 below.

10. Kurt Waldheim in a speech on November 7, 1986, quoted from Mayrzedt and Hummer (note 5), 145, translation Paul Luif.

11. It is clear that Kreisky's involvement in the Israeli-Palestinian conflict also had personal reasons. On Kreisky's foreign policy see especially Erich Bielka, Peter Jankowitsch and Hans Thalberg eds., *Die Ära Kreisky. Schwerpunkte der österreichischen Außenpolitik* (Vienna-Munich-Zurich: Europaverlag, 1983).

12. Bruno Kreisky: "Für Österreich ist heute die Neutralität die in höchstem Maße adäquate Außenpolitik", quoted from *Die Zeit in der wir leben. Betrachtungen zur internationalen Politik*, ed. Manuel Lucbert, 2nd ed. (Vienna: Fritz Molden, 1978), 73.

13. Since in the 1950s there were only very few visits abroad, one visit of the Austrian foreign minister in some Asian countries in 1958 is responsible for the high share of Asia in 1956/58.

14. Paul Luif, "Strategic Embargoes and European Neutrals: The Cases of Austria and Sweden," ed. Vilho Harle, *Challenges and Responses in European Security.* TAPRI *Yearbook 1986* (Aldershot: Avebury, 1987), 174-188.

15. Helmut Kramer, "Wende' in der österreichischen Außenpolitik? Zur Außenpolitik der SPÖ-ÖVP-Koalition," *Österreichische Zeitschrift für Politikwissenschaft* 17 (1988): 117-131.

16. See Joszef Antall, "Neutralität ist ein überholtes Konzept!," *europa* 5/6 (1990): 4-7, and "Ungarns Antall rät Wien: `Gebt Neutralität auf'. `Ungarn im Schlepptau Österreichs in die EG'," *Der Standard*, 19 August 1990, 1.

17. For a typical example see the article of the ÖVP foreign policy spokesperson Andreas Khol, "Neutralität - ein überholtes Instrument österreichischer Sicherheitspolitik?," in *Österreichisches Jahrbuch für Politik 1990*, 677-709.

18. These are basically the EFTA countries; see below.

19. Most specialists in international law maintained that a neutral has to pursue a independent foreign policy. As a member of the EEC it could not do so, even if a neutrality clause would have been accepted by the EEC. See especially Karl Zemanek, "Wirtschaftliche Neutralität," *Juristische Blätter* 81 (1959):249-251.

20. Sweden and Switzerland; Finland was from 1961 to 1985 associated member; only in 1986 it became full member of EFTA. Ireland remained outside EFTA. It joined the EC in 1973.

21. See Paul Luif, "Decision Structures and Decision-Making Processes in the European Communities' Relations to the EFTA Countries: A Case Study of Austria," *Österreichische Zeitschrift für Außenpolitik* 33 (1983): 139-160.

22. The quotations are from Article 30 of the Single European Act.

23. See the article "Gratz gegen neue Eg-Diskussion: `Energien werden verzettelt'," *Die Presse*, 2 December 1985.

24. Andreas Khol, "Im Dreisprung nach Europa: Kooperation - Assoziation - Union," *Europäische Rundschau* 13 (1985): 29-45.

25. See Alois Mock, "Außenpolitische Erklärung," Manuscript, May 11, 1988.

26. This is the content of the "Outline of the Austrian Integration Policy" which was approved by the government on December 1, 1987.

27. See the interesting article "Kernelemente von Österreichs EG-Annäherung. Unzureichend geklärte Neutralitätsprobleme," *Neue Zürcher Zeitung*, 28 August 1988, 21.

28. Jacques Delors, "Statement on the Broad Lines of Commission Policy. Strasbourg, 17 and 18 January 1989," *Bulletin of the European Communities*, Supplement 1/89, 17.

29. Ibid., 18.

30. "EG-Beitritt: Delors betont Skepsis. `Glaube nicht, daß Österreich den ganzen Weg mit uns gehen will'," *Der Standard*, 25 January 1989, 1,

31. Ibid.

32. See the articles "`Zielkonflikte vermeiden'. Jankowitsch zu aktuellen Fragen", *Wiener Zeitung*, 25 January 1989, 4, and "Jankowitsch-Reaktion: `Die EG wird nervös'", *Kurier*, 26 January 1989, 2.

33. "Vranitzky für engere Kooperation EFTA-EG. Positive Reaktion auf das Angebot Delors'", *Der Standard*, 30 January 1989, 2.

34. Heinrich Mathis, "Graf: `Brief nach Brüssel' erst nach Efta-Aussprache mit Delors", *Der Standard*, 2 February 1989, 11.

35. For a detailed enumeration of the reasons which led to Austria's membership application see Paul Luif, "Austria's Application" (see first note).

36. Heinrich Schneider, *Alleingang nach Brüssel. Österreichs EG-Politik,* (Bonn: Europa Union Verlag, 1990), 95.

37. The agreement of the parties was published as "EG-Parteivereinbarung vom 26. 6. 1989," *Wiener Zeitung*, 29 June 1989, 5.

38. Österreichische außenpolitische Dokumentation. Texte und Dokumente (January 1990): 74, translation Paul Luif.

39. Thomas Mayer, "Ein Fragezeichen begleitet Mock bei der Übergabe des EG-Briefes," *Der Standard*, 18 July 1989, 4.

40. Otmar Lahodynsky, "`Wir haben nichts gegen Österreich.' Belgiens Aussenminister Mark Eyskens hat aber Angst vor der Neutralität," *Die Presse*, 20 July 1989, 3.

41. The text of the Soviet aide-memoire is taken from "`Keine außergewöhnliche Aktualität'. Österreichs Reaktion auf Moskaus Aide memoire ist Gelassenheit - Nur die Grünen sagen: Ein Denkzettel," *Der Standard*, 11 August, 1989, 5 (translation Paul Luif).

42. Waldemar Hummer and Michael Schweitzer, *Österreich und die EWG. Neutralitätsrechtliche Beurteilung der Möglichkeit der Dynamisierung des Verhältnisses zur EWG* (Vienna: Signum Verlag, 1987)

43. These are the words of Article 224 EEC Treaty.

44. See Karl Zemanek, "Austria and the European Community," in *German Yearbook of International Law - Jahrbuch für Internationales Recht* 33 (1990): 157.

45. Andreas Unterberger, "Vranitzky beschleunigt EG-Annäherung: Bekenntnis zur Politischen Union. Klares Ja Österreichs zu intensivierter Integration," *Die Presse,* 11 October 1989, 1.

46. "Aide memoire der österreichischen Bundesregierung vom 16. Februar 1990," *Österreichische außenpolitische Dokumentation. Texte und Dokumente* (April 1990): 16-18.

47. *Erklärung der Bundesregierung vor dem Nationalrat von Bundeskanzler* Dr. Franz Vranitzky. 18. Dezember 1990 (Bundespressedienst, Vienna 1990), 17.

48. "Erklärung von Außenminister Mock aus Anlaß der Tagung des europäischen Rates vom 14. und 15. Dezember in Rom, Wien, am 16. Dezember 1990," *Österreichische außenpolitische Dokumentation. Texte und Dokumente* (February 1991):59.

49. Benedikt Kommenda, "Über den Golf in die Gemeinschaft. Österreich ist den Zwölf nähergerückt," *Die Presse,* 5 March 1991, 18.

50. *Austria's Application for Membership.* Commission Opinion, Brussels, 1 August 1991 (=SEC(91) 1590 final).

51. Otmar Lahodynsky, "Ein neuer Nettozahler für die Gemeinschaft," *EG-Magazin* 9 (September 1991):30.

52. Commission Opinion (see note 49), 28/29.

53. "Das große Aufatmen in Wien: Regierung sieht Neutralität nicht zur Diskussion gestellt. Das 'Avis' der Europäischen Geneinschaft wird von Österreichs Politikern durchwegs positiv aufgenommen," *Die Presse,* 2 August 1991, 4.

54. Public opinion poll by Fessel GfK/IFES, November 1990/January 1991, n=2000.

55. The only party from which "loud" voices can be heard in favor of abandoning neutrality is the FPÖ.

**APPENDIX 1: Official Visits of Austria's President, Chancellors and
Foreign Ministers Abroad
(Shares of Regions in Percent)**

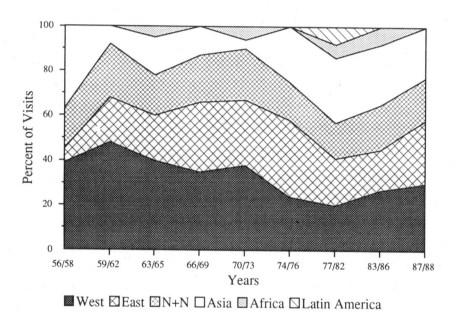

■ West ⊠ East ⊠ N+N □ Asia ▨ Africa ◩ Latin America

Note: "West" = NATO countries plus Australia, New Zealand and South Africa;
"East" = Warsaw Pact plus Albanis; "N+N" = European neutrals and nonaligned.

Sources: Paul Luif, "Neutrality and External Relations: The Case of Austria," in
Cooperation and Conflict, 21, No. 1(1986), 28, and additions from the *Außenpoli-
tischer Bericht*, 1985 to 1988.

**APPENDIX 2: Austrian Exports to Selected Groups of Countries
(Share of Total Exports in Percent)**

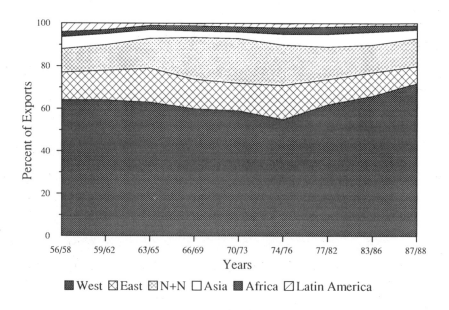

■ West ⊠ East ⊠ N+N □ Asia ■ Africa ⊠ Latin America

Note: For definitions of the regions, see APPENDIX 1.

Sources: Statistische Nachrichten, various volumes, and author's calculations.

**APPENDIX 3: Austria's Exports to the Integration Groups in Europe
(Percentages of Austrian Total Exports)**

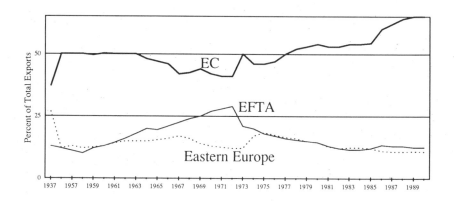

EFTA Eastern Europe EC

Sources: Statistisches Handbuch der Republik Österreich and *Statistische Nachrichten*, various volumes.

Austria and European Integration after World War II

Oliver Rathkolb

Whereas the most recent debates about Austria's integration into the European Community (EC) focus mainly on economic matters, it is important to analyze the economic, political and military aspects of integration in their total complexity. The European community is not only aiming to integrate the economies of its member states but also to coordinate social developments and to bring about political union of the EC members. From the military perspective, nine of the twelve full EC members belong to the Western European Union (WEU), an international organization that should strengthen the role of Europe within the North Atlantic Treaty Organization (NATO). An analysis that combines the unforeseeable developments within the EC aiming towards a stronger political and military union with the economic aspects of European unification should give us a fuller picture of the process.

History has little to offer in the political debate about Austria's integration, which has been occuring since 1988 against the backdrop of dramatic change: the end of the Cold War, the dissolution of the Soviet Union, and the democratic revolt in East Central Europe. On the other hand, various arguments from the late 1950s and 1960s have reappeared in the recent debates. Austria's neutrality is no longer a product of the Cold War, but is now a strong pillar of the relatively new "Austrian identity" (compared with the strong pro German sentiments before 1945). In public opinion polls conducted in September 1991 57 percent of Austrians were not prepared to change their neutrality status even if this meant exclusion from the EC.[1] Twenty-eight percent favored changing neutrality, if that were the prerequisite to join the EC; only 4 percent were prepared to give up neutrality outright. When asked in

January 1992 to choose between abolition or continuation of neutrality 96 percent chose neutrality, and only 2 percent were prepared to give it up.[2] As early as 1965, 82 percent of Austrians were against joining the EC if neutrality would be endangered.[3]

These figures are evidence that ever since Austria became a neutral state in 1955 neutrality has become a constituent element in the Austrians' sense of nationhood. Certainly the concept of neutrality—seen from a geopolitical angle—has changed considerably. But one must be aware that Austrian attitudes in 1992 are the results of developments over almost four decades. Therefore, it is not just historical self-analysis to examine the debates about European integration in the late 1950s and early 1960s.

The following analysis will concentrate on the development of policies towards integration with Western Europe after World War II, concentrating on the relationships between the international situation, Austrian neutrality and the first drive towards closer integration. European integration in a broad sense is not limited to the EC but includes other international organizations as well:

The *Organization for Economic Cooperation and Development* (OECD), established in 1961 replacing the Organization for European Economic Cooperation (OEEC) of 1948 to promote economic and social welfare amongst its member states, and to stimulate and harmonize efforts on behalf of developing countries.

The *North Atlantic Treaty Organization* (NATO) created in 1949 as a Western European, Canadian and U.S. military "security league... with such regional and collective arrangements as are based on continuous self-help and mutual aid, as affect its national security."[4]

The *Council of Europe*, formed in 1949 to "achieve a greater unity between its members for the purpose of safeguarding and realizing the ideals and principles which are their common heritage and facilitating their economic and social progress." (Although the Parliamentary Assembly of the Council of Europe is only entitled to propose actions to bring European countries closer together especially the European Convention on Human Rights of 1950 has already created obligatory jurisdiction.)

The *European Free Trade Association* (EFTA), established in 1960 to reduce customs duties and quantitative restrictions between members on industrial products; in free trade agreements with the EC in 1973.

From a historical perspective, Western European integration concerns Austria's relationship with OEEC, and the EEC in the economic sphere, with NATO, in the military sphere, and the Council of Europe in the political sphere.

From the beginning of the debate over Austria's participation in the European Recovery Program, it was clear that this decision had major political implications for the East-West conflict. In a top secret memorandum, drafted shortly after the Austrian government—including the only Communist cabinet member—had decided to participate in the 1947 Paris negotiations for the implementation of the Marshall Plan,[5] Secretary of State George C. Marshall was informed that this decision marked a formal change for U.S. occupation policies in Austria:

> In view of the changed strategy inherent in the European Recovery Program it is deemed advisable to review this policy for Austria, and to consider the solution of the Austrian problem in the framework of the general situation in Western Europe and specifically in relation to the European Recovery Program. Austria's participation in the European Recovery Program and in the Interim Aid program over strong Soviet objections and the further consolidation for the U.S. political position in Austria has made that country the easternmost Central European bulwark of the European Recovery Program. Conversely, abandonment of Austria to potentially complete Soviet penetration would drive a wedge between Italy and Western Germany, expose the Southern flank of the U.S. zone of Germany, and threaten the position in depth of the European Recovery Program in France and in England, besides depriving us of a useful wedge between the Slavic states of Jugoslavia and Czechoslovakia and an excellent observation post of Soviet operations in the Balkans.[6]

The decision to go to Paris was made after conflict in the Austrian Coalition-Government over foreign policy priorities.[7] Soviet disapproval of the Marshall Plan threatened Soviet opposition in the Austrian State Treaty negotiations. Nevertheless, the Council of Ministers decided on 8 July 1947 to cooperate in establishing the ERP organization in Paris.[8] The conservative Austrian Foreign Minister Karl Gruber of the People's Party quickly overcame his original fear that pro-ERP decision would destroy the chances for a quick conclusion of an Austrian Treaty. Prominent Socialists, including even the right-wing Social Democrat and "Cold Warrior" Vice Chancellor Adolf Schärf, continued to emphasize Austria's formal neutrality in the Cold War. Although the Socialist party disagreed with U.S. economic policies, after intensive discussions in the party and the Socialist dominated Trade Union movement, the Socialists accepted the reformist concept of ERP aid that focused on a "mixed economy,"[9] they were also prepared to accept repercussions on the level of the great power conflict on the Austrian situation. In the official Paris negotiations Gruber ordered diplomatic caution ("*auf sanften Pfoten gehen*"[10]) and restraint during the negotiations but asked to exploit opportunities without taking sides in the great power conflict.

This extremely cautious and somewhat opportunistic approach to

European integration should be considered a basic policy line, although in 1948 and 1949, with the Prague *coup d'état* and the growing international tensions and conflicts about Berlin, Austrian Conservatives and Socialists took a distinct pro-Western ideological position. On those occasions when a possible chance for a State Treaty existed, the Austrians expressed their inherent political ambivalence to a position of de facto neutrality. It was not by accident that the Great Coalition Government (the last Communist minister had resigned in late 1947) was prepared to stand up to Soviet protests after the signing of the OEEC treaty on 16 April 1948, since at that time there was no treaty solution in sight. But although the Soviets protested, they did not use the alleged violation of the Second Control Agreement to tighten military controls in their zones of occupation, to separate Austria along the Enns-border-line, or to blockade Vienna, which was under quadripartite administration.

De jure, all of Austria was included in the bilateral ERP agreement of 2 July 1948 between Austria and the United States as a result of interventions by both the U.S. Military High Commissioner and his principal diplomatic advisor[11] who feared the partition of Austria. De facto, however, the Soviet zone of occupation obtained only a minimum of the total ERP aid,[12] which in 1953 was around 18 percent.[13] Even such minimal aid to the Soviet sector of Austria was criticized in the U.S. Congress as "red aid." A very strict system of licensing and screening of Austrian exports, established during 1948 and 1949,[14] resulted in total Austrian governmental cooperation. After the Korean War Austria observed the Cocom-embargo de facto.[15]

A geo-strategic analysis of Austria's participation in the OEEC shows that the original links of the Austrian economy to Eastern Europe were considerably reduced during the Cold War. For its cooperation with the West Austria received plentiful ERP funds. Eastern imports were reduced to 8 percent in 1955 (compared with 32 percent in 1937). In spite of the USIA (Soviet owned firms that had formerly been German property) connections, exports to the East fell from 28 percent in 1937 to 8 percent in 1955. Imports from OEEC countries rose from 40 percent to 75 percent, exports from 53 percent to 71 percent.[16]

Whereas Austria tried to gain from the investments under OEEC supervision as much as possible, she reduced her role in other Western European integration projects—such as the Council of Europe—to the position of silent observer. From the first preparatory meetings in 1948, an Austrian parliamentary delegation, headed by the ÖVP representative Eduard Ludwig, cooperated in the Council debates. But the Foreign

Department of the Chancellery expressed a number of reservations about full-fledged membership. Austria should be represented in all meetings and events aiming at European integration (i.e., Western European integration) but should not take any initiatives due to its precarious international position between East and West. Furthermore, many Austrian diplomats at the time did not believe that a "European Parliament" and a "European Constitution" were realistic goals for the near future.[17]

A lack of concern for the "European idea" existed in the Foreign Department; Foreign Minister Gruber was much more interested in the United Nations than European integration; it also extended the beginning to the Socialist parliamentary group in the Austrian National Council, which did not send a representative to the first meeting of the Parliamentary Assembly in August 1949 in Strasbourg.[18] It is obvious that in the late 1940s and early 1950s the Austrian government did not plan to become deeply involved in the Council of Europe and Soviet pressure cannot be blamed exclusively for this lack of infatuation with the European idea. Austria's offical status with the Council of Europe started as that of an "informal" member and changed in late 1951 to "observer" status.[19] Neither the French nor the British governments wanted Austria to become a full member because of possible negative consequences for Austria's relationship with the Soviet Union. The Austrian government itself feared negative effects on its efforts to conclude a State Treaty.[20]

The Austrian Cabinet did not decide to apply for full membership in the Council of Europe until February 1956. The ÖVP-Chancellor Julius Raab dragged this discussion out both because he feared Soviet protests portraying the Council of Europe as a branch of NATO and because he had negative feelings towards the *"Straßburger Sandkastenspiel"*[21] and the *"Europabastler."*[22] Pressure by Socialists (since 1953) and ÖVP-parliamentarians, however, helped overcome the chancellor's dilatory approach.

Austria's full participation in the Council of Europe did not mean that it was on her way to become a full-fledged member of the European club. Some of the "Austro-Europeans" like the Socialist Karl Cernetz or the Conservative Barthold Stürgkh pressed in this direction; they wanted Austria to become a member of the European Coal and Steel Community (ECSC) as well. Established in 1952, the ECSC was the first step toward the United States of Europe because it created a common, unrestricted market for coal and steel and thereby became the precondition for the European Common Market coming into existence in 1958.

The key foreign affairs decision makers in the Great Coalition, however, had agreed long before the declaration of permanent neutrality in 1955 on other foreign policy priorities. The first goal was to work towards full participation in the United Nations. The "*Montanunion*,"as the ECSC was often called at that time, was given lower priority. After 1955 the neutrality argument was certainly strengthening this long-range concept. Obviously, the Foreign Office viewed the supra-national principle of the original Schuman Plan, the basis for the ECSC, as negative. The Ministry for Trade and Commerce, however, tried to emphasize the positive economic aspects of the *Montanunion* and the fact that after the establishment of a common market for coal in 1953 by the "six" Austria suddenly was excluded in bilateral trade with these member-states of the *Montanunion*.[23]

From the end of 1951, experts in the Ministry for Trade and Commerce asked for negotiations. But not until October 1952 was the "*Hohe Behörde*" (the High Authority, the executive body of the ECSC) confronted with the Austrian plans. An "Austrian observer" would be sent to Luxemburg, but would not specify the form of cooperation. After the accreditation of an Austrian representative in Luxemburg in May 1953, the aim was to conclude a special arrangement, especially one covering trade tariffs. When in October 1954 these unilateral negotiations failed Austria stopped her efforts toward a "special agreement" with the ECSC and decided to wait and see what the "six" would offer in the future.[24]

After the phase of no negotiations (December 1954 - early 1956), the Austrian representatives reported to Vienna. In June 1956 the Foreign Department made it quite clear that Austria's "political status," prevented it from joining the common market at the moment.[25] This statement is striking, in the light of Austria's tendencies to be a de facto "secret ally" of the West, not only ideologically but also militarily.[26] Austria's growing ties with the West in practice meant the gradual rearmament of an Austrian army "nucleus" under U.S. supervision since 1949 and even cautious advances by individual Austrian politicians towards NATO-membership before 1953. Although Chancellor Julius Raab did change Austria's inflexible pro-Western foreign policy under Gruber in 1953 and 1954, he allowed certain sections of the "secret ally program" to continue even after 1955, which was against the spirit of the neutrality law. Some examples from the post-1955 period prove that the neutrality law—in a narrower legal sense—was not broken, but that Austria took part in or tolerated military and intelligence programs favoring the Western Alliance. Such programs were extremely problematic from the perspective of neutrality policy:

* Rearmament of the Austrian army with U.S. financial assistance and under U.S. guidelines (which from the U.S. perspective initially meant "to be of direct assistance to the defense of NATO area in the event of general war"[27]);

* U.S. and NATO Transit over Austrian territory of military "soft supplies" (ammunition, and the like);

* Military overflights (several hundreds between 1955 and 1958 and during the Lebanon Crisis of 1958);

* U.S. Escapee Program from Eastern Europe in order to obtain intelligence information;

* Cocom, resulting in economic warfare against Eastern Europe and the Soviet Union.[28]

Thus, in a number of cases—even as far as strategic questions were concerned—Austria was openly oriented toward the West. On the other hand, Chancellor Raab tried to continue a special type of "*Ostpolitik*." He tried to reduce the reparations owed to the Soviet Union under the Austrian State Treaty and he worked hard at filling Austria's neutrality with substance to improve its credibility in case of conflict. Therefore Austria's post-1955 foreign policy was always very mindful of the limits of Soviet willingness to accept Austria's pro-Western inclinations.

During ten years of intensive negotiations with Soviet officers, diplomats and experts over to the Austrian State Treaty it had become clear that what the Soviets feared above all was a new "*Anschluß*" and the development of a new overbearing German power in Central Europe. Even an indirect economic "*Anschluß*" to the Federal Republic—in light of various and tight pro-Western policies, was unacceptable for the Soviet Union and its extreme security interests. As a consequence of Austria's "secret ally" tendencies and open pro-Western ideological and cultural policies, the economic margin in the Cold War was extremely small.

Therefore, Austrian politicians and diplomats (from both leading parties) were reluctant to test Soviet good will in the field of European integration except in the case of the Council of Europe. After the debate about the "European Defense Community" in 1954, the Council had lost the character of a tight military or close political union. When in July 1956 Great Britain proposed a "greater European" solution by developing plans for a "free trade zone" within the framework of the OEEC, Foreign Minister Leopold Figl and others welcomed this effort to build a larger free trade area beyond the small European community of the six. Perhaps this approach was even seen as a possibility for later full membership in the ECSC, as Figl indicated in Strasburg.[29]

The events in Hungary in 1956, however, proved that the Soviet Union still was prepared to react with full military strength and brutality against immediate threats to their security interests and sphere of influence. Therefore in 1957, Austria intensified its cooperation with the other neutrals (Switzerland and Sweden), concerning the integration in Europe.[30]

After the signing of the treaties of Rome on 25 March 1957, the Socialist State Secretary in the Foreign Office Bruno Kreisky summed up the various pros and cons about full Austrian integration in the Montanunion states:

Pro integration:

1. Integration would enhance production methods by increasing foreign trade, automation, use of atomic energy and research;
2. The common market would help initiate political integration;
3. Economic cooperation would help to overcome bilateralism in Europe (OEEC and ECU, European Currency Unit);
4. The common market is important for Austria because in 1956 Austria exported 49.9 percent into Western European countries and imported 50.6 percent of its total imports from there;
5. Common customs tariffs would lead to protectionism and would endanger non-member countries such as the Scandinavian states, Switzerland and Austria.

Contra integration:

1. Existence of politically stable and prospering small states (Switzerland, Sweden, Netherlands, Belgium) argues against integration;
2. The primary aim of the Montanunion integration process is to establish a politically and militarily unified Europe, but the Common Market leads to discrimination against all other states; One could overcome these effects by creating a free trade area and initiating special economic measures favoring outsiders;
3. Harmonization of political economies;
4. Integration would create problems for agriculture;
5. Integration is not compatible with neutrality policy;
6. As far as underdeveloped countries are concerned, "Europe is not enough"; one should work towards international solidarity and international economic integration; "A Swiss politician said that "Switzerland cannot live with Europe alone!" With regard to European integration one has to say: "Europe cannot live with Europe alone!"[31]

In addition to these economic and geopolitical arguments, State

Secretary Kreisky, inspired by the legal department of the Foreign Office (Stephan Verosta and later Rudolf Kirchschläger), brought the neutrality question into the debate, especially after his appointment to Foreign Minister in 1959. Kreisky was aware that a free trade area would have been the only form of economic integration compatible with Austria's neutrality policy at the time. He brought his party, the SPÖ, in line with observing Austrian neutrality in all negotiations about European integration and backed chancellor Raab's course towards an integration through a large free trade association within the framework of the OEEC.[32] Despite heterogeneous positions, the SPÖ (with the exception of the "European" Karl Czernetz) favored the Free Trade Association during 1956 and November 1958. Within the OEEC, an intergovernmental committee, headed by the British State Minister Reginald Maudling ("Maudling Committee"), would work out a concept for this larger Free Trade Area.

After the "Maudling Committee" talks failed in November 1958, internal debates in the Socialist party created two lobbies. On the one hand experts of the Austrian Chambers of Labor—one of the Socialist think tanks in Austria's chamber system and social partnership—and experts of the Trade Union movement favored bilateral negotiations of Austria with the EEC; on the other hand, Kreisky, along the line of the reports of Fritz Kolb, a Socialist diplomat with the "high authority" of the European Coal and Steel Community, developed a common approach for Scandinavians, Britains, Swiss and Austrians. Early in 1959 Kreisky modified these ideas and proposed a "small free trade zone" consisting of Sweden, Denmark, Norway, Switzerland, Great Britain, Austria and Portugal.[33]

Chancellor Julius Raab backed Kreisky's views. After the lost elections of 1959, when Kreisky became Foreign Minister, Raab declared that Austria was prepared to join the seven non-EEC States in Stockholm.[34] Undoubtedly, Raab influenced by conservative interest groups in his own party (the peasants movements, small trade and commerce), held to the course of independent neutrality, favoring the United Nations and reducing engagement with the Council of Europe and the EEC. Like the Chamber of Labor, the Federation of Austrian Industrialists favored direct Austrian "solo" negotiations with the EEC.[35] Raab and his followers in the ÖVP overruled the Industrialists and the ÖVP Minister of Commerce, Fritz Bock, who favored closer relations with the EEC.

Within the Socialist Party, the chairman Bruno Pittermann and the head of the Trade Unions, Franz Olah, sided with Kreisky, but with a different set of arguments. Pittermann launched ideological attacks against the EEC, which he saw as a *"Bourgeois bloc"* favoring *"Kartellkapitalismus"* in Europe.[36] Kreisky focused on neutrality and the risks of a future German domination of the Austrian economy.

After 1959 Austria had to deal once more with the geopolitical perceptions of the two superpowers which were not in line with Austria's interests regarding European integration. In January 1959 the Soviet ambassador in Vienna, Sergej G. Lapin, made it clear that a bilateral association with the EEC would reduce Austria's sovereignty and would incorporate Austria's economy into the military bloc of NATO, which in turn would contradict Austrian neutrality policy.[37] These interventions continued in the autumn of 1959, indicating that an *"Anschluß"* (annexation) of Austria by the EEC would be interpreted as a violation of article IV of the State Treaty, explicitly prohibiting the *"Anschluß an Deutschland."*[38]

Foreign Minister Kreisky realized the far-reaching consequences of the Soviet security concerns and insisted the neutrality remain the guiding principle for Austrian foreign policy. Kreisky realized that the Soviets would try to prevent a "German power increase" as result of Austria's joining the EEC (53 million Germans in the EEC plus 6 million Austrians). He knew that the French had the same reservations. Therefore Kreisky asked for coordination and cooperation from the other European neutrals to harmonize their interpretations of neutrality. The first question in the negotiations, according to Kreisky, should be whether the neutrals could accept integration. Kreisky argued "The question of Austria's relationship with the EEC will become without a doubt the toughest touchstone for Austrian neutrality policy" (*"Die Frage des Verhältnisses Österreichs zur EWG werde sohin der bisher schwerste Prüfstein der österreichischen Neutralitätspolitik sein"*).[39]

Kreisky's efforts to coordinate a neutral approach toward the EEC, however were heavily critized by the Kennedy Administration. George Ball, the Under Secretary, feared that a close association of the neutrals would change the original geopolitical identity of the EEC as an anti-Soviet and anti-Communist union. After high-level talks between Great Britain and the United States in January 1962, the State Department described a possible association of the neutrals with the EEC as "not a desirable solution," because "it would tend to impair the effectiveness of the EEC" and could be used as a precedent for other countries, thereby isolating Finland.[40]

These deep concerns were openly articultated in 1961. Great Britain had started bilateral negotiations with the EEC. Austria, like Sweden and Switzerland, had presented a letter to EEC President Ludwig Erhard proposing negotiations under article 238 of the treaties of Rome ("association").[41] The United States was not prepared to accept Austria's reservations about treaty making power in foreign trade and suspension of provisions of the treaty of association in case of military conflicts as a consequence of Austria's permant neutrality.

During talks between President John F. Kennedy, Chancellor Gorbach and Foreign Minister Kreisky the United States echoed Soviet concerns by stating that an association could create problems as documented in intelligence evaluations from Czech sources. The Soviet Union could interpret an association under article 238 as an open violation of the State Treaty. Therefore, President Kennedy asked to take the Soviet concerns into consideration and favored quiet diplomacy to solve commercial problems.[42]

In the internal briefing papers for the President, the real U.S. military concerns were partly cloaked in economic arguments (namely, the creation of a new preferential system would affect the interests of the U.S. directly), which should drive Austria into a bilateral agreement similar to the 1956 agreement between the High Authority of the Coal and Steel Community and the Austrian Government.[43] In the internal decision making process, however, the real reason was postulated: "Association of the neutrals would impede the political integration of the EEC".[44]

Foreign Minister Kreisky was held "responsible for the Austrian position on association and on the tactics of solidarity with the Swiss and Sweden".[45] As early as 7 June 1961 he informed U.S. Secretary of State Dean Rusk about the Neutrals' plans for special EEC association to stabilize the integration after the United Kingdom's steps towards full participation in the European Community:

> It is equally obvious that the non-comitted countries of Europe could not follow this way [of the United Kingdom and others], as the institutional arrangements and the supranational character of the Community as well as the intensity of its integration would imperil their international political status.
>
> The undisturbed continuity of this status, however, lies not only in the interest of these countries but equally so in the paramount interest of Europe and the West. As the recent years have shown, the neutrality of these countries is nothing sterile but is fulfilling an active and constructive function in the interest of the free world.
>
> A subordination of these countries to the supranational structure of the EEC resulting in majority decisions in the whole field of economic and commercial policy would be clearly inconsistent with their legal obligations. This would

undoubtedly shake the general international confidence in them which is the sole warrant for their continued existence and function.[46]

The Austrian side, too, was fully capable of using the Cold War weapon—but in reverse—by trying to convince the U.S. government "that Austria is an integral part of Western Europe and must participate in the integration movement to the fullest extent consistent with its neutral status if the country is not to be isolated, abandoned, and drawn toward the Soviet Bloc."[47]

Soviet interventions against Austria's association were confined to threats, which became more obvious in 1962 and 1963. Nikita Khrushchev declared that Austria's incorporation into the EEC would have a negative impact on Austria and her status of neutrality, since the EEC was an instrument of NATO. Although the Soviet Union understood Austria's situation, Khrushchev argued he had to issue a warning not to violate the State Treaty or Austria's neutral status.[48]

In 1963 the Soviet threats vis-à-vis the Austrian Government were repeated and intensified. The Kremlin warned Austria about the "negative consequences on our bilateral relations and for Central European developments." The Soviets made it clear that the situation was becoming very serious indeed Soviet ambassador Awilow in Vienna used the words "I implore you, the situation is indeed grave." ("*ich beschwöre Sie, die Situation ist wirklich ernst*"), when he intervened and talked to Kreisky on 22 May 1963.[49]

The Austrian Foreign Minister took these concerns very seriously. Kreisky emphasized in cabinet meetings that one had to take the Soviet fears into account. He warned against using the propaganda argument that Austria was not viable without close ties to the EEC, which would mean an economic *Anschluss* with Germany from the Soviet perspective. In 1963 he again favored a free trade solution and a treaty with the EEC which would calm down the French concerns with regard to Great Britain.

Within the coalition, the ÖVP slowly began to change their party position after Julius Raab left office in 1961. Raab had always made it clear that he was favoring a strict neutrality policy in accordance with Kreisky's views. Raab did not want Austria "to starve as a consequence of strict neutrality policies" ("*daß Österreich nicht in Neutralität verhungert*"), or, to become economically isolated. Yet Raab was not prepared to endanger Austria's neutrality for "a mess of potage" ("*um ein Linsengericht*").[50]

The changes in the Austrian government 1963 reduced the power of

Kreisky's Foreign Office in the integration negotiations and strengthened the ÖVP Minister of Trade and Commerce, Fritz Bock. The new
Austrian government started to work towards direct bilateral negotiations to join the EEC. The question of Austria's integration became a key
issue of the new government. The EEC agreed to work out a study
concerning the possible arrangement with Austria and started exploratory talks.

In Austria, this approach continued to be subject to fierce debates, even
within the various ÖVP lobbies.[51] In secret discussions with Bock,
Kreisky tried to continue a strict "neutrality first" policy. Kreisky warned
explicitly against restrictive interpretations of Austria's neutrality; for
him neutrality was not just a military concept. To reduce Austrian
neutrality to its bare-bone military aspects would be as dangerous as a
singular emphasis on the customs union with the EEC. Western and
Eastern Europeans might once again remind Austro-German of the
customs union project before World War II.[52] Kreisky warned against a
"strictly economic" perspective advocated by the director of the Austrian
Institute for Economic Research (*Österreichisches Institut für
Wirtschaftsforschung*) Franz Nemschak, who always tried to prove that
an agreement with the EEC was the only chance for Austria's future
economic survival.

As to Bock's position, Kreisky agreed to start exploratory talks; but
Kreisky blocked the custom unions project, which was intensively
pushed by the Germans, arguing that they only wanted to save the poor
Austrians. He underlined that one should stop undermining Austria's
economic and political viability—a customs union with the Federal
Republic was not the key for Austria's economic survival.[53] Bock, on the
other hand, saw Austrian neutrality in a more narrow sense than Kreisky.
He limited neutrality to the military sphere, not accepting restrictions on
neutrality policy in peace times. But Bock was prepared to keep the
Soviet concerns in mind and to stick to the European Free Trade
Association (EFTA) membership—even during the exploratory talks
with the EEC.[54]

In the 1960s, besides Soviet, American and domestic concerns regarding the possible EEC integration, Austria was also confronted with
French complaints. These were expressed on the highest level by
President De Gaulle and were related to his permanent antipathy toward
the United Kingdom's integration approach. De Gaulle disliked Austria's
coalition with Great Britain in the EFTA and saw a special role for the
Austrians as "*Danubiens*" in a larger European context.[55] Between 1960

and 1962 De Gaulle himself seemed inclined to favor a unilateral association of Austria with the EEC, respecting Austrian sovereignty and its status of neutrality. In 1962, Austria, from De Gaulles' perspective, was *la clef de l'Europe*[56] and should function as some kind of "show-window" for the EEC toward the Communist satellite states in Eastern Europe. In 1962, during an official visit by Chancellor Gorbach and Foreign Minister Kreisky, the French President remarked that he was disappointed that Austria had not yet developed concrete association plans. In 1963, however, the *Quai d'Orsay* indicated the risks of such a decision because of possible Soviet intervention.[57]

De Gaulle, who wanted a clear decision, especially criticized Austria's active participation in the EFTA. Eventually, Austria's policy of playing EFTA melodies and trying to sing with the EEC, brought the French government into the anti-EEC association camp, favoring a strictly neutral Austria, which, moreover was useful in the process of detente and a future all European integration process.[58] De Gaulle's policy of detente towards Eastern European countries certainly had much higher priority than Soviet negative reactions to the EEC-association question. In this spectrum Austria was important as "a Danubien country opening the way into the East *(Donauland...und weil es den Weg nach Osten öffnet).*[59] In 1967 the French Foreign Minister Couve de Murveille emphazised that France was primarily interested in stability in East Central Europe and therefore favored non-integration for Austria, not only as a result of Soviet security interests, but also as a means of containing growing German economic influence in the area, which had repercussions for the internal EEC stability.[60] The new Austrian ÖVP Chancellor Josef Klaus tried to revive the Austrian drive into the EEC in 1964. Till 1967 exploratory talks and negotiations were continued striving to bring about a special arrangement between the EEC and Austria, and even introducing a de facto customs-union resembling an economic union.[61]

An Italian veto, however, based on differences with Austria over the South Tyrol question, finally stopped these negotiations. They were resumed in November 1969. In 1972, after the signing of two interim agreements and two global agreements with the European Community on 30 June 1967, Bruno Kreisky, who had advanced to Chancellor, spoke in the National Council of the final bridging ("*Brückenschlag*") between EFTA and EEC. He also spoke of the changes in the import-export structure as a result of Austria's exclusion from the "Common Market".[62] Even the Federation of Austrian Industrialists has accepted this effect as "better inner European diversification of Austrian foreign trade" ("*bessere*

innereuropäische Streuung des österreichischen Außenhandels").[63] In
1959, Austrian exports into EFTA countries amounted to ÖS 2.9 billion,
and in 1970 to ÖS 21 billion, raising the EFTA percentage of Austria's
exports from 11.6 percent to more than 28 percent. During the same time,
exports into EEC countries rose from ÖS 12.4 billion to 30.6 billion, a
decline from 49.3 percent in 1959 to 38.7 percent in 1970. The change
was not so significant for imports: EEC imports declined from 57.2
percent to 55.9 percent, EFTA imports rose from 11.7 percent to 19.6
percent.[64]

The 1972 solution was based partly on the negotiations of the 1960s
but was primarily a free-trade-zone-solution respecting Austria's absence from political bindings. In an official note, the Soviet Union
stressed the importance of the State Treaty and Austrian neutrality, but
did not oppose EFTA's association with the EEC and asked for consultations on the bilateral trade relations.[65]

Paul Luif has analyzed the economic background studies from the
1950s and 1960s, most of which advocated Austria's immediate integration in the EEC by stressing economic arguments. Luif concluded that
these studies failed to foresee the real economic developments and
overestimated the negative aspects of Austria's non-association with the
EEC.[66]

From a historical perspective, it is interesting to note that similar
discussions have arisen in Austria over the last two or three years as a
consequence of the EC plans to create a closed common market by 1993.
Once again, a large number of economic experts try to prove that Austrian
viability depends on the complete integration into the EC; some even try
to demonstrated the opposite.[67] As has been pointed out, all "precise"
economic prophecies of the 1950s and 1960s that Austria could not
survive without joining the EEC have been wrong.

Since 1991, information brochures have tried to persuade the voters
for or against the EC integration of Austria. Austria's acceptance into the
EC would result in a plebiscite, changing large parts of its constitution.[68]
Although in the 1960s most legal experts agreed that Austria's neutrality
had not been compatible with the charter and aims of the EC, in the most
recent debate the majority voted for legal compatibility.[69]

As most recent public opinion polls show, the Austrian public has
become very sensitive about the question of neutrality, which is consti-
tuting an important pillar of Austrian identity.[70] We are still confronted
with this question even though the Cold War has ended. Instead, regional
and internal conflicts have erupted on Eastern and Southeastern Euro-

pean soil. Although the external structures have changed considerably, Austrian neutrality has been gaining new functions. And there still exist a number of other continuities, dating back to the first debates about Austria's position in the European integration of the 1950s and 1960s such as the relationship between France and Germany (especially after German unification), as well as a possible "German-Austrian" super-power within the EC (with the German economy controlling 38 percent of foreign capital in Austria[71]). Fifty percent of Austria's imports came from the FRG, and 30 percent of the exports go to Germany. These facts already have disturbed the French Government. With regard to Austria's neutrality reservation in the letter to Brussels in 1989, EC officials and state governments alike point out the possible future development of the EC into a tighter political and military union. This aim will certainly be strengthened as a result of the war in Yugoslavia and other regional conflicts.

The key question for Europe, will be whether it is able to cope with the enormous economic and social problems—intensified by nationalistic internal quarrels—in East Central Europe and the successor states of the Soviet Union.[72] And in this European conflict—which could end in a new separation of Europe into rich and poor European states along old Cold War lines—Austria again "is in between." In this context, Austria has to decide carefully about the adaptation of her international position and foreign policy to the broad changes of the geopolitical environment. There are no signs, however that these "greater European" views are enlarged to include the North-South-dimensions despite a growing world-wide interdependence on a number of levels. Whether Daniel Burstein's forecasts in *Euroquake*, that Austria will join the EC but remain neutral and therefore stay outside the new EC defense union,[73] will become true or not is unpredictable. From historical experience, however, it seems that Austria's "long shadow of neutrality" will continue.

NOTES

1. Sozialwissenschaftliche Studiengesellschaft, Pressekonferenz (Vienna, 1991), 5.

2. *Profil*, 13 January 1992, 16.

3. Sozialwissenschaftliche Studiengesellschaft, 33. Bericht (Vienna, 1965), 15.

4. John Paxton, ed., *Statesman's Year-Book. Statistical and Historical Annual of the States of the World for the Year 1977-1978* (London, 1977), 39.

5. Manfried Rauchensteiner, *Die Zwei: Die Große Koalition in Österreich 1945-1966* (Vienna, 1987), 106-108.

6. Geoffrey Keyes (US High Commissioner in Austria) to George C. Marshall (Secretary of State), undated, George C. Marshall Foundation, National Archives project, xerox.

7. See Günter Bischof and Josef Leidenfrost, eds., *Die Bevormundete Nation. Österreich und die Alliierten 1945-1949* (Innsbruck, 1988).

8. Wilfried Mähr, *Der Marshallplan in Österreich* (Graz, 1989), 81-172. New Austrian material is used by Florian Weiß, "Auf sanften Pfoten gehen. Die österreichische Bundesregierung und die Anfänge der westeuropäischen Integration," Master's thesis, Munich, 1989, 17-31, and by Martin Hehemann, "Die SPÖ und die Anfänge der europäischen Integration bis zur Grüdung der EFTA," Master's thesis, Münster, 1990, 27-31. Both studies are available in the Bruno Kreisky Foundation, 1050 Vienna, Rechte Wienzeile 97.

9. Fritz Weber, "Die österreichische Sozialdemokratie zu Beginn des Kalten Krieges," in *Der Marshall-Plan und die europäische Linke*, ed. Othmar Nikola Haberl and Lutz Niethammer (Frankfurt Main, 1986), 184.

10. Amtsvermerk, Besprechung Gruber (Foreign Minister) und Vollgruber (ambassador), 8 July 1947, Zl. Amerika 2, 107.651 pol./47, Bundeskanzleramt, Auswärtige Angelegenheiten [Federal Chancellery, Foreign Affairs], hereafter cited BKA, AA, Archiv der Republik, Vienna [Archives of the Republic], hereafter cited AdR.

11. Günter Bischof, "Between Responsibility and Rehabilitation: Austria in International Politics, 1940-1950," Ph.D. diss, Harvard University, 1989, 509-520.

12. Arno Einwitschläger, *Amerikanische Wirtschaftspolitik in Österreich 1945-1949* (Vienna, 1986), 125-132.

13. Weiss, Auf sanften Pfoten, 112.

14. Einwitschläger, *Wirtschaftspolitik*, 80-88.

15. Oliver Rathkolb, "Historische Bewährungsproben des Neutralitätsgesetzes 1955 am Beispiel der US-amerikanischen Österreich-Politik 1955 bis 1959," in *Verfassung: Juristisch-politische und sozialwissenschaftliche Beiträge anläßlich des 70-Jahr-Jubiläums des Bundes-Verfassungsgesetzes*, ed. Nikolaus Dimmel and Alfred-Johannes Noll (Vienna, 1990), 136.

16. Einwitschläger, *Wirtschaftspolitik*, 31.

17. Amtsvermerk, II Pol., Zl. 116.881/48, Box 67, BKA, AA, AdR.

18. Ludwig (head of delegation) to Gruber (Foreign Minister), 15 August 1949, 3, II pol., Box 103, Int.2, Zl.80.108 pol 49, Bes 103, II pol, BKA, AA, AdR.

19. Wolfgang Burtscher, "Österreichs Annäherung an den Europarat von 1949 bis zur Vollmitgliedschaft im Jahre 1956", in *Österreich im Europarat 1956-1986: Bilanz einer 30jährigen Mitgliedschaft*, ed. Waldemar Hummer and Gerhard Wagner (Vienna, 1988), 40-46.

20. Jenewein (Austrian Observer) to Heinrich Schmid (ambassador), 12 February 1952, Bes, 197, II Pol, BKA, AA, AdR.

21. Burtscher, Österreichs Annäherung, 48.

22. Lujo Toncic-Sorinj, *Erfüllte Träume: Kroatien - Österreich - Europa* (Vienna, 1982), 228.

23. More details in Weiss, Auf sanften Pfoten, 80.

24. Ibid., 87-97.

25. Ibid., S.153

26. Gerald Stourzh, "The Origins of Austrian Neutrality," in *Neutrality: Changing Concepts and Practices*, ed. Alan T. Leonhard (Lanham, 1988), 38-40.

27. Rathkolb, Historische Bewährungsproben, 126.

28. Rathkolb, Historische Bewährungsproben, 124-130.

29. *Wiener Zeitung*, 24 October 1956.

30. Weiss, Auf sanften Pfoten, 158.

31. Notes by Bruno Kreisky, undated, Folder: European Integration, Stiftung Bruno Kreisky Archives (cited hereafter SBKA).

32. More details in Hehemann, SPÖ, 128 ff.

33. Hehemann, SPÖ, 124.

34. Hans Mayrzedt and Waldemar Hummer, *20 Jahre österreichische Neutralitäts- und Europapolitik (1955-1975), Dokumentation*, Vol. I (Vienna, 1976), 328.

35. Paul Luif, "Die internationale Politik der Österreichischen Volkspartei," in *Schwarz-bunter Vogel. Studien zu Programm, Politik und Struktur der ÖVP*, 149.

36. Hehemann, SPÖ, 149.

37. Bruno Kreisky, Bericht an den Ministerrat, 10 June 1963, 3, Folder: European Integration, SBKA.

38. Ibid.

39. Protokoll über die Abteilungsleitersitzung auf Schloß Wartenstein, 6 July 1961, Projekt BMWF 1990/91, 11, SBKA.

40. Platzer (ambassador) to Bundesministerium für Auswärtige Angelegenheiten, 14 March 1962, Folder USA, SBKA.

41. More details in Paul Luif, *Neutrale in die EG? Die westeuropäische Integration und die neutralen Staaten* (Vienna, 1988), 95.

42. Bruno Kreisky, *Im Strom der Politik: Der Memoiren zweiter Teil* (Vienna, 1988), 176.

43. Briefing Paper for President's Meeting with Austrian Chancellor, 26 April 1962, Declassified Documents Collection 1978,B,393 (Original in the Johnson Library, Austin Texas).

44. Ibid., III, Discussion.

45. Ibid., II, Talking Points.

46. Kreisky (Foreign Minister) to Dean Rusk (Secretary of State), 7 June 1961, Folder USA, SBKA.

47. Briefing Paper, III Discussion, 2 (see note 43).

48. Kreisky, Bericht, 4; vgl. auch Kreisky, *Im Strom der Politik*, 177.

49. Kreisky, Bericht, 6 and 5.

50. Cited after Luif, *Neutrale*, 99 (article by Raab in the *Österreichische Neue Tageszeitung*, 6 December 1959).

51. Ibid., 100.

52. Auszug aus der Verhandlungsschrift Nr.8 über die Sitzung des Ministerrates am 28. Mai 1963, 18, Box EWG, SBKA.

53. Ibid.

54. Ibid., 19-21.

55. Oliver Rathkolb, "De Gaulle 'im Spiegel österreichischer Außenpolitik und Diplomatie 1958/59-1965," in *Jahrbuch für Zeitgeschichte 1990/91*, ed. Österreichische Gesellschaft für Zeitgeschichte (Vienna 1991), 87.

56. Ibid., 88.

57. Kreisky, Bericht, 2.

58. Rathkolb, De Gaulle, 91.

59. Josef Klaus, *Macht und Ohnmacht in Österreich. Konfrontationen und Versuche* (Vienna, 1971), 319.

60. Toncic-Sorinj, *Erfüllte Träume*, 379.

61. Luif, *Neutrale*, 97.

62. Erklärung von Bundeskanzler Dr. Kreisky in der Sondersitzung des Nationalrates vom 25.7.1972, Box Speeches 1972, SBKA.

63. Rosmarie Atzenhofer, "Österreichische Integrationspolitik seit 1948: Zwischen EG-Diktat und dem Streben nach Unabhängigkeit," in *Der un-heimliche Anschluss: Österreich und die EG*, ed. Margit Scherb and Inge Morawetz (Vienna 1988), 83.

64. Erkärung Kreisky, 10.

65. Atzenhofer, Integrationspolitik, 88. Compare Manfred Rotter, "Austria's Permanent Neutrality and the Free Trade Agreement with the EEC: Strategies to Reduce Dependencies," in *Small States in Europe and Dependence*, ed. Otmar Höll (Vienna, 1983), 306-318.

66. Luif, *Neutrale*, 111.

67. Fritz Breuss, Fritz Achebeck, *Die Vollendung des EG-Binnenmarktes. Gesmatwirtschaftliche Auswirkungen für Österreich: Makroökonomische Modellsimulationen* (Vienna, 1989), trying to underline the need for full participation; see also *Ausweg Europa? Wirtschaftspolitische Optionen für Österreich*, ed. Beirat für gesellschafts-, wirtschafts- und umweltpolitische Alternativen (Vienna 1989) arguing against an EEC integration of Austria.

68. E.g. as pro-EEC brochure compare *EWR ABC: Auswirkungen des Europäischen Wirtschaftsraums auf Österreich* (Vienna, 1991); as a continuing warning, see press information service *Informationsdienst Österreich und Europa*, 1989-1991 ff.

69. Compare *Österreich und der EG-Binnenmarkt* (Vienna, 1988), 31f.

70. More details and references in Helmut Kramer, "Öffentliche Meinung und die österreichische EG-Entscheidung im Jahre 1989," *SWS-Rundschau* 31 (1991): 191-202.

71. Wilhelmine Goldmann, "Kapitalverflechtung Österreich-Deutschland: Österreich als Partner oder Commis?" in *Österreich und Deutschlands Größe. Ein schlampiges Verhältnis*, ed. Oliver Rathkolb, Georg Schmid, Gernot Heiss, (Salzburg, 1990), 167. Compare also *Wem gehört Österreich wirklich?* ed. Wilhelmine Goldmann, Elisabeth Beer, Brigitte Ederer, Roland Lang, Miron Passweg and Rudolf Reitzner (Vienna 1991).

72. Thomas Nowotny, *Europtimismus - oder warum das Abendland nicht untergeht* (Vienna, 1991), 225-261.

73. Daniel Burstein, *Euroquake: Europe's Explosive Economic Challenge Will Change the World* (New York, 1991), 344f.

EC Membership and the "Velvet" Revolution: The Impact of Recent Political Changes on Austria's Economic Position in Europe

Felix Butschek

Which Austria in which Europe?

It is comparatively easy to answer questions about the effects of Austria's envisaged membership in the European Community. While present data suffice to analyse the problem, the historical perspective is needed to provide meaningful answers. Whatever political structure will be found to integrate the Eastern European countries into a union, these nations have already left their former economic systems, organizations and interrelations behind, and are increasingly concentrating their economic activities on the West. This is especially true of Austria's neighbors, the East Central European countries, the "successor states," of the Habsburg Monarchy—Czechoslovakia, Hungary, Poland and what used to be "Yugoslavia". Thus, the Austrian position in a new Europe can no longer be analyzed in the framework prevailing before 1989, but has to be considered under the new circumstances, resulting from the changes of 1989, which will have considerable effects on Austria's regional economic position.

To understand the ambivalent influences to which Austria will be exposed in the 1990s, one has to look back to the early industrialization of the nation, which developed in a political context quite different from the one of today. Present-day Austria was in the nineteenth century part of the Austrian-Hungarian monarchy, a leading European power of 51 million inhabitants in her late period. The monarchy included—leaving aside the regions of the Hungarian crown—the present Austrian territory,

Bohemia, Moravia and the rest of Silesia where conditions for industrialization were similar to those in most Western and Central European countries. But it also included provinces where such conditions were lacking such as Galicia, Bukowina, Dalmatia and the coastal area, which together accounted for more than a third of the population. In these areas, industrialization started only around 1900. The moderate economic expansion of this state led not only contemporaries but later also many historians to assume that industrialization started late and was hesitant. This relatively slow growth however was the result of the regional-sequential nature of the industrialization process. What was typical for the whole of Europe also held for developments in the monarchy which, like a microcosm, reflected the European conditions on its own soil.[1]

The relatively slow economic growth of the monarchy is, therefore, partly a statistical phenomenon of its uneven regional development. Even if its industrial areas expanded as fast as the West and Central European economies, average growth inevitably had to lag, as more than a third of the population did not participate in the expansion process.[2] A comparison with the Western and Central European countries is therefore not entirely valid. While it is true that these countries also exhibited regional disparities and sometimes a gap between Western and Eastern parts[3], they did not comprise large, territories of such strikingly different economic and social structure as found in the monarchy. Nevertheless, the territory that is today's Austria developed in a way very similar to the other countries of Western and Central Europe. This similarity is confirmed by economic analyses estimating national income back to 1830.[4] This research shows a growth path not unlike that of the rest of Europe.

Towards the end of the Habsburg Monarchy, today's Austria represented an economic area whose state of development corresponded with that of Central Europe. But Austria's economic status interrelated with the national economy of the whole monarchy. This meant that the major trade occurred with the other regions of that economic unit. No statistics exist on the monarchy's internal economic exchanges except on the trade with Hungary—and this was considerable. It amounted to 40 percent of the total exports of the Austrian half of the empire. Although Germany was the main foreign trading partner, only a comparatively small share of exports from the present Austrian territory went there.

Although the political dissolution of the Habsburg Monarchy proved to have far-reaching economic consequences—the sheltered markets were lost—Austria continued to enjoy prosperous relationships with external trading partners. In 1924, when most postwar troubles were overcome, Germany was Austria's most important trading partner with a share of 13 percent, Czechoslovakia, Yugoslavia, Italy, Poland and Hungary, played significant roles as well: these countries together received nearly half of Austria's exports. On the import side, Czechoslovakia was by far the most important country. Given the economic strength of Germany, one can infer from these figures the close economic interrelations of the Austro-Hungarian Monarchy, which determined the regional position of the Austrian economy up to 1938 (see appendix 1).[5]

On the other hand, it was precisely the close interrelations of the now-dissolved monarchy—in addition to the immediate consequences of the war—that caused Austria's first major economic setback. After the war, gross domestic product fell far below the level of 1913. The nation needed time to reestablish old trade relationships, or to generate new ones. Even in the upswing that occurred after the postwar difficulties, the GDP hardly topped that of 1913. In the cyclical peak of 1929, it surmounted the prewar level by only 5 percent.[6]

The Great Depression caused a second major setback. In the trough of the recession, real GDP fell to 81.5 percent of the 1912 level; industrial value added attained only 60.9 percent. In 1933, 557,000 people, or 26 percent of all workers and employees, were unemployed. As in other European countries, there was some recovery after 1934. But the recovery could not offset the negative effects of the Great Depression, let alone those of World War I. By 1937, GDP was still down to about 90 percent of the 1913 figure and the rate of unemployment remained at 21.7 percent.[7]

In spite of the political transformation, economic changes were not dramatic, although one would have expected a shift of Austrian economic activity from east to the west, as the relative importance of a country's foreign trade flows depend mainly on geographical distance, demographic size and level of economic development (per capita GDP).[8] But specific events kept these changes in a narrow range. Germany's share of foreign trade increased until the beginning of the 1930s; with the rising political troubles and the introduction of the new economic order, Germany lost ground again as an Austrian trading partner until 1937. The market shares of Western countries showed a tendency to increase, but only within narrow limits. In 1937 the successor states (including Romania) still received 31.5 percent of Austria's total exports. Thus, the position of the Austrian economy in the European context was relatively stagnant and to a high degree bound to the traditional Eastern markets.

With the occupation by the German *Reich* in 1938, the *"Ostmark"* economy boomed. German armament and expansionary economic policy fuelled economic growth and promoted a considerable redirection of trade to Germany. According to estimates, "Austrian" trade with Germany trebled while the exports to other countries decreased by 24 percent.[9] During the following war years the relationship between Austria and Germany became even closer.

Separation from the East: Integration into the West

The end of the World War II brought many fundamental changes for Austria's economic and political position in Europe. Peace for Austria meant a separation from Germany, but it was not this event alone that caused the German share of Austrian exports to fall to a minimum. In a time of still regulated foreign trade with differing levels of destruction and reconstruction in Europe pure economic forces were not always decisive. In 1948, the year of the German *"Währungsreform"*, when Western Germany took the first steps towards future sovereignty, its share in Austria's exports was 5.8 percent. Prime export markets for Austria after the war were Italy (17 percent) and Switzerland (13.3 percent). But the former successor states also gained importance. A little less than one fifth of Austria's total exports went to the successor states. With 7.5 percent, the CSR reached the same share as before the war. Yugoslavia also approached this level.

But 1948 was a watershed for economic postwar development. Europe splintered apart: the Western countries united economically under the so-called "Bretton Woods" system, which instituted the coordination of market economies by the free flow of goods, services and payments, while the Eastern European countries united under central planning. For political reasons, and later economic ones, trade between east and west decreased for the duration of the Cold War. This decrease was especially significant for Austria. Because parts of Austrian industry under Soviet occupation (USIA) had been directed toward the Eastern markets, Austria reached the highest European share in trade with the Soviet satellites. But this trade never amounted to more than 15 percent (including the U.S.S.R.) The former successor states gained shares between 1 and 2.5 percent, altogether about 8 percent.

During the 1950s Austria became firmly integrated into the system of Western economies. Austria was included in Western reconstruction policies from the beginning of the post-war period and received support from many sources. It became a member of the IMF (International

Monetary Fund), the World Bank and GATT (General Agreement on Tariffs and Trade). The European Recovery Program (Marshall Plan), was of crucial importance for the Austrian economy. It meant the definite inclusion in the group of Western democratic, industrialized countries, even though the eastern parts of Austria were under Soviet control. The Marshall Plan provided sufficient foreign aid, to permit reconstruction of the Austrian economy without all the limitations the nation had to face after World War I.[10]

This period of Western European reconstruction and integration under the auspices of Bretton Wood lasted until 1960. It lead to the most dynamic economic expansion ever experienced in Europe. A major contribution to this buoyant growth was the increasing international division of labor. Austria's export quotas rose from 19.0 percent of the GDP in 1950 to 31.1 percent in 1970. These years brought an economic miracle; the Austrian GDP more than trebled, reaching nearly the size of the German one. In 1960, 26.8 percent of Austrian exports went to Germany, 16.6 percent to Italy and two thirds to OEEC countries. Forty percent of imports came from Germany and 70% from Western Europe (see appendices 2 and 3).

The Stages of European Integration

Austria's next period was marked by the treaties of Rome and Stockholm. The former created the European Economic Community (EEC) into two trading blocks. The European Free Trade Association (EFTA) followed in 1960. In spite of the very close economic interrelation with the EEC countries, Austria's reasons joining the EFTA were political. The Austrian government considered it impossible for a neutral country to become a member of a customs union, losing its treaty-making power and option to quit—bearing in mind the position of the Soviet Union. As a consequence of this political decision, a certain reallocation of Austria's position in the European economy took place.

As both trading blocks removed internal tariffs and the EEC built up a common external one, considerable redirections of trade flows occurred. In this *First Phase of Integration*[11] the export shares of the EEC countries (the Federal Republic of Germany and Italy) decreased while the percentages of the EFTA countries (Switzerland and Great Britain) rose considerably. This swing was not so clearly expressed on the import side. Here, the share of the FRG even increased slightly. It should be stressed, however, that the gains in EFTA exports could not compensate for the losses of those with the EEC. Total foreign trade growth slowed down, the share of Austrian foreign trade in the Organization for Economic Cooperation and Development (OECD) countries decreased, and it was held that these obstacles to foreign trade were one reason for the comparatively weak performance of the Austrian economy during the 1960s in period of structural crisis.

After the recession of 1967-68, a new upswing set in which was to become the longest boom in Austrian postwar history, hardly affected by the mild international recession of 1971-72. The boom was brought about by buoyant exports of industrial manufactures, implying sizable gains of market shares in the trading partner countries. Obviously Austrian industry had overcome its problems and successfully adjusted to international demand. But one decisive reason for this favorable performance was that discrimination of exports was no longer rising, as the rearrangements of tariffs had been finished at this time. During the first half of the 1970s no dramatic changes in shares of foreign trade were visible.[12]

Since 1973 Austria's conditions for foreign trade improved additionally. After an Interim Agreement in 1972 with Austria, the EEC and EFTA concluded a Free Trade Agreement. In this *Second Phase of Integration*, which removed to a considerable degree the economic divisions in Western Europe, the growth of Austrian foreign trade gained further momentum and its share in that of OECD Countries reached its climax 1974 with 1.36 percent. The new situation did not mean a complete redirection of trade flows. Great Britain lost the importance in Austrian trade it had as an EFTA country, while Switzerland preserved it. But the importance of the Federal Republic increased dramatically. In 1990, its share of Austrian exports reached 36.7 percent and of imports already 43.7 percent.

The decision by the EC countries to complete the internal market by 1992 gave further momentum to the integration process. This action caused consequences which went far beyond the goals that were set in Brussels. It set in motion activities that promised to transform an economic association into a political union, and it loosened the coherence of EFTA. Austria was the first EFTA country to apply for memberhship in the EC in August 1989. Although this step was not appreciated at first by the other EFTA members, nearly all of them are considering the same policy. Sweden was the next to present its application.

Out of a rather complicated constellation arose the European Economic Space (EES). On the one side was the interest of the EFTA countries to participate in the most recent dynamics of European integration on the other side a tendency in the EC Commission to prevent applications for EC membership by too many EFTA countries. In the fall of 1991, after tough negotiations, the EC Commission concluded that the first goal of the EES could be reached; this will certainly not prevent the majority of EFTA countries from applying for full membership.

The high esteem attributed to this new EC activity by economic agents is apparent in the sudden investment boom following the announcement of the internal market. This remarkable increase was one important reason for the acceleration of economic growth which made it possible to overcome the stagnation in the first half of the 1980.

Another Step on a Familiar Road

The preceding considerations should have demonstrated that European economic development after World War II was characterized by a permanent process of integration which also determined Austria's position in this area. So in spite of the far reaching consequences of the EC decision to complete the internal market, no fundamental changes for the future development of Austria's economy should be expected. The argument for an Austrian membership in the EC remains the same, because Austria is economically already part of it. In 1990, 64.5 percent of Austrian exports went to EC countries, and 68.3 percent of its imports came from these countries. It was only political reasons that caused the Austrian government to prefer EFTA membership in the 1960s. As the political constellations started to change toward the end of the 1980s, economic considerations—especially the EC decision to establish the internal market—assumed greater importance for the Austrian governments.

There is no doubt that Austria's membership in the Common Market will have economic consequences. The Austrian Institute of Economic Research has studied these effects in several studies very closely.[13] The results of these research projects correspond basically with the "avis" elaborated by the EC Commission in Brussels. So the expected economic consequences seem to be undisputed.

The first area of change is trade policy. Austria would have to adopt the European Community's regulations, including an extension of preferential trade with certain less developed countries and the lowering on average of tariffs on imports from third countries (from currently 4.9 percent to some 4.2 percent). There will be no changes of tariffs in trade with EC countries because all of them have been eliminated by the Free Trade Agreement of 1972. Considerable effects are only to be expected by the removal of the non-tariff barriers that will be part of the internal market.

The consequences of all these changes will vary very much according to the sector of the Austrian economy affected. The open sector—industry—will not experience decisive changes. This sector is now almost completely integrated. Research shows that one fifth of Austrian industrial enterprises are currently harmed by non-tariff barriers. The removal of frontier controls and the opening up of public procurement will certainly provide additional export possibilities for Austrian industrialists. On the other hand competition will intensify in the home market for the same reasons. But all these changes will occur in a limited range.

Sheltered sectors of the Austrian economy—such as banking and insurance, construction, domestic trade and especially agriculture—will be strongly affected. These economic branches either receive massive government subsidies or operate in a market controlled by legal and administrative restrictions. Their adjustment burden will be comparatively large; to survive they will have to become internationally competitive. With the Free Trade Agreement of 1972, Austria adopted the EC regulations concerning cartels, monopolies and subsidies in the open sector. But EC membership will enforce the removal of state monopolies such as tobacco, alcohol and salt. Some adaptations of the structure of Austrian subsidies to the EC pattern might also become necessary.

Taxation policy will have to be altered significantly also. The most recent tax reform, in force since the beginning of 1989, may be considered a step in the right direction of EC taxation principles. The reform included a reduction of marginal rates of personal and corporate income taxes along with exemptions from personal income taxation and the introduction of a withholding tax on income from interest. But further adjustments would be necessary, most importantly, the lowering of value added tax rates. Following current proposals of the EC Commission, Austria would have to abandon its rate for "luxury goods" (32 percent), and lower its reduced rate from 10 percent to 9 percent. The regular rate of 20 percent causes no problems. To compensate for the loss in tax receipts resulting from such adjustments, direct taxation would have to be increased. In the long run, this would bring the Austrian tax structure—now biased towards indirect taxes—more in line with the average tax structure within the EC.

Of course, membership in such a highly integrated economic union will restrict the freedom of monetary policy in Austria. However, given the hard currency policy pursued, this will be a loss in theory rather than in practice. Monetary policy has for more than a decade been oriented toward keeping the exchange rates stable vis-à-vis the Deutschmark. There would be no incentive to change this policy.

The Austrian Institute of Economic Research evaluated the total quantitative effects of an Austrian EC membership. This study followed the methodology which the Cecchini Report applied in its assessment of the macroeconomic consequences for the EC of the completion of the internal market[14] and produced its results by using an econometric model of the Austrian economy.[15]

As the Cecchini Report expects an additional economic growth of 4.5 percent for the EC within 6 years after the completion of the internal market, Austria will in any case benefit from this activity. If it remains outside the EC, an additional growth of 1.6 percent will occur: in case of membership, this effect will amount to 3.6 percent. The inflation rate will be 5.2 percent lower and employment 1.6 percent higher than in a status quo scenario without the internal market. On the other hand, in the case of EC membership, the price for the high performance of the goods and labor markets will be deficits in the internal and external balance because Austria will have to render net payments of roughly 12 billion Austrian Schillings. The price reductions will provide considerable welfare for the large majority of the population even as they harm entrepreneurs in the presently sheltered sector of the Austrian economy.

Although the Treaty of Rome did not deal with social questions, there is considerable uneasiness among the Austrian population on the social effects of EC membership: people fear "social dumping." These fears seem groundless, however. Articles 48 to 51 of the Treaty of Rome deal only with the free movement of labor. Originally the EEC conceived social progress only as a consequence of higher economic growth of full employment and at the best, of higher mobility (Art.117, Par.1).

Although this position is logical from the point of view of economic union, the lack of social security regulation is problematic in the EC. This is especially true since the fears over EC enlargement in Southern Europe about social dumping also arose within the Community. To check this widespread feeling, a Charter of Social Rights was accepted by the European Council in December 1989. The Charter provides a certain framework for minimum standards.[16] Similar feelings have surfaced in Austria, as a downward in social standards is expected. Fears have been voiced not only by the people but also by the Austrian government in its report on integration to the Austrian Parliament.[17]

It is very doubtful, however, that these fears are justified, not only with respect to the lack of social regulations in the Treaty of Rome but also because the share of social expenditures in Austria does not significantly exceed the EC average.

An important step towards the realization of EC membership was made by the formation of the "European Economic Space." Of course, its regulations differ from those of EC, but it provides some of the EC advantages and the possibility of gradual adaption. The EES does not allow absolutely free mobility of goods and persons because this construction is no customs union. Border controls are upheld. EFTA members cannot directly interfere in the development of EC regulations, they have to accept the relevant legislation.

Integration effects are provided by opening public procurement to all member countries as well as by the liberalization of financial services. Analysts therefore also expect from Austria's EES participation positive effects for Austria's economic development. GDP growth is expected to be higher by 2.3 percent within 6 years after completion of the internal market by than it would be if Austria remained outside the EES. Inflation will be lower by 3.5 percent and employment higher by 1.1 percent (see appendix 4)[18].

Although the medium range effects on the Austrian economy seem substantial enough, the more important, long-range ones have to be seen in two directions. First, Austria's membership not only means the breaking up of non-tariff trade barriers and the exposition of the sheltered sector to international competition, but a general deregulation according to EC rules. These changes extend far ahead of those made in other countries in the 1970s and 1980s because of the still prevailing deeply rooted mercantilistic tradition of Austria's economic institutions. It should be stressed that this deregulation has been publicly recommended for many years, but the Austrian government was too weak to remove the hidebound barriers to economic activity. It was predominantly international pressure in the course of the integration process that forced the government to undertake steps toward liberalizing the economy. EC membership means a visible change, because EFTA left the internal rules of its members untouched. Austria has to perform a double step: first to adapt to the, "old" EC rules and second to adapt the new ones in connection with the internal market. The institutional structure of the Austrian economy will have to change in the future.

The second point is a counterfactual argument: remaining outside the EC will, as the simulation research of the Austrian Institute of Economic Research shows, prove no dramatic consequences. But, as all EFTA members seem to understand if a country is excluded from the growing number of European Institutions and Cooperations, it remains outside the stream of European thinking that will characterize the future. An eventual falling back behind the European growth pattern may lead to detrimental effects on the economic and social stability of a country.

Reorientation towards Mitteleuropa?

So the advantages and drawbacks of Austria's EC membership as well as its position in the Europe of the future seem comparatively clear. But according to what has been said before, it is also apparent that the political changes in the East will have a considerable impact on the Austrian economy.

Two extreme possibilities can be excluded. The Eastern neighbors will hardly gain the trade position they had between the wars as former members of a national economy. On the other hand their marginal position of the postwar era will not continue. The probable share of the Eastern neighbors in Austria's foreign trade will depend on the time these economies will need to introduce a working market system. But the intensity of foreign trade depends also on the income level, and in this respect, the economic planning system had fatal consequences on these countries.

According to the west-east gradient of industrialization, the state of economic development of the successor states differed considerably. This pattern determined the income level before World War I. Between the wars the highest income could be found in Austria and Czechoslovakia; in Hungary and Poland, it was a third lower. World War II changed this pattern considerably in so far as the CSR remained the country with the highest income of this group, but Austria had fallen back decisively: in 1948 its income level reached only two thirds of the Czechoslovak one and equaled that of Poland. The postwar development overturned this hierarchy again. As far as the data allow a comparison, one can see that toward the end of the 1980s Austria had gained by far the highest income of all successor states. The income per capita of Czechoslovakia has fallen back to approximately half as much as Austria's. Hungary and Poland reach still lower levels (see appendix 5)[19].

The change of the economic system along with the fact of a comparatively low income means an obstacle to a proper foreign trade. For the next decade the probable membership of Austria in the EC will determine the foreign trade structure, but in the following years the picture will change. With a working economy and increasing income, the former successor states will gain that share of Austrian foreign trade that can be expected of a neighbor country. This trend will increase with the tendency of the last decades away from mere trade to industrial cooperation.[20] There are considerable possibilities here: think of a Middle European industrial agglomeration containing Vienna, Brno and Bratislava! The latest figures suggest that future development in this direction is a real possibility. Despite the falling GDP and stagnating foreign trade in these countries, Austrian exports to its Eastern neighbors are already booming.[21]

Conclusion

It should be clear that the present and future position of Austria in the European economy can be understood only against the historical background. The early phases of industrial development saw present-day Austria as part of the Austro-Hungarian Monarchy with a considerable share of its trade going into Eastern Europe. This situation did not change substantially between the wars, although a reorientation to its Western neighbors should have been expected.

The splitting up of Europe after World War II changed this traditional pattern completely: Austria became a participant in the ongoing integration process of the Western European countries, and trade with the Eastern shrank to a minimum. Austria's most recent step toward EC membership must be seen, therefore, as one on a familiar road. The impact of this membership on the Austrian economy is expected to be significant and positive but will remain within limits. Long range effects are even regarded as more important than medium ones. Welfare gains are expected as a result of more intensive competition, especially in the Austrian service sector. The removal of non-tariff barriers and the opening up of public procurement will have favourable effects on industry.

In the next decade, Austria's interrelations with the Western European economies will reach its climax. But in the following years a reorientation towards the Eastern neighbors will take place. This new Austrian position may possibly be *mitteleuropäisch*.

NOTES

1. David F. Good, "Modern Economic Growth in the Habsburg Monarchy," *East Central Europe* 7 (1980): 251.

2. Felix Butschek, "Der österreichische Wachstumsrückstand," *Beiträge zu Wirtschaftspolitik und Wirtschaftswissenschaft* (1972); Richard L. Rudolph, "Quantitative Aspekte der Industrialisierung in Cisleithanien," in *Die Habsburgermonarchie 1848-1918*, ed. Adam Wandruszka and Peter Urbanitsch, Vol I (Vienna, 1973), 245; David F. Good, *The Economic Rise of the Habsburg Empire* (Berkeley-Los Angeles-London, 1984).

3. Knut Borchardt, "Regionale Wachstumsdifferenzierung in Deutschland im 19. Jahrhundert unter besonderer Berücksichtigung des West-Ost Gefälles," in *Wirtschaft, Geschichte und Wirtschaftsgeschichte: Festschrift für F. Lütge*, ed. W. Abel (Stuttgart, 1966).

4. Anton Kausel, "Österreichs Volkseinkommen 1830 bis 1913: Versuch einer Rückrechnung des realen Brutto - Inlandsproduktes für die österreichische Reichshälfte und das Gebiet der Republik Österreich," in *Geschichte und Ergebnisse der zentralen amtlichen Statistik 1829 bis 1979*, ed. Österreichisches Statistisches Zentralamt (Vienna, 1979); Anton Kausel, N. Nemeth, Hans Seidel, Österreichisches Volkseinkommen 1913 bis 1963," *Monatsberichte des österreichischen Instituts für Wirtschaftsforschung*, 14. Sonderheft (Vienna, 1965).

5. St. Karner, J. Kubin, M. Steiner, "Wie real war 'Mitteleuropa'?" *Vierteljahresschrift für Sozial - und Wirtschaftsgeschichte* (1987).

6. Kausel, Nemeth, Seidel, "Österreichisches Volkseinkommen," 5.

7. Felix Butschek, *Die österreichische Wirtschaft im 20. Jahrhundert* (Vienna-Stuttgart, 1985), 48.

8. H. Linnemann, *An Econometric Study of Internal Trade Flows* (Amsterdam, 1966), 34.

9. Felix Butschek, *Die österreichische Wirtschaft 1938 bis 1945* (Vienna-Stuttgart, 1978), 47.

10. Butschek, *Österreichische Wirtschaft im 20. Jahrhundert*, 90.

11. Fritz Breuss, *Österreichs Aussenwirtschaft 1945 bis 1982* (Vienna, 1983), 79.

12. Butschek, *Österreichische Wirtschaft im 20. Jahrhundert*, 144.

13. Fritz Breuss, H. Handler, and J. Stankovsky (coordinators), *Österreichische Optionen einer EG - Annäherung und ihre Folgen*, WIFO Gutachten (Vienna, 1988); Fritz Breuss and F. Schebeck, "The Completion of EC's Internal Market and its Impact on the Austrian Economy, Macroeconomic Simulations," *WIFO - Working Papers* 31 (1989); M. Schneider, *Folgen der Integration für die österreichische Land - und Forstwirtschaft*, Studie im Auftrag des Bundesministeriums für Land - und Forstwirtschaft, WIFO (Vienna, 1988); P. Szopo, *Folgen einer Annäherung an die Europäischen Gemeinschaften für Wirtschaftsförderung und Wettbewerbspolitik in Österreich*, Studie im Auftrag des Bundesministeriums für Finanzen, WIFO (Vienna, 1988); Jan Stankovsky, *Bedeutung der Ursprungsregelung im Aussenhandel*, WIFO-Gutachten (Vienna, 1990); Helmut Kramer, "Strukturprobleme Österreichs aus der Sicht des Avis der EC-Kommission," *Monatsberichte des Österreichischen Instituts für Wirtschaftsforschung* (1991).

14. M. Catinat, E. Donni, A. Italianer, "The Completion of the Internal Market: Results of Macroeconomic Model Simulations," Commission of the European Communities, Brussels, *Economic Papers* 65 (1988).

15. Fritz Breuss and F. Schebeck, "The Completion of EC's Internal Market and its Impact on the Austrian Economy, Macroeconomic Simulations," *WIFO-Working Papers* 31 (1989).

16. G. Casetti, "Die soziale Dimension des europäischen Binnenmarktes," *Die Volkswirtschaft* (1990).

17. Beitrag zum Integrationsbericht der Bundesregierung an Nationalrat und Bundesrat, Wirtschaftliche und Soziale Auswirkungen eines EG - Beitritts (mimeographed), 10 March 1989, 28.

18. Fritz Breuss and F. Schebeck, "Österreich im EWR, Gesamtwirtschaftliche Auswirkungen," *Monatsberichte des österreichischen Instituts für Wirtschaftsforschung* (1991), 285.

19. Felix Butschek, "Erste Auswirkungen des wirtschaftlichen Umbruchs im Osten auf Österreich," *Monatsberichte des österreichischen Instituts für Wirtschaftsforschung* (1991).

20. P.R. Kriegmann, "New Theories of Trade among Industrial Countries," *The American Economic Review, Papers and Proceedings* 73 (1983).

21. Butschek, "Erste Auswirkungen des wirtschaftlichen Umbruchs im Osten auf Österreich," 211.

APPENDIX 1: Regional Structure of Austrian Foreign Trade

EXPORTS	% SHARES OF TOTAL EXPORTS			
	1924	1929	1932	1937
Germany	13.1	15.7	16.5	14.8
Italy	10.1	9.0	9.9	14.0
Poland	9.7	4.8	3.6	4.3
Romania	6.5	5.1	3.5	5.6
Switzerland	6.6	5.7	8.0	5.1
Yugoslavia	10.3	7.7	7.6	5.4
Czechoslovakia	11.0	13.5	10.6	7.1
Hungary	8.8	7.5	9.3	9.1
France	2.5	3.4	4.1	4.3
Great Britain	4.3	4.5	3.6	5.3
U.S.	2.1	3.4	1.9	2.5
U.S.S.R.	0.9	2.8	1.3	0.6
Other Countries	14.1	16.9	20.1	21.9
World	100.0	100.0	100.0	100.0

IMPORTS	% SHARES OF TOTAL IMPORTS			
	1924	1929	1932	1937
Germany	14.9	21.0	20.0	16.1
Italy	7.2	3.6	4.9	5.5
Poland	7.5	8.8	7.6	4.6
Romania	2.5	3.8	5.8	6.0
Switzerland	5.6	4.4	3.5	3.2
Yugoslavia	4.4	4.0	7.7	7.9
Czechoslovakia	22.6	18.1	15.2	11.0
Hungary	11.7	9.9	9.8	9.0
France	2.3	2.7	2.0	2.8
Great Britain	2.8	2.8	2.5	4.5
U.S.	5.5	6.0	4.0	6.0
U.S.S.R.	0.3	0.8	1.2	0.3
Other Countries	12.7	14.1	15.8	23.1
World	100.0	100.0	100.0	100.0

Source: Bundesamt für Statistik

APPENDIX 2: Regional Structure of Austrian Foreign Trade 1955-1990

% SHARES OF TOTAL EXPORTS

EXPORTS	1955	1960	1965	1970	1975	1980	1985	1990
Germany	25.1	26.8	28.6	23.4	21.9	30.8	30.1	36.7
Italy	16.1	16.6	10.8	9.7	8.0	11.0	9.0	9.8
Switzerland	4.6	4.9	7.5	10.4	7.8	7.5	6.7	6.9
Great Britain	3.7	2.8	3.9	6.1	5.6	3.7	4.6	3.9
France	3.4	1.7	2.2	2.2	2.5	3.5	4.0	4.8
Netherlands	3.9	3.0	3.8	2.9	2.5	2.6	2.4	2.9
Sweden	1.7	2.6	3.2	4.4	4.2	2.6	1.9	1.8
U.S.	4.9	4.4	4.2	4.1	2.5	2.2	4.7	3.2
Belgium-Luxemb.	1.9	2.0	1.3	1.2	1.6	1.5	2.3	2.2
Denmark	0.7	1.0	1.6	2.2	2.0	1.1	1.1	0.9
Norway	0.6	0.9	0.9	1.3	1.4	1.0	1.0	0.5
Finland	0.5	0.7	0.8	1.3	1.3	0.9	0.9	0.8
Japan	0.1	0.6	0.3	0.5	0.6	0.8	0.9	1.6
Bulgaria	0.6	0.7	1.6	0.9	0.9	0.7	0.8	0.3
Czechoslovakia	1.5	2.6	2.3	2.2	2.5	1.4	1.1	1.9
GDR	1.7	1.8	1.8	0.9	1.5	1.3	1.2	0.7
Poland	2.6	1.8	2.0	1.6	4.4	2.7	1.2	0.9
Hungary	2.2	2.4	2.6	2.8	3.6	2.2	2.6	2.2
Romania	0.5	0.9	1.4	16	1.2	1.1	0.3	0.2
U.S.S.R.	0.8	3.5	3.6	2.9	2.9	2.7	3.8	2.2
EC 86	56.9	55.4	52.7	48.9	46.4	56.2	56.1	64.5
EFTA 86	7.3	9.1	12.4	17.4	14.8	12.1	10.5	10.1
CMEA Countries	9.9	13.7	15.3	12.9	17.1	12.1	11.1	8.5
Other Countries	25.9	21.8	19.6	20.8	21.7	19.6	22.3	16.9

Source: Österreichisches Statistisches Zentralamt

APPENDIX 3: Regional Structure of Austrian Foreign Trade 1955-1990

% SHARES OF TOTAL IMPORTS

IMPORTS	1955	1960	1965	1970	1975	1980	1985	1990
Germany	35.4	40.0	41.8	41.2	40.0	40.8	40.9	43.7
Italy	8.0	8.0	8.3	6.5	8.1	9.1	8.2	9.1
Switzerland	4.3	4.3	5.5	7.4	6.7	5.0	4.5	4.3
Great Britain	4.5	5.0	5.5	6.8	4.0	2.7	2.3	2.6
France	4.5	3.7	4.2	3.5	4.0	3.9	3.6	4.2
Netherlands	2.7	3.2	3.2	2.9	3.0	2.7	2.6	2.8
Sweden	1.4	1.4	1.8	2.6	2.5	1.8	1.8	1.7
U.S.	10.5	7.3	4.4	3.4	2.9	3.4	3.7	3.6
Belgium-Luxemb.	1.9	1.6	1.7	1.9	2.2	2.1	2.1	2.9
Denmark	0.6	0.7	1.2	1.4	0.9	0.7	0.6	0.7
Norway	0.8	0.6	0.4	0.5	0.5	0.3	0.7	0.3
Finland	0.2	0.1	0.2	0.5	0.5	0.5	0.5	0.7
Japan	0.2	0.4	0.5	1.0	1.5	2.4	3.3	4.5
Bulgaria	0.3	0.5	0.6	0.3	0.3	0.2	0.2	0.1
Czechoslovakia	1.7	1.6	1.8	1.9	2.0	1.9	1.9	1.2
GDR	1.3	1.4	1.3	0.8	0.7	0.7	0.6	0.3
Poland	2.7	2.2	2.2	1.6	1.6	1.0	1.1	0.9
Hungary	2.2	1.9	1.5	1.7	1.5	1.4	2.0	1.6
Romania	0.7	0.7	1.0	0.8	0.7	0.4	0.4	0.1
U.S.S.R.	0.5	2.8	2.5	2.2	3.4	4.2	4.4	1.8
EC 86	58.8	63.3	66.2	65.4	63.4	63.1	62.1	68.3
EFTA 86	6.7	6.4	7.9	11.0	10.3	7.6	7.6	7.1
CMEA Countries	9.4	11.2	10.8	9.4	10.2	9.7	10.7	6.0
Other Countries	25.1	19.1	15.1	14.2	16.1	19.6	19.6	18.6

Source: Österreichisches Statistisches Zentralamt

**APPENDIX 4: EC's Internal Market
Impact on Austria's Real GDP**

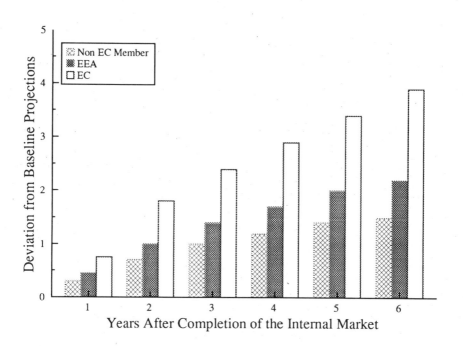

APPENDIX 5: Gross National Product in Europe
PERCENT OF U.S. (U.S. = 100)

COUNTRIES	1938		1947		1948		1985	
	$	%	$	%	$	%	$	%
NW Europe								
Denmark	316	60.7	276	41.5	307	45.0	12,254	74.3
Ireland	252	48.4	247	37.1	287	42.0	6,704	40.6
Norway	255	48.9	248	37.3	253	37.0	13,897	66.2
Sweden	367	70.4	413	62.1	413	60.5	12,639	76.6
Great Britain	378	72.6	363	54.6	401	58.7	10,915	84.3
W Europe								
Belgium-Luxemb.	275	52.8	255	38.4	278	40.7	10,680	64.8
France	236	45.3	207	31.1	228	33.4	11,455	69.4
Netherlands	323	62.0	219	32.9	250	36.6	11,269	68.3
Switzerland	367	70.4	451	67.8	441	64.6		
Germany							12,179	73.8
Middle/NE Europe								
Austria	179	34.4	96	14.4	130	19.0	10,729	65.0
CSR/CSSR	176	33.8	165	24.8	195	28.6	6,000	36.4
Finland	178	34.2	151	22.7	173	25.3	11,442	69.4
Hungary	112	21.5	82	12.3	98	14.4	5,062	30.7
Poland	104	19.9	114	17.1	141	20.6	3,977	24.1
S and SE Europe								
Bulgaria	68	13.1	51	7.7	66	9.7		
Greece	80	15.4	58	8.7	62	9.1	6,001	36.4
Italy	127	24.4	100	15.0	105	15.4	10,841	65.7
USA	521	100.0	665	100.0	683	100.0	16,494	100.0

Note: 1938, 1947, and 1948 amounts measured in 1938 prices.

Source: United Nations, *Economic Survey of Europe in 1948* (Geneva, 1949); Organization of European Economic Development, *National Accounts*, Vol. 1: *Main Aggregates, Purchasing Power, Parities Supplement* (Paris, 1987); United Nations, *International Comparison of Gross Domestic Product in Europe, 1985* (New York, 1988); J. Langr, "On the Discussion of the GDP Levels in the CSSR," *Politicka Ekonomie*, 37 (1989).

The Transformation of Austria in the Context of New Europe

Manfred Prisching

Austria is experiencing a completely new international constellation through the opening of East European borders and through the integration of the European countries in the European Community. A certain rearrangement of institutions is called for, a process of adaptation to the new circumstances, to the "New Europe".

The problems connected with this process and the factors shaping Austrian society and the mentality of its people are the subject of this essay: I want (1) to sketch some of the developments of this turbulent century to clarify the problems confronting Austria;[1] (2) to provide a short survey of economics, politics and society in Austria, together with some central data; and (3) to point to some publications that offer interesting approaches to the problems discussed.

From Civil War to Consensus

After World War I, Austrian democracy was born as the result of military defeat, without national autonomy, in a context of economic disaster, within multiple international pressures.[2] After World War I the consciousness of Austrian nationhood was weak. While the loyalty of the successor states of the Habsburg Empire was based on national affiliation, the inhabitants of the small German-speaking country "Austria" had difficulty in defining themselves according to language or culture.[3] For obvious reasons the Austrians considered an association with Germany (*Anschluß*)[4], but the association was forbidden by the victorious Allies. After Austria's absorption by Nazi Germany, the idea of an association died. Today, about 80 percent of Austrians think either that Dachau, and they had realized that the democratic order could be an Austrian nation exists or that the country is on the way to becoming one. Today relations with Germany are free of problems.[5]

Between the wars, many European countries threatened by ideological strife were "saved" by national dictatorships and emergency regimes. Austrian authoritarianism was a mixture of conservative and quasi-fascist attitudes, Christian reform ideas, holistic and organic theoretical models, movements of national revolutionaries and anti-Austrian and pro-German groups. But, in contrast to Germany, neither programmatic racism nor a totalitarian cult of the *"Führer"* existed. The intention was to enforce *Gemeinschaft* from above, because it appeared that the inner order was being destroyed by para-military groups fighting against each other in the streets. Governability was to be secured by tactics and compromise towards fascist Italy and national socialist Germany and by a strong hand within the country.[6]

The Social Democrats were ambivalent toward Austria. They proclaimed their belief in defending democratic institutions, but they used a language of radicalism that terrified the bourgeoisie. They also maintained the vision of transforming the capitalist system into a socialist system by way of social revolution. They did not consider this a utopian perspective for the future but a transformation which should take place soon. The idea that the revolution would come soon contributed to the hesitancy of the socialists but made them resist any cooperation with the bourgeoisie.[7]

The citizens of Austria daily experienced the malfunctioning of democracy. The conflicting political groups could not advance towards even minimal consensus. Political order disintegrated into self-interest. Civil war was imminent. This experience seemed to signal that democracy could not work.

After 1945, however, everything changed. Austria acknowledged its advantages as a small country and stopped doubting its viability. Democratic institutions gained acceptance. A "civic culture" began to develop. Politics were de-ideologized. Austria became the only successor to the Habsburg empire where free elections took place from 1945 until the end of the 1980s. The consensus among political groups now exceeds those of most other countries.[8] How can this contrast with the period between the wars be explained?

The high level of consensus in Austrian politics stems from the starting phase of the Second Republic.[9] First, the representatives of inimical political groups had met each other in the Nazi concentration camp in Dachau, and they had realized that the democratic order could be destroyed by a fundamentalist policy. The socialists abstained from their polarizing political strategy, and the church from any political activity. In fact, a position of neutrality developed in the church. The conservatives were ready to accept social reforms. Secondly, the practical problems of reconstruction after the war also generated pressure toward consensus. In the period after World War II, Austria was working just to secure its subsistence level; there was little space for ideological party politics, which was quite different from the situation after World War I, when economic difficulties led to political polarization. Furthermore, for a period of ten years, Austrian politicians were forced to show a consensual position towards the representatives of the occupation armies, until the State Treaty was signed in 1955 and the occupation forces withdrew.[10] This necessity united Austrian parties. Even the nationalization of German industries in Austria, which was to prevent them from being seized by the allied powers, was a common decision. Finally, the rapid growth that began after the withdrawal of the allied forces mitigated distributional conflicts because it allowed the position of all social groups to be improved. Essential conflict potentials were eliminated.

Another element of consensus is the traditional Austrian mentality. There is a relatively strong attitude towards regional and economic protectionism on the right side of the political spectrum; there are also strong ideas of economic protectionism and social reformism originating from the nineteenth century on the left side.[11] Mental relics from the premodern period have been condensed to an orientation of traditional privileges (including titles); compared to other countries, there is an aversion against geographical, social and socio-psychological mobility; traditional mechanisms of distribution (like social "connections") dominate. Actually, Austria is not a competitive society; rather, positional warfare between power groups shapes political life.[12] In the 1990s, in the course of an increasing internationalization of life, this situation will presumably change.

The consensual attitudes support two special institutions of the Austrian political system that cannot be explained if one ignores this historical background. It shapes the cooperation of the two big parties, the Grand Coalition, and that of the large interest groups, the Social Partnership.[13]

In comparison with other countries,[14] postwar Austria has a highly concentrated party system (two parties unite about three quarters of the votes), a high percentage of party members, a high identification with parties. The coalition government of the People's party and the Social

Democratic Party in the Grand Coalition[15] held from 1945 to 1966: it is a good example of a "pillared concordance democracy."[16] After the grand coalition broke down, there were some experiments with governments by the strongest party as well as small coalitions. Since the mid-1980s the Grand Coalition has been resurrected to solve pressing problems. For some critics this constellation has generated too much consensus. As early as the 1960s they critized this "sovereignty of the parties" that displaced the "sovereignty of the people." The rise of third parties, called the Liberal or "Freedom Party" and the Green Parties, may be explained by the disgust of voters with the domineering power cartel of the "big" parties.

Social Partnership is the other crucially important cooperative institution of the Austrian system.[17] Social scientists tried to analyze how this complicated system worked and came to realize during the years of economic crisis in the mid-1970s that corporatist systems withstood economic shocks better than pluralist systems which had to face more severe economic troubles.[18] The economic and social partnership is a system of concordance based on the consensus of large social groups, namely labor, capital and farmers. It tries to achieve the unanimity of the representatives or overcome the vetoes of all social partners. Many questions of social and economic policy, then, are decided by these interest groups; government and parliament merely execute their decisions. This model secures relief for the political machinery because controversial issues may be transferred to the social partners for settlement, thus giving the (often informal) committees strong influence. Furthermore, the model is based on a comprehensive and state-promoted system of chambers and interest organizations that are closely linked with political parties, parliament and government administration, partly in institutionalized form, partly through personal multiple functions. The system mainly works by maintaining informal procedures and by voluntarily observing certain economic and distributional principles, such as a productivity-oriented wage policy. An essential core of the decision-making system is surrounded by institutions that are influenced or regulated by the social partners, like social security institutions, committees and advisory boards, courts and funds.

The consensus seems to have been eroding during the last few years. This is true for the party system as well as for the system of social partnership. Political culture in Austria is becoming similar to that of most modern Western democracies; some observe a fundamental change of paradigm.[19] The de-concentration of the party system and the growing relevance of new parties such as the Greens may be a result of the replacement of the postwar generation of politicians who share the common fateful experiences of the First Republic and World War II. Citizens' recognition that changing majorities in government do not fundamentally alter their daily existence might also be contributing to the change. This stronger interconnection with other European countries in the "New Europe" will reinforce "normalization" of political life.

Some characteristics of this ongoing process include the following[20]: (1) Parties are being de-ideologized; they are becoming catch-all-parties. Statements of their representatives are becoming more and more diffuse. As in the U.S., the personality of the top candidate is considered a main criterion for voting behavior; and single-issue decisions of voters are increasing. (2) A process of partisan dealignment can be observed, and voter volatility is growing.[21] (3) The political process is becoming ritualized; politics are being enriched by show elements (pseudo politics). (4) The political scenery is increasingly splitting apart and fragmenting, and new parties are emerging. These small parties add radical positions to the parliamentary process. They have an agenda-setting function even though they are overburdened by conceptual and administrative work. (5) More and more citizens are staying away from politics because of a disgust with politics, parties and politicians. This withdrawal has been spawned by a series of political scandals in Austria, which came to the notice of the public in the 1980s, such as scandals of adulterated wine and the illegal sale of military goods by State Industries, a criminal murder story set among friends of high-ranking socialist politicians, and finally the Waldheim affair. (6) The political apathy of citizens is increasing, not least because of the working of the political machinery which, according to the economic figures, must be considered successful but which seems to run by itself.

The system of social partners is facing pressures to make adaptations. The majority of workers (about 60 percent) are members of the Austrian Trade Union Federation (ÖGB), but their share is declining. While voters agree in principle on the cooperation of interest groups[22], they consider it more and more an undemocratic and bureaucratic apparatus with sclerotic consequences for the political and economic dynamics of Austria. The corporatist organization no longer mirrors the reality of a pluralist society where class relations have dissolved and homogeneous interests of identifiable social groups no longer exist. The internationalization of economic life restricts the possibilities of interest policy. Thus, reforms are demanded, such as the structural democratization of the institutions of social partnership (like chambers and associations), the dissolving of personal interconnections of interest group representatives with the political sphere—generally considered as an accumulation of privileges—and the elimination of obligatory membership in the chambers. Today every farmer, entrepreneur and worker in Austria has been forced to be a member of his legal interest organization.[23]

This process of dissolution will be accelerated in the "New Europe." The parties are not able to develop a consistent idea of long-term policy because they have lost their traditional identities without successfully constructing new ones. They have become loose associations of different interest groups.[24] This is not necessarily a difficult situation, but it is a challenge for Austria where the political parties have penetrated and dominated public and private life with unusually high intensity. There are even politically influenced sport associations, kindergartens, fishing clubs, cultural societies, automobile clubs and burial-funds in Austria. As parties dominate all areas of life, voter expectations are high that these powerful machineries will solve all problems that may arise. While the idea of a "minimal state" is not applauded in Austria, the increasing uneasiness with the pervasive party state is growing.

From Existential Doubts to the Economic Miracle

Austria is one of the richest countries on earth, but among the rich countries it is one of the poorer ones. Gross domestic product (at current prices and purchase power parities) is $12,506 per capita (1988); this is approximately the standard of Italy, Belgium or the Netherlands.[25] After World War I the economy stagnated, and the world economic crisis finally stopped growth impulses. After World War II, the social product was roughly at the level it had been in the monarchy at the beginning of the century.[26]

Austria's comfortable position today is based on the enormous economic growth process after World War II, often referred to as the "Austrian economic miracle." As early as 1948/49, the rationing of most goods could be abolished, not least because of U.S. economic aid; the American "politics of productivity" also became the ideological model for economic reconstruction. Economic growth from 1955 to 1989 amounted to 259 percent, similar to German developments. The structural turning point of 1945 may have contributed to the enormous growth, but so did the faster economic development of the reconstruction period (the fourth or fifth long wave in a Kondratieff-paradigm of economic history).

During the postwar period fundamental structural changes took place. (1) The export quota of the social product was increased from 7 percent to 25 percent; industrial products conquered greater shares while the percentage of exported raw materials and food was cut by half. (2) The export quota of 1.3 percent of the world market remained stable. The balance of payments was kept under control. A strong integration in the European Community took place; two thirds of Austrian foreign trade is now oriented towards the EC; the most important connections exist with Germany. (3) Tourism assumed a central position in Austria's economy; income from tourists amounts to $1,350 U.S. per capita,[27] one of the highest rates in the world. (4) The expansion of the welfare state has continued during the last decades. A quarter of national income is devoted to this purpose. The risks of modern economic life are covered by a system that provides insurance for health, accident and unemployment; it also secures old age pensions and family benefits. Almost all citizens are covered by the social security net, and if social security entitlements are insufficient, social welfare benefits guarantee a minimum level of existence. The expansion of these programs must be explained by demographic developments, the expansion of the groups of entitled persons, and rising costs; these have been the most relevant factors for rising government expenditures.

In today's world Austria is one of the most advanced welfare states. Public expenditures amount to 43 percent of the social product (1988), which is approximately the same level as the Netherlands, Belgium and Norway; Denmark and Sweden are higher with about 50 percent, the U.S. and Japan are lower with about 30 percent. There are pressures to expand the public share of national income. Austria's public debt places it in the middle range of industrial countries: with a net deficit of about ÖS 63 billion per year and an accumulated financial debt of about ÖS 860 billion compared with a gross domestic product of about ÖS 1,800 billion (1990).[28] In the 1980s the OECD-countries have tried to freeze the dynamic expansion of their budget deficits, and during the last few years Austria has taken part in this effort. Austria has made no attempt, however, to overcome the economic crisis at the expense of the socially deprived, as has been practiced by other countries. Financial restrictions have also generated concerns about a crisis of the welfare state[29] and of over-provision by the state, but most Austrians agree that the welfare programs providing a safety net in risky times should remain intact.[30]

The interpretation of the instruments and achievements of economic policy have changed during the decades since World War II. (1) From the

1950s to the early 1970s politicians believed in their capacity to regulate the economic process (by means of a "bastardized-Keynesian" model). They even tried to proceed from crude regulation of the economic process to "fine tuning," and they were convinced that they had finally overcome capitalist business cycles. (2) Societal reform ideas were connected with this vision of the future. The democratization of all sectors of life was also emphasized by the students' movements arriving in Austria at the end of the 1960s, but compared to other countries, in a weakened version. (3) When in most industrial countries unemployment rates and inflation rose in the mid-1970s, Austria's politicians thought that they could dive through the cycle by employing fiscal policy and supporting state industries for employment stabilization. "Austro-Keynesianism," as the economic policy in the second half of the 1970s became known, comprised economic incentives by government expenditures, structural policy and subsidies on the supply side, as well as a currency policy aimed at stabilizing prices. (4) This strategy reached its limits in the early 1980s when businessmen became used to economic stimulation and budget deficits exploded. In the turbulences following the oil crisis, the ideas about technocratic regulation of the economy turned out to be illusions. (5) At the same time citizens realized new policy deficits. The apocalyptic picture painted by the *Club of Rome* became a bestseller. With their sharpened sensibility, Austrians detected more and more environmental scandals and ecological dangers.

Consequently, Austrians developed a new paradigm of policy. They were no longer ready to believe the politicians with their slogans of business as usual. The unplanned consequences (especially environmental ones) of the politics of productivity and annual growth rates became a political issue. Since the 1970s, the international trend towards a market-oriented policy—proclaimed in the U.S. and implemented in Great Britain—has enhanced skepticism toward state regulation. This ideological wave of economic liberalism arrived in Austria in a watered down version, even though one of its most famous proponents, Nobel prize winner Friedrich von Hayek, is Austrian.[31]

This change in economic thinking has had three consequences. First, it is the premise that the structures of the "New Europe"—with free mobility of persons, goods, services and capital—will be accepted by the majority of Austrians. Second, Austrian state industry had produced bigger and bigger deficits, which the state had to subsidize at the tune of ÖS 60 billion during the 1980s. Reforms were delayed because the enterprises had been considered a bulwark of Socialist economic policy.

With the new liberal economic paradigm, fundamental restructuring has finally become possible; this has resulted in a shrinking of the workforce and has brought about healthy enterprises. Third, the basic trust in paternalistic, welfare oriented government has been consistently decreasing in Austria; more attention is paid to the problem-solving capacities of the market and the functional advantages of self-organized groups.[32] However, the Austrian government is cautious with programs of privatization; this caution is a reasonable policy, as some of Britain's negative experiences show.[33] Deregulation and marketization, on the other hand, have been considered positive ideas since the beginning of the 1990s. This attitude represents a radical shift from the one that dominated at the beginning of the 1970's and is an appropriate disposition for the start of a "New Europe."

In any case, the Austrian interpretive model of political economy shows particular ambivalences. This will make it difficult to come to terms with the conditions prevailing in the "New Europe." On the one hand, a strong skepticism has developed, a disgust with political life, which in the perspective of most citizens seems to be shaped by corruption and scandals, by relations of social protectionism and unlegitimated political privileges.[34] On the other hand, naive optimism remains in existence—an optimism that makes people call for the helping hand of government whenever problems arise. This may be a late consequence of Austrian "Josephinism," a term relating to the most radical period of enlighted reform from above in Austrian history.

The new economic situation is also influenced by the opening of the Eastern European borders. Austria is no longer situated in a quiet corner at the southeast margin of the European economic space. Instead, it has now been moved into the center of a new Europe that is restructuring. The relevance of the Eastern European countries as economic partners must not be overestimated. One has to look at the figures: The external trade of the OECD countries with the whole of Eastern Europe amounts to 2.3 percent of exports and 2.9 percent of imports (1987); even their trade with the less developed countries is twice as high. Nevertheless, the following consequences can be foreseen: (1) The modest purchasing power of Eastern European markets will not increase dramatically during the next years, and strong competition will exist for the few resources among western enterprises. (2) Austria's "bridge services" will not be indispensable, because direct contacts between East and West will take place via different institutions. (3) In the future, increased migration of lower income industries will take place not only to the south, but also to the east.

(4) Large investments will be needed in Austria to build up the infrastructure toward the east, an infrastructure that has been superfluous until now because of dead borders. (5) Western governments will have to make substantial financial aid available to the former socialist countries; Austria is prepared to participate in these efforts.

From the Island Model to International Integration

Austria is an affluent, stable and democratic small nation. The separation from surrounding territories with other ethnic populations after World War I has had positive effects; the Austrian government has been fortunate in not having to deal with the problems in Croatia and Bosnia, in Cracow and Hermannstadt.[35] Like other small European states, such as Switzerland, Denmark or the Netherlands, Austria has escaped the arrogance of power.[36] On the one hand, Austria's size leads to restricted autonomy; in a time when international leverages are growing, small states can often do nothing more than duplicate the measures of big nations.[37] On the other hand, Austria has the option of "free-riding"; for small countries, obligations are restricted too. Small nations are exempted from many of the concerns of big nations. In its currency policy, for example, Austria has done nothing more than follow the course of Germany and peg the Austrian Schilling to the exchange rate of the German Mark.

After regaining her independence in 1955, neutral Austria was situated in a relatively sheltered zone in spite of central European Cold War tensions until the 1980s. It was no longer the *porta orientis* as it had been in the nineteenth century. There were indeed memories of the neighbors, the lingering sound of the common past, but the bordering countries were no longer an element of present life. So Austrians looked to the west, where the economic activity had shifted. In the eighteenth and nineteenth centuries, the centers of economic activity had shifted to the east, to the surroundings of Vienna, where the population was concentrated and where the most important traffic routes lay. After the breakdown of the monarchy the trend was reversed. Vienna was unpopular. Annexed to Germany, new industries were established in western Austria. After the war, reconstruction started taking off faster in the western occupation zones than in the eastern part of the country occupied by the Soviet army. Cut off from eastern Europe by the "iron curtain," the western provinces oriented themselves to the West and profited again from their geographical proximity to the fast-growing parts of Central Europe. An economic west-east differential developed concerning welfare and economic dynamics.

A certain change in intellectual geography has also taken place during the last twenty years in connection with the term *"Mitteleuropa."* The idea of Central Europe had not been attractive to the nationalities that considered themselves as having escaped from the "Habsburg prison" after World War I. After the period of national socialism the idea had been even more discredited. But starting in the 1970s, Austrian cultural policy promoted the model of a stronger connection among the Danubian states, and this notion found some resonance in several neighboring countries.[38] For writers such as Milan Kundera, György Konrad and Leszek Kolakowski, the idea was appealing as a bastion against Soviet communism, and it produced a reassessment of the Habsburg monarchy, with some nostalgic features.[39] Now, after the fall of the borders, the appeal has faded. Today, eastern-oriented romanticism has been eliminated and "Central Europe" signifies (regional) good neighborly policy. A nostalgic attitude would not help the Eastern European countries; they aspire to matching West European standards.

Since the fall of the Iron Curtain, Austria has looked also to the west. During the Kreisky era in the 1970s, Austrian foreign policy was "global" and "interventionist"; Austria offered her services as a neutral state and as a mediator on the international scene. In the 1980s, Austria withdrew to Europe because of changed conditions, including an emphasis on a "realistic politics of neutrality."[40] The application for membership in the European Community is one of the consequences of this shifting of interests, and the integration of the European market is the immediate impulse for the "letter to Brussels" which was delivered on 17 July 1989. Shortly after this act, a phase of Europe-centered euphoria followed in Austria. Since then, however, a process of reassessment has started as the disadvantages of an EC membership on some issues (land possession by foreigners, protection of the environment) and in some sectors (agriculture) have become more obvious.[41] Austrian attitudes towards an EC accession have polarized since the time of application; while half of the population has consistently supported membership, the number of opponents has grown from 13 percent (April 1987) to 42 percent (January 1989).[42]

One element shaping Austrian identity during the last decades is particularly relevant for membership of the EC—Austrian neutrality. Austria has committed itself to eternal neutrality,[43] but this position in international law collides with the intention of EC members to melt toward a political union with a common security and foreign policy. Neutrality has come to be part of Austrian self-confidence; since 1955 it has been considered part of Austria's particular role in the international arena. Neutrality has vitally strengthened Austrians' belief that they represent a nation; therefore, 70 to 80 percent of Austrians would rather dispense with EC membership than renounce neutrality.[44] On the one hand, a fundamentalist position takes shape. The opponents of EC membership use neutrality as an unsurmountable barrier to the European Community. On the other hand, observers who consider EC membership advantageous for Austria warn of "neutrality fetishism;" the political scenery in Europe is changing, so traditional neutrality is no longer reasonable. The function of neutral territory to guarantee a buffer zone between the superpowers is obsolete. For the vision of a United Europe, which could become an instrument for keeping the peace by other institutions, neutrality is an obstacle; at the least, it needs a new interpretation.[45]

The consequences of potential membership in the European Community are difficult to estimate, especially since the EC countries themselves do not know what the final design of their political and economic cooperation will look like. In fact, Austria is already intimately connected with the EC; 63 percent of exports go to EC countries, 68 percent of imports come from there (1987). Strong economic impulses are expected from the common market. Austria will profit from it even as a non-member, which is not to say that higher advantages can be expected for membership.[46]

A complementary remark is necessary. The EC is not only an economic entity. A rising number of people are concerned about how European unity might be constructed without threatening the special national features of the individual European countries, namely Europe's great multiplicity, the differences of cultures and behavioral patterns which this multiplicity comprises.[47] Austria has never been a paragon of ardent nationalism like France. Austrians are used to multiple affiliations abroad and social plurality at home albeit never realized without conflicts. The vision of a monotonous and uniform European culture makes Austrians uneasy.[48] The new formula for mitigating those concerns is "unity in diversity," but this is no more than a vague hope, not a yet detailed and viable concept.

From Dead to Open Frontiers

Austria is an ethnically mixed society. It is situated where, some centuries ago, the Bavarian and the Slav populations merged. The intensity of immigration to Austria, especially to Vienna, during the last decades of the monarchy, from Hungary, Bohemia, Italy and Poland can easily be proven by reading an Austrian telephone directory, not to speak of the influences of different nationalities on Austrian cooking or theater. The Neapolitan influence on architecture and opera, the French influence on the language cannot be ignored. Vienna has been an ethnic and cultural melting pot for a long time.

The immigrants have been integrated, but the consequences of living together with them remain perceptible in mentality and behavior. Austrians are ascribed a high degree of empathy: to be able to delve into another person is crucial in a multi-ethnic society. It is said that Austrians, particularly the Viennese, are characterized by multi-layered behavioral patterns and by semantic ambivalence. They understand overtones and insinuations, hints and irony; they are charming and friendly. But there is also slackness, skepticism and self-irony, opportunistic behavior and weakness of the character, a permanent hesitancy—traits which may better be understood by imagining a multi-ethnic society where appropriate behavioral rules are never certain.

Mobility has been quite remarkable in the past decades. More than 10 percent of the Austrian population were born outside the frontiers of Austria, and 5 percent have a foreign citizenship. Since the end of World War II, Austria has absorbed many political refugees: immediately after the war, about 400,000 ethnic German refugees from Eastern Europe; in 1956/57 180,000 Hungarians; in 1968/69 many citizens of Czechoslovakia, and in 1981/82 thousands of Polish people. Since the 1970s Austria has operated as a turnstile of sorts for Jewish emigrants from the Soviet Union, who usually stay in Austria only for transit to other countries. Austria's favorable economic situation has brought many foreign workers into the country, especially from Turkey and Yugoslavia. At the end of 1990 about 260,000 foreigners (among 3 million employed workers) were legally working in Austria.[49] Their temporary jobs tend to become permanent, and many manage to stay in Austria. The second generation, which has grown up in Austria and cannot relate to the country of origin, is especially likely to stay.[50] Since 1945, 650,000 persons have settled in Austria permanently, while the whole population today is about 7.6 million inhabitants.

Austria's demographic development resembles that of most other industrial nations.[51] (1) The population has increased from about 5 million to more than 7.5 million people during the past hundred years. The birth rate and the death rate have declined. Life expectancy has dramatically increased and is 72.1 (for men) and 78.8 (for women). The population "pyramid" is becoming a "mushroom," with a broad cap and a thin trunk. (2) The number of marriages is decreasing, divorce rates are growing. While the core family produced an excess of births up to the 1960s, the population has been stagnating for several years and is going to shrink. The smaller age cohorts are already entering the age of parentage, so that the number of births is decreasing further. The group of families with more than three or four children is almost extinct. The average size of households is decreasing too, and there are more and more one-person or two-person households. (3) Rising life expectancy and decreasing birth rates are the reasons for an aging of the population; the share of people over 60 will rise from about 20 percent to 32 percent (in 2030). This tendency will mean severe financial problems for old age social security and the generous system of public health. One thousand persons (between 15 and 60) pay for 300 aged persons now; they have to pay for approximately 650 aged persons in the year 2035—according to an extrapolation with medium assumptions. The group of persons over 75 is increasing even faster, and they will need special care programs.[52] (4) The question of how to take care of elder persons will be aggravated by the rising employment rate of women which is, at about 60 percent, still relatively low in Austria.

The "New Europe" will not change these trends fundamentally. Three forecasts can be made. First, when Austria will be a member of the European Community it will be part of a geographic space where free mobility for citizens of all EC countries is guaranteed. This will produce new shifts in population statistics. Second, there is not only rising pressure for immigration from Eastern European countries, but also from countries of Southern Europe, North Africa, and the Middle East, and countries even farther away. When the Soviet Union opens its borders, many will ask for permission to emigrate to the developed West European countries. Austria will have to design a reasonable, long-term immigration policy. This need not necessarily have to be a policy of restrictions, but definitely a policy of putting up criteria for immigration. If the Austrian population is to be stabilized, immigration of about 25,000 people per year should be allowed. It would slow down the process of population aging, produce economic growth and improve the viability of the social security system.[53] Third, strong immigration has cultural consequences, as some major European cities—like London or Paris— are already experiencing. Xenophobia and intolerance will grow, and racist movements may create some problems in the future, as the fall 1991 election campaign in Vienna has already shown. Growing tensions with the integration of foreigners can already be observed in certain urban districts of Vienna, where foreign workers concentrate and send their children to school.

From a Traditional to a Post-Industrial Society

When one thinks of fin-de-siècle Vienna, what springs to mind is a fertile ground for creative modern culture. Some historians even praise the Habsburg monarchy for promoting cultural innovation, in spite of all its peculiar and contradictory structure.[54] Today, much attention is being paid to the arts, fashions and architecture of this period; moreover, Viennese fin-de-siècle literature, philosophy and psychoanalysis are also much admired. Many famous names such as Arthur Schnitzler, Sigmund Freud, or Otto Wagner come to mind. Other developments such as bureaucracy, law, economy, technology and medicine are rather neglected, however.[55] Since the turn of the century, Austria has implemented a comprehensive process of modernization. I can sketch only some categories.[56]

Structure of employment

Austria is becoming a service economy in accordance with the Fourastié-model. The number of employed persons in the primary sector (agriculture) has declined from about 50 percent in 1890 to 33 percent in 1951 and about 7 percent today. In the secondary sector (industry) the share of about 27 percent in 1890 increased to 38 percent in 1951 and decreased since the early 1970s to about 35 percent. The tertiary sector (services) has risen from 23 percent in 1890 to 29 percent in 1951 and further to about 58 percent today. The number of blue collar workers is declining, the number of white collar workers rising. In the "New Europe," traditional demarcations between the professions will diminish faster. If Austria joins the EC, declining prices in food products and a lower price level in the trade sector are expected. Peasants living on many very small farms in Austria will face special pressures from competitive large agricultural units in the EC; 71 percent of Austrians expect grave disadvantages for the agricultural sector.

Inequality

"Class theories" no longer describe social reality; a differentiated middle class structure has developed. "Horizontal inequalities" are gaining relevance: inequality of social security, access to leisure time amenities, conditions of living and working, access to public goods, the supply of the health system, etc. Women are disadvantaged, as they are in most countries, with regard to their income and career chances; they are burdened by the double strain of holding down jobs and household duties and by a higher level of hidden unemployment—in spite of a European wave of legislation to promote the rights of women. Foreign workers present a new social stratum below the indigenous hierarchies, and their immigration will increase. Families with more than 3 or 4 children often approach the poverty level. In the "New Europe" the income level of Germany (which is slightly above the Austrian) will be reached. While the Austrian tax system is only slightly progressive, government expenditures contribute to a redistribution of income; this structure can be maintained.[57] A reduction of welfare programs with redistributional effects does not appear to be necessary.

Education

In the sixties, an educational catastrophe was proclaimed in Germany, and demands for an expansion of the system of education were also heard in Austria. The government attempted to close the deficit of teachers and qualified workers, and started an expansion program for secondary schools and universities. The effort was legitimated by the demands of the economy as well as by the "right to education" for all citizens. Gifted children (as well as children from agricultural areas and from lower strata) were supported by the government, and programs for the mass marketing of higher education showed some success. Trends toward reaching higher qualified certificates exist and will be strengthened in the "New Europe." Some general remarks concerning educational problems: (1) The trend towards secondary schools (which pupils leave at age 18 instead of 15) is strong, especially in urban areas. The number of university students rose from 13.888 in 1955/56 to 40.889 in 1969/70 and to 164.746 in 1989/90; the quota of students compared to the population of the same age group is 14.6 percent (compared to: Switzerland's 14.9, Germany's 18.9, Sweden's 22, U.S.'s 24). (2) Because of different organizational conditions, international comparisons are not reliable; for the certificate of a German *"Fachhochschule"* or the American Bachelor of Arts (which count as post-secondary education) can often be compared with Austrian certificates at the secondary level in certain types of schools. In adapting to international structures of education, Austria will develop shorter post-secondary courses and restructure secondary schools to become post-secondary. (3) The orientation toward Europe will produce an internationalization of studies.[58] However, in the future, university education will be supplied at no cost to students. (4) Demographic development will reduce the numbers of pupils from 1981 to 2011 by 30 percent; the free capacities of teachers and buildings will be used for improving the quality of education. The increase of foreign pupils will demand special programs. (5) An attempt is being made to improve competition between schools, competition that will enhance quality of education rather than lower intellectual standards for getting certificates.

Mass media

The government monopoly over radio and television still exists in Austria, but in fact the industry is perforated by satellites, cable television and by broadcasting across the frontiers. In the next few years the market of electronic media will be liberalized, and there will be full competition from private suppliers. In the field of print media, Austria is characterized by an especially high concentration of newspapers—in fact, two thirds of the population get their news from three major newspapers. German corporations are gaining more and more influence, and anti-trust legislation will attempt to prevent a further concentration.

Religion

Rising income and education accelerate the process of eroding religious attitudes, as in other industrial nations. Traditional Catholic beliefs, which dominate in Austria, are diminishing.[59] Confessional contradictions are disappearing. Attendance at church services is declining, from a third of church members (1945) to a fourth today. The number of people leaving the church has risen, from 10,000 to 35,000 per year in the same period. The number of priests has decreased. A more selective religious belief is developing.

Value change

Concerns about technical and economic progress are growing in many industrial countries. In Austria there were conflicts about building new power stations and in a referendum a fully equipped nuclear power plant was voted down by the population and consequently has not gone on line. These concrete events signal more fundamental changes. "Eco-oriented" people are seeking new life styles that are totally different from those of modern industrial society.[60] Social scientists have described these social phenomena with terms like "the silent revolution," "post-materialism" or "post-modernism." However, these changes might not signify a post-materialist change of values, but rather an accumulation of values: the proponents do not disdain the goods of industrial society, but they want to acquire them and others all in a better quality. Visions of the new life style remain vague. The only obvious fact is that these visions negate existing society. Adherents of far-eastern messages of salvation, or of the new-age movements, present extreme versions of the new attitudes; on the other hand, Yuppies prize such things as money, career, and life style.

New social movements

Small groups have become the vanguard of ecological consciousness, and the environment in which they work is impossible to survey; what is emerging is a mixture of new social movements, citizens' committees, sects, and new small parties. These developments are similar to those in other countries, but there are time lags in the dispersion of green-alternative issues in the European Community. Austria has ecological laws and control measures that are stricter than those of most European countries. Fifty-four percent of Austrians fear that membership in the EC would have negative effects on these rigorous ecological standards.[61]

A special Austrian concern is trans-Alpine transit traffic between Germany and Italy with its rising load of exhaust emissions. During the last two decades EC traffic has increased from 3 to 20 million tons per year; the number of trucks crossing the Brenner Pass has increased from 800,000 in 1976 to 1.4 million today. The shifting of this truck traffic to the railroads is one of the most difficult issues of conflict with the neighboring countries. The EC will expect the creation of the common market to be accompanied by a further increase of transport services.

Conclusions

1. Austria has a consolidated national identity, and this awareness of nationhood concerns also its relations with Germany. For participating in the process of European integration Austria will have to redefine her neutral status under international law. The shifting of certain responsibilities to Brussels will open the chance to compensate for this act of Europe-wide centralisation by strenghtening federalism through a constitutional reform in Austria.

2. In the last decades, a strong system of political consensus has developed in Austria; this is proved by the cooperation of the two great political parties in the Grand Coalition and by the Austrian version of a corporatist system, the Economic and Social Partnership. Political culture in Austria, however, will have to adapt to Western European standards, which means that the special stability of political relations will be eroded. Austrians are characterized by a special mixture of disgust with political parties and politicians and of high aspiration levels concerning paternalistic government policy in all problems of life.

3. The Austrian economic miracle has produced a high level of complacency. The Austrian economic structure has been modernized, the

welfare state has been expanded. Economic policy in the 1970s was successful in stabilizing employment and price levels, but "Austro-Keynesianism" had to be substituted by a policy of reconstruction in the 1980s. A market-oriented economic policy has been emphasized during the past few years, but economic liberalism is being applied with great sensitivity and in a watered down version.

4. As a small nation, Austria has limited room for action in its foreign policy, but it is also little burdened by international obligations. The idea of "Central Europe," which has found some resonance in neighboring countries to the East, has transcended the frontiers of the country, as well as the application for membership in the European Community, the most important international policy decision for the rest of the century. Austria already has strong interconnections with EC-countries, especially with Germany.

5. Austria, particularly eastern Austria, has been an ethnically mixed society since the time of the monarchy. After World War II Austria integrated many political refugees. The potential of foreign workers has risen with economic welfare. The pattern of population development is similar to that of other industrial societies, so Austria will have to develop a reasonable immigration policy to come to terms with rising numbers of immigrants from Eastern Europe, from North Africa and from the Middle East.

6. Austria's social structure shows the average pattern of modernization; a shifting of employment from the primary to the tertiary sector, moderate inequality with redistributional measures, strong expansion of the system of higher education, loss of relevance for the churches, a value change emphasizing post-materialist and ecological concerns, and a demand for more participation articulated by new social movements, citizens' committees and newly arising parties.

NOTES

1. To understand some of the problems Austria has to solve in the "New Europe" one needs to go back at least to developments at the beginning of the century; as an example, the conflicts arising in Yugoslavia, one of the succession states of the Habsburg monarchy, go back to the "Balkans question" which stressed political relations in the second half of the 19th century, and to explore their roots one has to go back some centuries.

2. Eduard März, *Österreichische Bankpolitik in der Zeit der großen Wende 1913-1933. Am Beispiel der Creditanstalt für Handel und Gewerbe* (Vienna: Verlag für Geschichte und Politik, 1981); Eduard März and Fritz Weber, "The Antecedents of the

Austrian Financial Crash of 1931," *Zeitschrift für Wirtschafts- und Sozialwissenschaften* 103 (1983): 497-519; Gerald Schöpfer, "Möglichkeiten einer aktiven Konjunkturpolitik im Österreich der zwanziger Jahre," *Geschichte und Gegenwart* (1983): 24-46.

3. For a survey of Austrian history see Robert J. W. Evans, *Das Werden der Habsburgermonarchie 1550-1700. Gesellschaft, Kultur, Institutionen* (Vienna-Cologne-Graz: Böhlau, 1986); Hanns Leo Mikoletzky, *Österreichische Zeitgeschichte. Vom Ende der Monarchie bis zum Abschluß des Staatsvertrages 1955* (Vienna- Munich: Austria-Edition und Österreichischer Bundesverlag, 1964); Charles A. Gulick, *Österreich von Habsburg zu Hitler* (Vienna: Forum Verlag, 1976); Walter Pollak, ed., *Tausend Jahre Österreich. Eine biographische Chronik*, 3 vols. (Vienna-Munich: Jugend und Volk, 1973); Erika Weinzierl and Kurt Skalnik, eds., *Österreich - Die Zweite Republik*, 2 vols. (Graz-Vienna-Cologne: Styria, 1983); Erich Zöllner, *Geschichte Österreichs. Von den Anfängen bis zur Gegenwart*, 6th ed. (Vienna: Verlag für Geschichte und Politik, 1979).

4. Actually, the background of the striving towards the German nation is more complicated. The rise of nationalism in the nineteenth century may be traced back to ideas of romanticism, with visions of *"Volk," "Volksgeist"* and language. After the defeat of bourgeois-liberal revolution in 1848, it was no longer possible to admit progressive reform ideas, and they were replaced by the idea of a liberal and national union with Germany. But already at the end of the century the "Austrian" was opposed to the "German": The essential components of Germanhood within the "Austrian" were acknowledged, but the multiple additional elements of Austria's culture were emphasized. Moritz Csáky, "'Historisches Gedächtnis' und Identität," *Geschichte und Gegenwart* 10 (1991): 131-144; also Peter J. Katzenstein, *Disjoined Partners. Austria and Germany since 1815* (Berkeley: University of California Press, 1976); Felix Kreissler, *Der Österreicher und seine Nation. Ein Lernprozeß mit Hindernissen* (Vienna-Cologne-Graz: Böhlau, 1984); William T. Bluhm, *Building an Austrian Nation. The Political Integration of the Western State* (New Haven: Yale University Press, 1973); Georg Wagner, ed., *Österreich. Von der Staatsidee zum Nationalbewußtsein* (Vienna: Österreichische Staatsdruckerei, 1982).

5. For problems of Austrian identity see also Alfred Ableitinger, "Der 'Deutschlandkomplex' der Österreicher in der Ersten Republik," *politicum* 1 (1980): 9-17; Ernst Bruckmüller, *Nation Österreich. Sozialhistorische Aspekte ihrer Entwicklung* (Vienna-Cologne-Graz: Böhlau, 1984); Friedrich Heer, *Der Kampf um die österreichische Identität* (Vienna-Cologne-Graz: Böhlau, 1981); Robert Kann, *Das Nationalitätenproblem der Habsburgermonarchie*, 2 vols., 2nd ed. (Graz-Cologne: Böhlau, 1964).

6. Wolfgang Etschmann, *Die Kämpfe in Österreich im Juli 1934* (Vienna: Österreichischer Bundesverlag, 1984); Gerhard Jagschitz, *Der Putsch. Die Nationalsozialisten 1934 in Österreich* (Graz-Vienna-Cologne: Styria, 1976); Gottfried-Karl Kindermann, *Hitlers Niederlage in Österreich* (Hamburg: Hoffmann und Campe, 1984); Helmut Konrad, ed., *Sozialdemokratie und Anschluß* (Vienna-Cologne-Graz: Styria, 1978); Ludwig Reichold, *Kampf um Österreich* (Vienna: Österreichischer Bundesverlag, 1984); Walter B. Simon, *Österreich 1918-1938. Ideologien und Politik* (Vienna-Cologne-Graz: Böhlau, 1984).

7. Norbert Leser, *Zwischen Reformismus und Bolschewismus. Der Austromarxismus als Theorie und Praxis* (Vienna-Frankfurt-Zürich: Europa Verlag, 1968).

8. Alfred Klose, *Machtstrukturen in Österreich* (Vienna: Signum Verlag, 1987); Heinz Fischer, ed. *Das politische System Österreichs*, 3rd. ed. (Vienna-Munich-Zürich: Europaverlag, 1982).

9. Manfried Rauchensteiner, *Der Sonderfall. Die Besatzungszeit in Österreich 1945-1955* (Vienna-Cologne-Graz: Styria, 1979).

10. Gerald Stourzh, *Geschichte des Staatsvertrages 1945-1955. Österreichs Weg zur Neutralität*, 2nd ed. (Graz-Vienna-Cologne: Styria, 1980).

11. Alexander Vodopivec, *Die Balkanisierung Österreichs. Folgen einer großen Koalition* (Vienna-Munich: Molden, 1966).

12. Friedrich Fürstenberg, "Sozialkulturelle Aspekte der Sozialpartnerschaft," in *Sozialpartnerschaft in der Krise. Leistungen und Grenzen des Neokorporatismus in Österreich*, eds. Peter Gerlich, Edgar Grande and Wolfgang C. Müller (Vienna-Graz-Cologne: Böhlau, 1985), 29-39.

13. Peter A. Ulram, *Hegemonie und Erosion. Politische Kultur und politischer Wandel in Österreich* (Vienna-Cologne-Graz: Böhlau, 1990); Melanie A. Sully, *Political Parties and Elections in Austria* (London, 1981).

14. Klaus von Beyme, *Parteien in westlichen Demokratien* (Munich, 1984).

15. Manfried Rauchensteiner, *Die Zwei. Die Große Koalition in Österreich 1945-1966* (Vienna: Österreichischer Bundesverlag, 1987).

16. A. Wandruszka, "Österreichs politische Struktur," in *Geschichte der Republik Österreich*, ed. Hans Benedikt (Vienna: Verlag für Geschichte und Politik, 1954), 289-485; Gerhard Lehmbruch, *Proporzdemokratie. Politisches System und politische Kultur in der Schweiz und in Österreich* (Tübingen, 1967).

17. Dieter Bös, *Wirtschaftsgeschehen und Staatsgewalt* (Vienna-Freiburg-Basle: Herder, 1970); Alfred Klose, *Ein Weg zur Sozialpartnerschaft. Das österreichische Modell* (Vienna: Verlag für Geschichte und Politik, 1970); Thomas Lachs, *Wirtschaftspartnerschaft in Österreich* (Vienna: Verlag des Österreichischen Gewerkschaftsbundes, 1976); Peter Katzenstein, *Corporatism and Change: Austria, Switzerland and the Politics of Industry* (Ithaca-London: Cornell University Press, 1984); Bernd Marin, *Die Paritätische Kommission. Aufgeklärter Technokorporatismus in Österreich* (Vienna: Internationale Publikationen Ges., 1982); Anton Pelinka, *Gewerkschaften im Parteienstaat. Ein Vergleich zwischen dem Deutschen und dem Österreichischen Gewerkschaftsbund* (Berlin: Duncker & Humbolt, 1980); Gerald Schöpfer, ed., *Phänomen Sozialpartnerschaft* (Vienna-Cologne-Graz: Böhlau, 1980); Reinhard Christl, *Sozialpartnerschaft und Beschäftigungspolitik in Österreich* (Frankfurt-Berne-New York: Peter Lang, 1990); Peter Gerlich, et al., eds.: *Sozialpartnerschaft in der Krise. Leistungen und Grenzen des Neokorporatismus in Österreich* (Vienna-Graz-Cologne: Böhlau, 1985).

18. Ulrich von Alemann, ed., *Neokorporatismus*, (Frankfurt-New York: Campus, 1981).

19. David Campbell, "Der politische Paradigmenbruch in Österreich. Bürgerinitiativen und Volksabstimmungen als demokratiepolitische Phänomene", *SWS-Rundschau* 31 (1991): 211-222.

20. Peter Gerlich and Wolfgang C. Müller, eds., *Zwischen Koalition und Konkurrenz. Österreichs Parteien seit 1945* (Vienna: Braumüller, 1983); Anton Kofler, *Parteiengesellschaft im Umbruch* (Vienna-Cologne-Graz: Böhlau, 1985); Anton Pelinka and Fritz Plasser, eds., *Das österreichische Parteiensystem* (Vienna-Cologne-Graz: Böhlau, 1988); Fritz Plasser: *Parteien unter Streß. Zur Dynamik der Parteiensysteme in Österreich, der Bundesrepublik Deutschland und den Vereinigten Staaten* (Vienna-Cologne-Graz: Böhlau, 1987); Fritz Plasser and Peter A. Ulram, *Unbehagen im Parteienstaat* (Vienna-Cologne-Graz: Böhlau, 1982); Fritz Plasser, Peter A. Ulram and Manfried Welan, eds., *Demokratierituale. Zur Politischen Kultur der Informationsgesellschaft* (Vienna-Cologne-Graz: Böhlau, 1985); Christian Haerpfer, "Gesellschaft, Wählerverhalten und Parteiensystem. Wahlverhalten in Österreich, der BRD, Belgien und Großbritannien 1974-1987," *Journal für Sozialforschung* 27 (1987): 173-187.

21. The portion of voters with party identification has been decreasing from 75 percent (1969) to 59 percent (1989); the share of floating voters is rising from 7 to 28 percent for persons under 30, from 13 to 24 percent for persons with higher education, from 10 to 23 percent for white collar workers and public officials.

22. In spite of a slight weakening of the positive estimation, 63 percent of Austrians consider the system of social partnership "favorable," 6 percent "disadvantageous," and 30 percent are indifferent (1990). 58 percent are against a dissolution of the social partnership, 13 percent would agree to it. Further empirical results may be found in Kurt Traar and Franz Birk, "Die österreichische Sozialpartnerschaft und ihr Umfeld. Eine demoskopische Bestandsaufnahme", *SWS-Rundschau* 27 (1987): 11-40.

23. Manfred Prisching, "Bestandsaufnahme dar Sozialpartnerschaft", *Wirtschaft und Gesellschaft* 17 (1991): 9-36.

24. Norbert Leser, "Transformation und Konvergenz im österreichischen Parteiensystem", in *Das österreichische Parteiensystem*, ed. Pelinka and Plasser, 367-384.

25. The GDP of $16,000 ranks below Germany or Sweden (with about $14-15,000), significantly below Switzerland ($16.700) or the United States ($19.558), but above Spain and the Southern European countries ($6-9,000).

26. Kurt Rothschild, *Austria's Economic Development Between the Wars* (London, 1947); Gustav Otruba, *Die österreichische Wirtschaft im 20. Jahrhundert* (Vienna, 1968); Gottfried Haberler, *Austria's Economic Development: A Mirror Picture of the World Economy* (Washington D.C., 1980); Felix Butschek, *Die österreichische Wirtschaft im 20. Jahrhundert* (Vienna-Stuttgart: Gustav Fischer, 1986); Hanns Abele, Ewald Nowotny, Stefan Schleicher, Georg Winckler, eds., *Handbuch der österreichischen Wirtschaftspolitik*, 3rd ed. (Vienna: Manz, 1984, 1989); S. W.

Arndt, ed., *The Political Economy of Austria* (Washington D.C., 1982); Helmut Kramer, Felix Butschek, eds., *Vom Nachzügler zum Vorbild. Österreichische Wirtschaft 1945-1985* (Vienna, 1985).

27. Austria's ÖS 16,000 may be compared with Switzerland (10,500), Spain (5,500), Sweden, Norway and Belgium (about 4,000) Great Britain 2,000, Germany and the U.S. (about 1,500). For the Austrian situation see Max Preglau et. al., *Fremdenverquer, Kosten und Nutzen des Tourismus am Beispiel Obergurgl* (Innsbruck, 1985).

28. The Austrian GDP in 1990 of ÖS 1.810 billion amounted to a per capita income of 235,000.

29. Egon Matzner, *Wohlfahrtsstaat und Wirtschaftskrise. Österreichs Sozialisten suchen einen Ausweg* (Reinbek. b.H.: Rowohlt, 1978); Egon Matzner et.al., *Der Wohlfahrtsstaat von morgen. Entwurf eines zeitgemäßen Musters staatlicher Interventionen* (Vienna: Österreichischer Bundesverlag, 1982); Manfred Prisching, *Krisen. Eine soziologische Untersuchung* (Vienna-Cologne-Graz: Böhlau, 1986).

30. Manfred Prisching, *Arbeitslosenprotest und Resignation in der Wirtschaftskrise* (Frankfurt-New York: Campus, 1988).

31. Friedrich von Hayek, *Law, Legislation and Liberty. A New Statement of the Liberal Principles of Justice and Political Economy*, 3 vols., 1973-79 (ed. in one vol. 1982: Routledge & Kegan Paul, 1982).

32. Christoph Badelt, *Sozioökonomie der Selbstorganisation. Beispiele zur Bürgerselbsthilfe und ihre wirtschaftliche Bedeutung* (Frankfurt-New York: Campus, 1980); Christoph Badelt, *Politische Ökonomie der Freiwilligenarbeit. Theoretische Grundlegung und Anwendung in der Sozialpolitik* (Frankfurt-New York: Campus, 1985).

33. Manfred Prisching, "Privatisierung als symbolische Politik," *Wirtschaftspolitische Blätter* 35 (1988): 408-416.

34. Christian Brünner, ed., *Korruption und Kontrolle* (Vienna-Cologne-Graz: Böhlau, 1981); Christian Fleck and Helmut Kuzmics, eds., *Korruption. Zur Soziologie nicht immer abweichenden Verhaltens* (Königstein: Athenäum Verlag, 1985).

35. Wolfgang Kraus, "Die demokratische Herausforderung. Motive eines neuen Aufbruchs," in Gerd Bacher, Karl Schwarzenberg and Josef Taus, eds., *Standort Österreich. Über Kultur, Wirtschaft und Politik im Wandel* (Graz-Vienna-Cologne: Styria, 1990), 827-840.

36. Gerald Stourzh, "Nach der deutschen Einheit: Österreichs Standort in Europa," *Europäische Rundschau* 18 (1990): 3-313.

37. This is an argument for membership in the European Community. As a non-member Austria would also have to adapt its legal system to the economic giant EC for competitive reasons, and as a member it has the chance to participate in the consultations.

38. Erhard Busek and Emil Brix, eds., *Projekt Mitteleuropa* (Vienna: Ueberreuter, 1986); Erhard Busek and Gerald Stourzh, eds., *Nationale Vielfalt und gemeinsames Erbe in Mitteleuropa* (Vienna-Munich, 1990); Erhard Busek and Gerhard Wilflinger, eds., *Aufbruch nach Mitteleuropa. Rekonstruktion eines versunkenen Kontinents* (Vienna: Edition Atelier-Herold, 1986).

39. Hans-Georg Heinrich, "Nachbarschaftspolitik - ein Mythos?", *Österreichische Zeitschrift für Politikwissenschaft* 17 (1988): 155-168.

40. Helmut Kramer, "'Wende' in der österreichischen Außenpolitik? Zur Außenpolitik der SPÖ-ÖVP-Koalition," *Österreichische Zeitschrift für Politikwissenschaft* 17 (1988): 117-131.

41. H. Glatz and Hans Moser, eds., *Herausforderung EG-Binnenmarkt. Kopfüber in die EG?* (Vienna: Service Fachverlag an der Wirtschaftsuniversität Wien, 1989); Paul Luif, *Neutrale in die EG? Die westeuropäische Integration und die neutralen Staaten* (Vienna: Braumüller, 1989); Heinrich Schneider, *Alleingang nach Brüssel. Österreichs EG-Politik* (Vienna, 1990); Manfred Rotter, "Soll Österreich den EG beitreten - Zur Multidimensionalität einer eindimensional gestellten Frage," *Österreichische Zeitschrift für Politikwissenschaft* 17 (1988): 169-181; Andreas Unterberger, "Probleme und Vorteile einer österreichischen EG-Mitgliedschaft," *Europäische Rundschau* 19 (1991): 43-54.

42. Membership of the EC being the dominating international issue in the mass media (together with the changes in the Eastern European countries), interest in international policy has risen dramatically in Austria. In 1981, 25 percent called themselves "very interested" or "rather interested" in international matters, in the year 1990, 56 percent; "less interested" or "not interested" were 48 percent or 19 percent, respectively. In 1981, 7 percent thought that they were strongly affected by international decisions, in 1990 the level increased to 20 percent, see Helmut Kramer, "Öffentliche Meinung und die österreichische EG-Entscheidung im Jahre 1989", *SWS-Rundschau* 31 (1991): 191-202.

43. Konrad Ginther, *Neutralität und Neutralitätspolitik* (Vienna-New York: Springer, 1975); Manfred Rotter, *Die dauernde Neutralität* (Berlin, 1981).

44. Kramer, "Öffentliche Meinung."

45. It is not only Austria which, on the way to the "New Europe," has difficulties with its identity; Switzerland is in a phase of self-reflection too, see e.g., Hugo Bütler, "Der europäische Aufbruch und die helvetische Identitätskrise," *Europäische Rundschau* 19 (1991): 3-9; for a comparison of the two countries Friedrich Koja and Gerald Stourzh, eds., *Schweiz - Österreich. Ähnlichkeiten und Kontraste* (Vienna-Cologne-Graz: Böhlau, 1986). In Austria, opinions are divided, in 1991, 46 percent of the Austrians do not feel the need to redefine neutrality, while 43 percent think that the neutral position should be adapted to the new circumstances.

46. Fritz Breuss and Jan Stankovsky, *Österreich und der EG-Binnenmarkt* (Vienna: Signum Verlag, 1988). In the meantime, there is also a parallel action under way, the construction of the European Economic Space, proposed by Jacques Delors.

47. Max Haller, "Grenzen und Variationen gesellschaftlicher Entwicklung in Europa

- eine Herausforderung und Aufgabe für die vergleichende Soziologie,"
Österreichische Zeitschrift für Soziologie 13 (1988): 5-33.

48. In 1989, 48 percent of Austrians thought that the EC has negative effects on national peculiarity and identity, 20 percent hoped for positive effects.

49. Austria maintained a very low level of unemployment in the years of economic crisis after 1975; but now the unemployment rate persists at about 5 to 6 percent (150,000 to 180,000 persons) in spite of solid annual growth rates and an increase in the number of employed. One of the reasons is the (partly illegal) immigration of foreign workers.

50. Hans Wimmer, ed., *Ausländische Arbeitskräfte in Österreich* (Frankfurt-New York: Campus, 1986).

51. In 1790, Austria (on the territory of today) had a population of 3 million, in 1890 5.4 million, in 1923 6.5 million, in 1951 6.9 million. Birth rates (births on 1.000 inhabitants) decreased from about 35 (around 1870) to less than 20 (in the 1920s) and they are above 10 today. Death rates declined from about 31 (around 1870) to 19 (around 1912) and are about 12 today.

52. Peter Findl, Robert Holzmann and Rainer Münz, *Bevölkerung und Sozialstaat* (Vienna: Manz, 1987); Günther Chaloupek, Joachim Lamel and Josef Richter, eds., *Bevölkerungsrückgang und Wirtschaft. Szenarien bis 2051 für Österreich* (Heidelberg: Physica Verlag, 1988).

53. Heinz Faßmann and Rainer Münz, "Einwanderungsland Österreich?" *Demographische Informationen* (1990/91): 85-91.

54. Peter Hanák, *Ungarn in der Donaumonarchie. Probleme der bürgerlichen Umgestaltung eines Vielvölkerstaates* (Vienna-Munich-Budapest: Verlag für Geschichte und Politik, 1984); Carl L. Schorske, *Wien. Geist und Gesellschaft im Fin de Siécle* (Frankfurt a.M.: Fischer, 1982); Peter Berner, Emil Brix and Wolfgang Mantl, eds., *Wien um 1900. Aufbruch in die Moderne* (Vienna: Verlag für Geschichte und Politik, 1986); Emil Brix and Patrick Werckner, eds., *Die Wiener Moderne* (Vienna-Munich, 1990); Allan Janik and Stephen Toulmin, *Wittgensteins Wien* (Munich-Zurich: Piper, 1987); Endre Kiss, *Der Tod der K. u. K. Weltordnung in Wien. Ideengeschichte Österreichs um die Jahrhundertwende* (Vienna-Cologne-Graz: Böhlau, 1986); William Johnston, *Österreichische Kultur- und Geistesgeschichte. Gesellschaft und Ideen im Donauraum 1948-1938* (Vienna-Cologne-Graz: Böhlau, 1974); Albert Fuchs, *Geistige Strömungen in Österreich 1867-1918* (Vienna: Löcker Verlag, 1978); Norbert Leser, *Genius Austriacus. Beiträge zur politischen Geschichte und Geistesgeschichte Österreichs*, 2nd ed. (Vienna-Cologne-Graz: Böhlau, 1986).

55. Wolfgang Mantl, "Wien um 1900 - ein goldener Stachel," in *Wien um 1900*, 249-257.

56. See for surveys Kurt Steiner, ed., *Tradition und Innovation in Contemporary Austria* (Palo Alto, 1981); Erich Bodzenta, *Die österreichische Gesellschaft. Entwicklung - Struktur - Probleme* (Vienna, 1980); Erich Bodzenta, Hans Seidel

and Karl Stigelbauer, *Österreich im Wandel. Gesellschaft, Wirtschaft, Raum* (Vienna-New York: Springer, 1985); Stephan Koren, Karl Pisa and Kurt Waldheim, eds., *Politik für die Zukunft* (Vienna-Cologne-Graz: Böhlau, 1984); Bacher, Schwarzenberg and Taus, eds., *Standort Österreich. Über Kultur, Wirtschaft und Politik im Wandel.*

57. The main redistributional effects are implemented by unemployment compensation, health transfers and family benefits. Generally, one might presume that higher disposable income is reduced by 25 percent, medium income by 5 percent, while lower incomes rise by 30 percent. For opinions about distribution see Gilbert Norden, *Einkommensgerechtigkeit. Was darunter verstanden wird. Eine Erkundungsstudie* (Vienna-Cologne-Graz: Böhlau, 1985).

58. As Germany applies a *numerus clausus* for admission to several university courses, Austria has to face the problem of how to enact measures that will prevent students excluded from Germany from studying in Austria.

59. Paul M. Zulehner, *Religion und Kirche in Österreich* (Vienna, 1973).

60. Günther Chaloupek and Joachim Lamel, eds., *Die zweifelnde Gesellschaft* (Vienna: Österreichischer Bundesverlag, 1983); Max Haller and Kurt Holm, eds., *Werthaltungen und Lebensformen in Österreich. Ergebnisse des sozialen Survey 1986* (Vienna-Munich, 1987); Leopold Rosenmayr, ed., *Politische Beteiligung und Wertwandel in Österreich. Einstellungen zu Politik und Wertwandel im internationalen Vergleich* (Munich-Vienna: Verlag für Geschichte und Politik, 1980).

61. New decisions of the European Court indicate that severe laws in ecology and consumer protection are allowed even if they surmount the general level in other countries, and that these aims count more than free trade of goods.

Security in Europe 1992

*Wolfgang Danspeckgruber**

Introduction

To analyse security, in the contemporary European environment we must examine the shifting meanings of the term over the last two decades. Since the 1970s, notions of security have focused on the survival of the state and the stability of its boundaries, and more on the individual citizen and his or her well-being. Issues such as the welfare state, enemployment, education, social programs, energy conservation, environmental protection and economic interdependence have become the major security concerns of the general public and the governments of Western democracies. This new focus has been made strikingly clear in the search for greater self-determination, sovereignty, and prosperity east of the Elbe from 1988 onwards. In the Europe of 1992, only economic stability and prosperity will provide peace and security.

Today's changing environment in Europe is creating a new differentiation of security perceptions and concerns, especially between the old (West European) and emerging (East European) democracies. The latter are still preoccupied with more traditional issues such as sovereignty, while Western Europe has already shifted attention to the concerns prevalent in a post-industrial or post-modern society.

Three developments have profoundly shaped the European security environment. While the Western sphere has begun to strive for industrial, economic, scientific and political integration, the integrated systems of CMEA and WTO have crumbled in the East. The ensuing centrifugal forces have not stopped in front of entire states such as Yugoslavia, the USSR, and even the CSFR. By the same token, global bipolar antagonism has given way to a monopolar structure, a reemerging balance of power, and regionalization.

The paper addresses issues of European security in 1992 from three different perspectives: it considers the evolving meaning of security in theoretical terms; next, it explores developments in European security resulting from geopolitics and the emerging security architecture; finally, it examines the implications for Austria.

Background

Today the post-World War II order has ceassed to exist, and the Cold War has enden. But the division between European states persists. The states may still belong to various organizations such as to the EC (European Community), the EFTA (European Free Trade Association), and, eventually, the European Economic Area (EEA); militarily to NATO (North Atlantic Treaty Organization) or to WEU (West European Union). But states may also just be in search of a new orientation of their foreign and security policy. Regarding the level of GDP, industrial development, financial capabilities, and national welfare, countries may simply be categorized between the rich and the poor.

Starting with the increasing power of the Polish labor movement *Solidarity* and the dissolution of the Hungarian Communist party, the political upheavals in Eastern Europe culminated in the crumbling of the Berlin Wall in November 1989, the "velvet revolution" in Czechoslovakia, and the execution of Romanian President Ceausescu and his wife in December 1989. The wave of revolutionary events led to the most important milestones for a new European order: the unification of Germany in October 1990, the official dissolution of the Soviet Union, and the ratification of the European Political Union (EPU) and the European Monetary Union (EMU), December 1991 in Maastricht.

These developments emerged from three sources that came together in the 1980s: the intention of the Reagan administration to bring the United States back to global economic and political leadership (as seen by President Reagan's Strategic Defense Initiative of March 1983); the ascent of Communist Party Secretary General Michail Gorbachev and his desire to reform Soviet society and the economy to retain Soviet power; and the EC's search for intensified economic-industrial and political integration.

In the mid-1980s, the EC's members, particularly France and Germany intensified and expanded their drive for greater cooperation and integration in the face of ever increasing Japanese and American industrial-technological competition in world markets. This European reaction resulted at once in the intensification of scientific and technological cooperation (EUREKA, ESPRIT and the like). By 1987, the Single European Act (SEA) was ratified, a program for the creation of a Single European Market (SEM) was launched; plans were announced to hold intergovernmental conferences (IGCs) to create a European Monetary Union (EMU) and a European Political Union (EPU) between the twelve EC states.[1] The first major result has been the agreement of October 1991 between the EFTA and the EC to create an EEA with nineteen member states. The treaty created the largest free trade area in the world.[2] The other step towards a European Union (EU) was the ratification of the EPU and EMU at Maastricht, December 1991.

In Eastern Europe, the search for self-determination of ethnic minorities that has until 1990 been repressed by centralized communist leadership has also found new ways of expression. New socio-economic and welfare agendas have surfaced together with new standards in environmental protection. However, long-suppressed animosities between ethnic minorities within certain states—notably Yugoslavia, former Soviet republics, and Czechoslovakia—have erupted, and in some instances caused open violence. Ethnic groups have declared their intention to shape their own destiny by expanding freedom and minority rights, or even by claiming full sovereignty. Former Yugoslav Prime Minister Ante Markovic has warned about the danger that, instead of the Europeanization of the Balkans, there might be a Balkanization of Europe.[3]

The interconnectedness of these developments may explain why so many events unfolded within so short a time in the late 1980s. Now, there are indications that international relations have passed from the Cold War to a "hotter peace," from an era of relative bipolar stability to a time of greater fluctuation, antagonism, and even tensions—not necessarily *between* states, but most certainly either *within* some of them, or between territories irrespective of national boundaries.[4] These new developments re-create old dilemmas: the Iron Curtain may have fallen, but the difference between Eastern and Western Europe may be maintained by yet another obstacle—a "Welfare Wall" as described by Hungarian Prime Minister Jozsef Antall.[5]

Theoretical Considerations
Interpretations of Security

The concept "security" and the accompanying questions of threat perception and crisis-interpretation and crisis-management have undergone substantial transformation. Arguably, technological progress, economic interdependence, and the changing role of ideology in international affairs have provided the key elements to the evolution of security. Richard Cooper characterizes national security as "the capacity of a society to enjoy and cultivate its culture and values".[6] According to Heinz Vetschera security means "the relative absence of threat."[7] Therefore, both the kind and intensity of threat (what, how much) and the object (state, person, values) are important.

One may differentiate three levels in analyses of security. On the *macro level*, discussions address security and threat issues that are continental or national in scope; on the *micro level* these issues are analyzed as regional, or communal concerns. On the *personal level*, individual perceptions, fears, and aspirations are explored. Certainly those have been exposed to dramatic change over the last years, from being subject to great ideological influence to becoming issue of personal liberation and realization. The contents of the latter however is profoundly different in the Eastern and Western European states. While in the OECD member countries "post-industrial" or post-modern concerns show prominently, the former Warsaw Pact states struggle to find their way to stable liberal, industrialized democracies. "Post-industrial" means a dramatic increase in the awareness of issues such as pollution, environmental protection, social services, reduction of negative influences of technology, high safety standards at work—ie a general "back to nature" trend. As a precondition for this development a state and society must have been exposed to industrialization, modernization, and social sophistication over a period of time. The liberal idea, the voluntary refrain from use of force and power are as important preconditions as an engrained political culture.[8]

Threats to security may arise from actual or perceived developments, from military affairs, technological-environmental catastrophes, ethnic strife, natural catastrophes, or even economic shortcomings such as poverty.[9] Technological progress has produced two fundamental changes. One is an enormous increase in entanglement, integration, and infrastructural interconnectedness in all three dimensions, along with the decrease in the effects and values of national boundaries, and hence of sovereignty. The other is technology's dramatic contribution to the educational sophistication of our societies. By increasing information, technology has deepened societies' awareness in foreign affairs, and thus has heightened their perception of threats and fears.

Traditional military and diplomatic aspects of security now go hand-in-hand with economic, socio-political, and environmental concerns. Contemporary security analyses must consider the end of the Cold War, of geopolitical rules like the roll back strategy, and the diminished role of ideology in international relations. Other emerging security issues include personal well-being, welfare, migration, and pollution on the more individual level, as well as ethnic and sociocultural, or religious concerns on the communal level. Historical evidence, supported by contemporary developments in the CIS (Commonwealth of Independent States), suggests that certain security issues may develop from the personal to the micro and macro levels. For instance, poverty results in widespread discontent, creating political problems, and eventually leading to national or regional instability with security implications. Uwe Nerlich argues that military security and the political order in Europe are substantially influenced by economic and social forces which also have created the recent evolutions. The Japanese concept of "comprehensive security"—already long employed by Europe's neutral states—is thus important in dealing with political, military, economic and social, as well as environmental tasks in a national and multinational context.[10]

Such new dimensions of security cause new crises and conflicts, and in turn create demands for new crises prevention and management. Even in the purely military dimension, issues have been extended to confidence- and security-building measures, arms and force control, and verification. NATO's awareness of non-military components such as environmental protection, migration, demography, and nationalism in the NACC indicate the international readiness for the expansion of the concept of security.

The search for greater personal liberty and a higher standard of living runs concomitant with the awareness of national self-determination. The Czech-Slovak example shows that the latter does not necessarily depend on the former. The Slovaks seem to react against a "big brother" with whom they share the house, but who conceals them from the world. Slovak nationalism is fuelled partly by economic grievance (though the net annual transfer of resources between the two is in the Slovaks' favor), partly by the fear for the future.[11]

Long suppressed rivalries may flare up also between groups of different national, religious, or historical background over philosophical differences and territorial desires. Such conflicts have multiplied all over Europe between groups of different ethnic orientation, religious beliefs, and national backgrounds. Examples can be found in the current strife in Yugoslavia between Serbs, Croats, Slovenes, and Bosnians, and in the former Soviet Union between the sixteen republics (resulting in their full sovereignty). But even intra-state conflicts over a prolonged period may charge the neighboring geographic area and political atmosphere to a degree that draws in outside powers or eventually leads to actual war (i.e. the potential danger of "Lebanonization"). As a result, any minor nationality conflict may become a major, even hostile, affair. Thus, the chance of solving conflicts through objective political discussions is reduced. In such an emotionally charged arena, any conflict may easily spray to other ares via ethnic links and geographical proximity. Modern communications may allow a dispersion of ethnic conflicts independent of neighboring countries.[12] This could be called a negative or reverse Domino effect.[13] Also, the difference between boundaries accepted by ethnic groups and those maintained between states suggest further geographical dispersal to ever wider neighboring areas.[14]

Unfortunately, instead of a *Europeanization* of the Balkans, we may face a *Lebanonization* of the Balkans and a *Balkanization* of Eastern-European affairs. *Balkanization* means the spreading of conflicts among groups with different or even antagonistic ethnic, religious, or historical backgrounds. *Lebanonization* implies the continuous clashes between such groups in one territory until complete exhaustion or intervention by an outside power. The latter could develop into a substantial conflict.[15]

The treatment of Slovenia and Croatia (which were diplomatically recognized by the EC in January 1992) and the recognition of the former republics of the Soviet Union may offer great incentives for other minorities.[16] Indeed, in Italian South Tyrol pressure mounts for greater self-determination. The same is true among Catalans and Basques in Northern Spain, Valones and Flamons in Belgium, Slovaks in Czechoslovakia, Hungarians in Rumania and Yugoslavia, Macedonians in Greece, Albanians in Serbia, Greeks in Albania, Poles in the Ukraine and for others scattered throughout the territory of Russia, Belarus, Lithuania and Latvia.[17]

In contemporary Europe forces of integration vie with forces of disintegration. The dangerous—and potentially negative—aspect of this development lies in the historically unfortunate coincidence between the push for greater integration towards a European Union on the one hand and increasing problems from the East on the other. The effects of economic chaos and demands for self-government and democratization meet a European economy partly in recession and a united Germany increasing its power while still digesting unification; this limits its potential for economic help. At the same time the chaotic economic situation in the former Soviet satellite countries gives rise to national feelings and discontent. All of this makes for a potentially explosive mixture.

Changes in the Use and Value of Terminologies

Theoretical discussions of security are subtly altering the meaning of concepts[18] such as "independence," "autonomy," and "sovereignty." The meanings of "crisis" and "conflict"are also changing. These terms represent historic concepts that have been adapted over the decades by international law. The geographical changes in borders, combined with the demands of modern economics, make certain aspects of old concepts such as "independence," "sovereignty" and "autonomy" irrelevant. The readiness among Western European populations to think in purely national terms has diminished since the 1970s, though there are now contradictory trends emerging about foreigners. For Eastern Europeans the same does not seem to hold true. Notions of nationalism, sovereignty, human rights, economic prosperity—namely all dimensions of an advanced industrialized society—are still new and partly in the making. Eastern Europe is far from grappling with the considerations of post-industrial society, awaiting instead a still-to-be created modern industrial state.

The chances of the Baltic republics or, say, Slovenia to obtain "old style" sovereignty are relatively bleak. In *realpolitik,* sovereignty may have been reduced to a mostly legal concept, with limited actual feasibility. Economic autonomy is virtually impossible and even in the political, legal, and administrative sphere, traditional autonomy of governments is unlikely to materialize.

New states seem to seek a much enhanced degree of ethnic-national independence from their traditional national sovereign (Czechoslovakia, Slovenia, Croatia, Ukraine, Georgia, and the like). On the other hand, all of them are ready to accept inclusion in a proper supra-national conglomerate. Lithuania and Latvia have also expressed interest in eventually joining a working Commonwealth of Independent Sovereign States (CIS).[19]

Regionalization

"Europe of the regions" has become a keyword in contemporary European affairs. This regionalization includes the emergence of subregions comprising several smaller states or parts of states, sharing infrastructural needs based upon ethnic, historical, geographic, and climatic similarities.

For regions of Central and Northern Europe, these tendencies represent the continuation of a natural development, arrested after 1914. They provide links among different subunits, mostly federal states or counties of existing states, and form functioning communities via stronger interaction in transport, energy, environment, and social infrastructure. These subregions will eventually challenge the notion of sovereignty oriented to purely national objectives, and will reduce the chances that exclusively state oriented dogmas (such as neutrality) will prevail. Regionalization also may carry with it advantagous and disadvantageous tunes. Infrastructural programs and cohesion bears positive elements for regional development; economic chaos and ethno-religious conflicts have the potential to disperse (ie. the "negative domino effect"), with considerable negative impacts. In light of EC/EU integration, the question remains whether subregionalization contributes to continental integration or runs counter to it.

In Europe, regionalization can be observed in the Danubian area, in the Nordic area around the Baltic sea, and in the Mediterranean area, between cantons of Switzerland, regions of France, and Germany. The "Regio Basiliensis" (region of Basle, Switzerland) has existed for 27 years and provides a historic example of successful regionalization below the legal state level. But new regionalization may also occur in the political-military sphere. In 1991, Hungary, Poland, and Czechoslovakia have formed the "Visegrad Group"—growing out of the "Bratislava Process."[20] This is an expression of increasing trilateral cooperation, with military and political implications.

The *ARGE-Alp-Adria*, and *ARGE-Donau-Länder* cooperations offer models of interaction between federal states and provinces. Perhaps the most prominent organization is the "Pentagonale." It commenced in 1989 between the countries of the former Habsburg Monarchy—Austria, Hungary, Czechoslovakia, Italy and Yugoslavia. Joined by Poland in 1991, it has become the "Hexagonale." In a recent meeting, it decided to accept Slovenia and Croatia and possibly also other Yugoslav republics as future members of the group.[21] The *Hexagonale*'s transnational projects aim at cooperation in transportation, telecommunications, education, environmental protection, and cultural affairs, along with support for small and medium enterprises.[22]

Demography and Personalities
Still another set of issues will exert strong influence on Europe's future

stability and architecture, namely the issues of the human attitudes, population movements, and demographic developments (including the personality dimension of leadership and political culture in European politics).

Human behavior and expectations, and their impact on international affairs represent a significant, sometimes overlooked factor. These factors are important for governments as well as for the beliefs and attitudes of populations. There is a dramatic shift in status, education, orientation and historic understanding of the current younger, soon-to-be leading generation. In the Western European countries, this generation has obtained great educational sophistication, along with postindustrial values, high welfare expectations, prosperity, and enormous freedom for leisure and travel. In the 1960s and 1970s the liberal, revolutionary spirit prevailed, advocationg greater personal, sexual, educational liberty. The welfare society and *Wirtschaftswunder* gave rise to a widespread social-democratic influence. The liberal movement began to lose momentum in the late 1970s, and early 1980s, following the emergence of the Green and Alternative (anti-nuclear and pro-disarmament) political parties along with a "new Cold War," and new economic problems. By the end of the 1980s, we were confronted with manifold challenges: great economic achievements and other forms of success, the end of the Cold War and the unification of Germany, the breakdown of the Iron Curtain, but also econcomic and professional problems, AIDS, and mass migrations into Western Europe. The younger West European generation, partly by having lived the yuppie lifestyle, and partly through self centeredness has so far never been exposed to real hardship or major crises. Historical awareness has fallen to the point that even Adolf Hitler has become a remote controversial figure. In the Yuppie generation the warning examples of both world wars and the difficult postwar periods have evaporated. The younger generations may have lost the sensitive prudence that the older generation of leaders has adhered to. Today most of this postwar generation has died or is retiring. This certainly will influence future leadership styles as it already influences mass politics and the media. Political opposition movements or protests are likely to take more conservative stands in the future.

Demographic patterns are shifting in Central and Northern Europe, where closed societies are finding it necessary to accommodate refugees from neighboring areas as well as from outside cultures. The changes in 1989 and 1990 have created a severe and unexpected challenge for the West European societies who have to absorb the effects in their personal sphere. These emerging movements have brought together different religions (Christian and Islamic for example) and religious subgroups such as those from the Catholic south and the Protestant north.

The massive immigration to Western Europe is causing fundamental challenges. François Heisbourg has described population movementes since 1945: displaced persons; the migration from southern Europe and the Maghreb; the clandestine immigration, guest workers, and refugees of the 1970s; the immigration into the EC and Eastern refugees of the 1980s.[23] The developments in the early 1990s leave both the extent and intensity of migration from the East open. Soon there may be increased inflows from the former Soviet Union, depending on the degree of economic chaos and possible civil strife. The potential developments include refugees from civil war striven Yugoslavia, and eventually from neighboring areas affected by this conflict. Many of the new refugees will be Muslim or Orthodox. Resulting problems may comprise rising crime, racial or religious tensions, and the intensification of ultra nationalist backlashes. Additionally, such an influx in Central and Northern Europe might have negative repercussions on inherent north-south tensions within the EC area and integration.

The role of personality in political leadership carries great importance, particularly in periods of change. For instance, British Prime Minister Margaret Thatcher, German Chancellor Helmut Kohl, French President Francois Mitterrand, Mikhail Gorbachev, and U.S. President George Bush were instrumental in shaping European affairs in 1988-90. Their mutual understanding and appreciation encouraged peaceful transitions. Also the personal relationship between Helmut Kohl and François Mitterrand has been instrumental in the push for European unification; it has been argued that the Maastricht summit of December 1991 might not have happened without them.[24] The question remains how changes in this leadership quintet will affect Europe's future. Mrs. Thatcher's departure from the once-dominant Kohl-Mitterrand-Thatcher troika has already affected England's future position vis-a-vis Europe. Presumably the British government's attitude toward Yugoslavia would also have been different in Thatcher's days. Successors of President Mitterrand and Federal Chancellor Kohl, in combination with a changed leadership structure in the CIS, may provide for yet more instability and unpredictability. Already the new leaders such as Boris Yeltsin, the decreasing popularity of Mitterrand and domestic problems for President Bush and Prime Minister John Major seem to influence their international credibility. Perhaps more conservative policies and actions may appear soon in Europe's top political management echelon, reflecting the above described changes in the attitudes and interests of the peoples.

Geopolitics

In contemporary geopolitics, several issues are relevant: integration, regionalization, and the eventual search for hegemony in the community of states; also, the dissolution of old national entities, and the formation of new central authorities (see the European Union, leading from national disintegration to regional re-integration).[25] Regional hegemonic concentration may evolve in a centripetal manner around major economic and industrial powers; its international effects can be either benevolent or malevolent. While disintegration may be observed in certain areas, re-integration, centering around strong countries, or even supranational structures, may surface elsewhere. Whatever the expressed form of power, direct or indirect, economic-industrial capabilities and success are prone to create political-strategic influence and to shape international perception.[26] Despite centripetal versus centrifugal gravitation to or from power centers, balance of power will again be prominent as a determining force between states, especially the less powerful ones in Europe.

Another argument envisages the relationship between the center and periphery of empires. If Brussels were to become the center of a working European Union—a "European Empire"—one could conclude that conflicts in the Balkans or on the Bosporus would be located on its periphery.[27] But contemporary technological progress (rapid communication and transportation), import of labor from the peripheral areas (guest workers), and mass tourism in the Mediterranean, have substantially changed that assumption.[28] Environmental considerations such as pollution may force metropolitan tourists from their regular places into the periphery of such a European empire (i.e. see the effects of pollution of the Mediterranean).[29]

In contemporary terms, one can argue that the relative decline of the hegemony of the two superpowers has facilitated the breaking up of old structures and permitted the unification of Germany. This may be reminiscent of the 1860s. Then, German and Italian unification was possible mainly because of the relative absence of English and Russian attention from the continent, following the Crimean war.

Ultimately, national cost-benefit analyses will decide about the continued existence of societies under the influence of a national hegemon, or a move out and into the orbit of a supranational entity. This could be summarized as disintegration of states in search of EC membership, or as centrifugal forces providing for new centripetal movements. Smaller and less powerful states will be exposed to centripetal forces and will gravitate toward the (economically-industrially and hence politically) more weighty ones, thereby forming areas of influence, while observing balance of power considerations between themselves. In North America this will eventually result in the NAFTA, the North American Free Trade Agreement between Canada, the USA, and Mexico; in the Pacific Basin this may create an economic industrial area around the powerful economic center, Japan. All this implies, however, that the general interest is once more focused on the historically relevant Eur-Asian continent, and only to a much smaller extent on Third World affairs.

In a world moving from bipolarity to multipolarity or indeed unipolarity with one remaining global power—the United States—nuclear weapons will still contribute to continued stability, as does a maximum flow of information.[30] Also the defensive means against a nuclear attack, such as a more moderate SDI, will be accepted to provide protection against new potential nuclear powers. One may see the emergence of seven great powers in the next millennium: the United States, Britain, France, Germany, Japan, China, and possibly the EU, depending on its development. But the Commonweath of Independent States—indeed Russia—can remain in this club only if it retains its major republics, or if it creates enough of a sphere of influence to keep them under its influence. If the CIS can hold on, two major strategic poles might emerge on the Eurasian continent: Brussels/Berlin and Minsk/Moscow.[31] Globally, a triangular constellation may evolve between a powerful NAFTA, Japan, and a European Union.[32]

Historically, Germany and Russia have always maintained a special bilateral relationship. The good-neighborly relations between St. Petersburg and Berlin, Russia and Germany (e.g. the *Dreikaiser Vertrag*, or the Rapallo Treaty) suggest that extensive political and economic-industrial interactions will develop between these countries, especially once German unification has been digested and the domestic situation between the Soviet republics has been clarified. However, the extent to which an eastward drive of Western values and capital may continue without creating tensions between the two adjacent rival powers and their spheres of influence, remains to be seen. This phenomenon is magnified by the necessity of East European economies to attract sufficient Western skills, technology, and financial support to raise their standards of living to those of the West to satisfy the expectations of their own people.

Britain's role in Europe also recalls the 1850s: in the long run the

British may prefer their strong Atlantic ties to their continental ones in order to avoid too much damage to their sovereignty due to European integration. Great Britain once again may become the balancer in European affairs between French, German, and Russian interests based on its "transatlantic spine" (i.e. the "special relations" with the U.S.). A first such indication can be detected in British policy of obtaining special concessions in the Maastricht summit for "opting out or buying into" EC social policies and the EPU.

Two non-continental powers are likely to influence European affairs—Japan and the United States. The latter, it is hoped, will continue to retain a minimum military presence on the continent. Each time in this century, after the United States had withdrawn from the European continent, it had to redeploy in an emergency.[33] Japan's role in Europe's economy—as a supplier of technological-industrial products, capital, and employment—is already substantial, and will presumably increase, especially in Eastern Europe.[34] Japan will search for greater international recognition of its economic-industrial achievements (such as permanent membership in the UN security council and membership in the CSCE) which will eventually also color its presence in Europe.

Europe and its Relevant Security Institutions

Four interrelated subjects must be addressed in any discussion about European security institutions: the conceptual framework; the European Political Union/Western European Union/North Atlantic Treaty Organization interaction; the Conference on Security and Cooperation in Europe; and the prospects for former Warsaw Treaty Organization members. Much, however, depends on the actual national implementation of the EC agreements signed at Maastricht in 1991.[35]

The political situation in Europe has been substantially influenced by Germany's rapid economic-industrial-technological advances. Pleasing, adjusting to, or competing with the new Germany will be central to European decision making, even though Germany is confronted with an array of problems and even certain constraints on national choices.[36]

Post-World War II Soviet predominance in Central and Eastern Europe may be replaced by Western influence. The essential question is whether a *Europeanization* or *Germanization* will affect this region. A symbolic quarrel may develop over spheres of influence in East-Central Europe between the "two B's": Brussels and Berlin. The move of the German government—or part of it—to Berlin will create economic and financial convulsions in the adjacent areas. All the new Eastern democracies (for instance Czechoslovakia, Hungary, Poland, Rumania for example), including the new CIS, will be in dire need of German expertise, investment assistance, managerial skills, and technology. A historic example of eventual relevance is offered in the DM-bloc of the 1930s in East-Central Europe.[37]

This development may lead to a dispute over primacy—which nation-state will be *primus inter pares*, and form the nucleus of a new hegemonic regional system. There are many indications that Germany will play that role.[38] Eventually, this may cause a twofold problem: antagonisms may arise between European states, or competing interests may emerge between them and the EU. This could happen between France and Germany, as well as with Russia and the other newly independent states like the Ukraine. Their existence suggests the re-emergence of multipolarity in the new Europe and resulting balance of power as well as alliance formation considerations.

Since 1990 the drive towards European integration has been confronted with new developments. The SEM with its four liberties (freedom of movement of goods, services, and finances), includes the freedom of movement of persons. This issue, a sensitive one for the small EFTA members Austria, Finland, Liechtenstein, and Switzerland, surfaced in the negotiations for the European Economic Area (EEA). In a time when the mood in many European countries, especially the Central European ones along with Italy and France, has started to turn against foreigners and immigrants, doubts may emerge over the idea of further integration. This could eventually reduce the official inclination towards giving up even more sovereignty to control one's borders, military, and currency. The immediate negative reactions in many European countries to a loss of national currencies to the ECU, following the Maastricht decision, have indicated that popular resistance may increase. This situation is perhaps aggravated by a slowing down of the European economy, possible reductions in the availability of jobs, endangered social standards, and demands for higher environmental standards.

It must be kept in mind that the conclusion of the Treaties of Rome in 1956 occured in a time marked by the bipolar antagonisms of the Cold War. This was also the case at the time of the first and second enlargements of the EC 1973 and 1982. Even in the 1980s, when the economic situation was favorable, Cold War tensions were strong. Despite the preoccupation with Germany, the orientation of the EC has been primarily external rather than internal. This orientation helped the EC explain the difficulties in dealing with such delicate semi-internal issues as the question of violent Yugoslav disintegration. The outcomes of the Maastricht summit have unfortunately coincided with the negative effects of *perestroika* and *glasnost*: economic chaos and increasing streams of refugees.

The European Political Community - European Political Union

The Maastricht summit brought an increase in the powers of the European Parliament, a greater push towards a common foreign policy, and the establishment of two additional pillars for the European Union. The new European Community will rest on three pillars: the first one is the Treaty of the European Community, expanded and amended, which provides a greater role for the EC in environment, education, consumer protection, public health and pan-European networks (roads, computer networks, power links, telecommunications). The second pillar is a Common Foreign and Security Policy (CFSP). It remains still outside traditional EC procedures. The treaty seeks to improve the present cooperation by setting out rules for joint action. Most decisions will be taken by unanimity, but governments can decide to take certain decisions by a majority vote. This section also creates an embryonic future common European defence policy, which must be compatible with the NATO alliance. The third pillar comprises the intergovernmental cooperation in immigration, asylum, and trans-border police operations. It includes Europol, the EC-wide police intelligence corps. Again unanimity is required.

Germany, France, and other federalists wanted the second and third pillars merged into a single European Community treaty rather than left to intergovernmental cooperation. They have now settled for this three-pillar arrangement in exchange for including in the treaty provisions a gradual integration of these matters into community procedures.[39]

The Western European Union

The Maastricht agreements have given the European Community a defense role for the first time. The CSFP "shall include all questions related to the security of the EU, including the eventual framing of a common defense policy which might lead to common defense." The WEU, whose members all belong to the EC, will be the EC's defense arm. The focus will be on assimilation of WEU principles into the EPC structure.

The WEU was the actual beginning of European defense cooperation in the 1950s. In 1991, the WEU has come to be perceived as the premier expression of a European defense will. The French and Germans have favored a revitalized and reinforced WEU as a defense arm of the EPU, under extensive influence of the commission. WEU headquarters are to move from London to Brussels. There are three levels of association: full membership, associate membership, and observer status. Greece is to become a member, while (neutral) Ireland will obtain associate membership. Eventually all twelve EC members should become members of the WEU. Even the non-EC and non-WEU-NATO members, Turkey and Norway, have attended WEU meetings during the recent Gulf crisis.[40]

The WEU is the "defense bridge" between NATO and the EC to "elaborate and implement decisions and actions of the Union which have defense implications." The WEU and EC Council of Ministers' Secretariat will cooperate closely, and efforts will be made to synchronize meetings of the two organizations and to harmonize working methods. The Commission will be regularly informed and consulted on WEU activities.

Progressive economic integration will have to be complemented by future moves in foreign, security, and defense policies, if the EC is to maintain its momentum. Eventually the EC may just write WEU mutual defense clauses into the EC treaties and take the rest of WEU over when its treaty expires in 1998. This future collective European security system may then also be acceptable to EFTA members and the neutral Ireland in the EC. Part of this reasoning is the looming threat that the United States will continue to reduce its involvement in European defense matters and that Europeans will be obliged to develop their own defense capabilities.

Recently the WEU has proven incapable of bringing the Yugoslavian civil strife to an end. This has indicated rather drastically the still-existing limitations of inner-European capabilities for crisis management and defense cooperation. One major cause for this is the original outside orientation of the WEU and NATO against a Eastern/Soviet threat rather than a focus on "intra-European" stability. Now, however, the WEU, as the defense element in European integration, debates incorporation of East European states. The WEU's parliamentary assembly in Paris has proposed that Hungary, Czechoslovakia, and Poland should take part in WEU organization in the future. Also the military industries of the three Eastern European countries could be drawn into West European arms manufacturing.[41]

NATO

Although NATO went through many crises over the last decade, today it appeals particularly to Eastern European states. The proven military capabilities of NATO, its stabilizing influence in Europe, and its ensuring of a continued American presence on the European continent is attractive to states currently in limbo. Despite the above-mentioned agreements on CFSP, NATO's obligations concerning European defense will not be undermined. Both the political and military role played by the European members in the alliance will be enhanced. NATO also will take on a more political role.

NATO had established a consultation mechanism, the North Atlantic Co-operation Council (NACC) with the 16 NATO members and the former Warsaw Treaty Organization (WTO) members—the Eastern European and CIS countries. NACC, however, falls short of the WTO states' persistent demand for membership. Nevertheless, it clearly indicates their greater desire to cooperate with NATO in enhancing European security and stability than with any other security institution such as the CSCE. This is due to NATO's credibility as a stabilizing force with a functioning structure and proven instruments of conflict resolution at its disposal. The cooperation envisaged will focus on security and related issues, such as defense planning, arms control, the conversion of defense production to civilian purposes, and scientific and environmental cooperation. NACC may become the military arm of CSCE which would create a security system from Vancouver to Vladivostok.[42]

Michael Doyle's argument that democracies never have conducted open war against each other might be yet another reason for the prestige of the NATO.[43] The envisaged regular meetings of the NACC represent a consultative mechanism that could eventually develop into a concert mechanism. Dieter Senghaas, for instance, has emphasized the need for continuous consultations, coordination, and concertation of a "joint-European domestic policy."[44]

Among East European democracies, trends towards alliance member-ship are predominant, whereas permanent neutrality is less attractive. Neutrality may both be counter-productive in the post-Cold War era and impossible to pursue due to lack of adequate resources and the absence of domestic stability and national consensus. Indeed, their striving for continued modernization through Westernization amounts to *the* precondition for successful and persistent democratization. Dangerous regional instabilities make involvement with outside powers seem preferable to shaky independent defense efforts. For geopolitical reasons the newly independent states such as Slovenia, Croatia, and the Baltics and the larger former Soviet Republics such as Ukraine may prove the exceptions.[45] For them, neutrality may be the only available status except a military alliance with or against an all powerful neighbor. Indeed, Ukraine and Belarus may eventually become Finlandized or Canadaised.[46] Another option would be the conclusion of a network of bilateral nonaggression and neutrality agreements between them and CIS.

The Conference on Security in Cooperation in Europe

As a result of the CSCE Paris Summit of November 1990 and the signing of the European Charter, the CSCE forms part of the European security architecture together with the EC/WEU and NATO/NACC. A certain amount of competition or overlaping may result. As now predicted, the CSCE will be an important negotiation forum for *all* of Europe, America, and the succession states of the Soviet Union. It would be unrealistic though, to expect CSCE in the near future to replace security organizations such as the WEU or NATO. On the contrary, the Yugoslavian crisis clearly has shown the limits of the current CSCE's capabilities. Also there exists widespread agreement not to let CSCE evolve into yet another bureaucratic leviathan such as Brussels with thousands of governmental officials. There is no reason to believe that the U.S. would ever accept majority voting in the CSCE. Today, the CSCE lacks the one all-important feature to help settle armed conflicts beyond the negotiating table—a credible, functioning armed instrument. On the other hand there are strong signs that CSCE will gain in attractiveness for the newly independent Soviet republics—for whom it might become the main forum for debate.

Despite that continued role of NATO, the CSCE has enjoyed an evaluation following the agreements of the Paris Summit of 1990. A number of CSCE institutions are in place: an enhanced program of consultation between foreign ministers and senior officials; a small permanent secretariat in Prague with some ten to fifteen officials; a small Conflict Prevention Center in Vienna; an Election Observation Office and process; and a parliamentary wing (the Assembly of Europe in Strassbourg), enabling members of parliament from the now thirty eight members to meet at regular intervals. The contemporary problems of bringing peace to Yugoslavia, however, have neither contributed to international credibility, nor to increased intra-European trust in CSCE. Now interests exist to create a CSCE security council and eventually an armed intervention contingent.

A European collective security system would enhance stability, especially if it were binding in the CSCE area. Over time, new East European democracies could develop into the position and role of today's Neutral and Non-Aligned (N&N) states. Some of them, in case of exclusion from NATO membership, may gladly jump into a new role as a buffer, bridge or arbitrator formerly held by the neutrals. On the other hand, if all European CSCE states alike agreed to conduct an orchestrated foreign and security policy in Europe—to become equal members in a European collective security system—that could de facto mean the "neutralization of Europe."[47]

For many reasons extensive participation by Japan in the CSCE should also be sought. Efforts should be undertaken to attract Japanese affiliation and investments, for without Tokyo's maintained industrial interest no long term modernization and industrialization of Central Eastern Europe *and* the former Soviet Union seems possible. Much of the technical, industrial and managerial know how for modern consumer-oriented industries is in Japanese hands. Moreover, much of the world's disposable capital is held in Japanese banks and industries. To ask only for money without broader offers to include Japan in the reshaping of general European evolution seems unwise.

Security in Europe 1992 and Neutral Austria
General

For a small, permanently neutral country like Austria in the geopolitical center of Europe, the transforming events since 1988 have been of crucial importance. Indeed, Austrian foreign relations have been put into the limelight with the accord of the EC's SEA. If it is said that Europe is experiencing the greatest changes since the conference of Yalta, it may also be noted that Vienna is going through the greatest changes in its geopolitical environment since the conference of St. Germain in 1919. Today, Austria is prepared voluntarily to reduce its sovereignty by acceding to the EC.

But the country has become once again a prime example for a state on the crossroads between EC integration and the democratic revolutions of Eastern Europe. The former asks for looking westward and reducing statehood in favor of supranational membership; the latter brings back the past and offers new historic opportunities while recalling the importance of maintaining sovereignty. All areas of Austrian foreign relations will be touched by these developments. Regarding Austrian security two factors stand out: the emerging tension between integrative and disintegrative forces discussed above and the specifically Austrian geopolitical/ historical situation. The most important question for Austrian national security still is her status of permanent neutrality.

Austria and Continental Security

The easing in the international nuclear strategic environment, the evaporated bloc antagonism and the conclusion of the CFE and INF agreements go hand in hand with a dramatic increase of tensions inside the states of East Central Europe. This has caused an increase in international awareness of the region, and indeed of Austria as its historic center as well as of Vienna as its old historic capital. Austria is squeezed geopolitically by three concurrent developments: the unification of Germany, the sudden democratization efforts of its Northern neighbor Czechoslovakia and Eastern neighbor Hungary, and the flaring up of strife in its South Eastern neighbors Yugoslavia, Rumania, and Bulgaria.

European political and military integration represents one of the prime questions for Austrian foreign policy today. The important issue, therefore, is Austria's relationship with EPC/EPU and WEU. Following the Maastricht summit a knowledgeable Austrian observer noted: "Things will become easier for a neutral country because the WEU is an organization outside of the EC."[48] Despite the question of whether the WEU will really remain "outside" the EC, Austrian foreign minister Alois Mock stated that Austria "will be an observer in the WEU just as in NATO," and that he does "not see any problems if this is formalized."[49] That declaration implies that neutral Austria as a potential EC member may also participate in EC foreign and security policy.

Austria may also have to play an important economic and political role between the rich Central and Northern members of the EC, the developing Eastern neighbors and the poorer Mediterranean countries. This has become very obvious by the continuous support of Austria's EC application by Italy, as well as during the EEA negotiations. After the fall of the iron curtain, apparently, Austria's traditional geopolitical position as a "revolving door" in the center of Europe is in the process of being recreated. For its Eastern neighbors, Vienna may continue to function as their snowplough on the icy road to Brussels.

Ever since the Helsinki Agreements of 1975, Austria has been devoted to the CSCE process. Austria has regarded this and the UN as its prime interest in international security policy. The most recent evolution of the conflict in Yugoslavia has shown drastically, how much the CSCE will have to adapt from being originally a Cold War institution. Whether

Austria can continue to set independent initiatives will depend much on the speed of Austrian membership in the EC. Once admitted, Austria will certainly have to follow the EPC line in th CSCE process.

This leads to another often overlooked issue: the military dimension of EC integration may eventually ask active transborder solidarity if Austria becomes a member. In case of an attack on or emergency in another EC country, this agreement may comprise sending forces or providing other forms of support far beyond anything neutral Austria has been asked for. Gustav Daeniker calls this the "military doctrine of the protected peace" and indicates the expectation of utility and active intra-European solidarity in security policy.[50] Instead of a *"Bundesheer light"* (a lightly armed federal armed force), which was widely discussed in 1990, credible integration will eventually require substantial military participation. So far WEU membership is not obligatory, but it may be required under certain conditions and international expectations. Furthermore, even the new NACC has begun to expand the term *security* to include non-military matters such as environment, migration, and economic stability. In these areas Austria may offer much, including its expertise with regional trade and domestic economic stability (i.e. the proven system of social partnership).[51]

On the non-factual level of continental security, Austria may have to disprove misguided perceptions about increasing German-Austrian integration and cooperation. A consistent and clear domestic policy line is required. EC membership at the earliest possible moment presents another effective guard.[52]

Austria and Regional Security

Many of the new security issues in Europe are of particular relevance for Austria, namely migration, environment, socio-economic stability and prosperity, and the search for self-determination. A number of conflicts are possible in Austria's neighborhood. A certain security vacuum has arisen; combined with economic and nationality problems, this may cause possible military conflicts in the CSFR and Hungary. There are also potential minority crises emerging in Romania (Transylvania and Northern Romania), the Hungarian minority in Slovakia, Albanians in Kosovo, Hungarians in Voivodina, and Makedonians in Greece. Ever since the days of the Habsburg Empire Austria has had strong links to these areas. More recently, many guest workers have come to Austria from this region.

The increasing importance of economic and social dimensions in security also transforms the role of a neutral state such as Austria from a military buffer to an active participant with obligations to smooth the modernization process of Eastern and Southeastern Europe. This new configuration replaces a one-sided military neutrality with new socio-economic tasks of non-military support to stabilize the region.

Two factors have complicated Austria's position in the 1990's: the potential large-scale East-West migration, and the requirement that small neutrals participate in out-of-area operations in a European security system. For Austria the issue of Eastern European refugees is a traditional matter that has obtained sudden relevance. In 1991, the country had to absorb the highest per capita number of immigrants in the Western world (some 28,000 have asked for asylum). In its Central European location, Austria was exposed to the onslaught of refugees from the East, and it was the first to deploy forces to stop the influx of illegal aliens. Any further catastrophic developments on the Balkans or in the CIS might trigger a multiplication of refugees to prosperous Austria.

European subregional developments are of special relevance for Austria with its intensive participation in the evolution of the Danubian region.[53] It is becoming a motor for economic and industrial develop-ment in this region and tries to provide stabilization measures. Austria is very active in various Alpine and Danubian cooperative schemes (*ARGE-ALP-ADRIA*, *ARGE-Donauländer*, and the *Hexagonale*). Austria may also have to serve as a link between an emerging security group, for instance the Visegrad group in the East, and the WEU/NATO group. Austria will perhaps even be drawn into greater East Central European security cooperation. Two agreements between Austrian, Hungarian and Czechoslovakian armed forces have already been signed.

Austrian National Security

Presumably, the most important aspect of security is stability and prosperity at home, which may project credibility and prestige abroad. The consensus between political parties is important in the conduct of foreign relations. The Austrian coalition government between Social Democrats (SPÖ) and Christian Democrats (ÖVP) has tried consistently to follow a common foreign policy line: in the Austrian application for EC membership 1989; in the transition phase in Eastern Europe; during the Gulf War; during the dissolution of the Soviet Union; and following the Maastricht summit. Perhaps the greatest difficulty was the recogni-tion of Slovenia and Croatia, where Foreign Minister Alois Mock of the

ÖVP was the first European politician to propose such a step. The Social Democratic Federal Chancellor Franz Vranitzky was more cautious and reluctant. These general agreements on security policy have threatened to break down on the issues of WEU participation, defense, treatment of refugees, and especially the future status of Austrian neutrality.

The final word in the Austrian integration debate will be spoken in a plebiscite. Austrians' principal desires to enhance their prosperity, stability, and security, are at stake. The analysis of advantages and disadvantages between heading towards Brussels or waiting cosily on the sidelines, will depend upon the national plebiscite. The danger of a looming potential "*Norwegenization*" should be a warning example. In 1973, Oslo obtained the green light from the EC for membership. But membership was rejected by the Norwegian people. There are indications that the general inclination for rapid integration is declining in Austria, at least in the polls.[54]

The recent disintegration of the Soviet Union even affected the second important pillar of Austrian security, the State Treaty of 1955. Some argue that the disintegration of the Soviet Union effectively eliminates one of the four signatory powers and guardians of the Austrian Treaty and its provisions. For many people, however, the State Treaty and Austria's neutrality ought to go untouched. The Yugoslavian civil war has shown the need for the maintenance of a small, efficient and modern armed force, perhaps smaller in numbers but greater in readiness and better equipped (such as a rapid deployment forces).[55]

The real issue is the future of Austrian neutrality, its interpretation, adaptation, and maintenance. Neutrality developed from a concept overshadowed by bipolar Cold War antagonism, to a concept of a more universal orientation in two major directions, namely protecting against conflicts between great powers and remaining neutral in regional conflicts. A new dimension may be added—the relationship with a major supranational continental organization. This is different from the issues the neutrals had to face regarding the choice between UN membership or continued neutrality in the 1950's. Only Switzerland saw major incompatibilities here, following its experiences with the League of Nations and Swiss differential neutrality. Today's EC membership may bring enormous economic advantages, which was certainly not the case with the UN. Moreover, the international sphere has changed considerably since the 1950s and 1960s.

One could generally argue that *intensive regionalization neutralizes national neutrality.* Consequently, Austrian neutrality may move from a bipolar orientation to a potential unipolar one vis-à-vis the U.S. and a regional one vis-à-vis Germany. Besides, the requirement to try to remain neutral in a regional conflict remains in place. If the European integration process continues at its speed and creates a functioning European security system, neutrality may be unneccesary. If integration slows down, or if a new European system emerges, favoring balance of power, then neutrality may offer an attractive alternative.

But even under successful integration, it is conceivable that a permanent neutral could enter into a contractual agreement with a European defense alliance. Such a defense agreement should be without reciprocity and could be compared to an armed guarantee. A model might be Article I of the Finno-Soviet treaty of 1948, or the Belgian neutralization treaty of 1834. The arrangement could provide for armed support of the neutral in case it comes under attack from a third power. In all other cases, the neutral would remain without obligation and would conduct its independent defense. Such an agreement would in fact produce very little change, since at this time it seems highly likely that Western European states would support neutral Austria in case of an attack.

EC membership should, therefore, remain compatible with a modified, adapted neutrality—at least as long as other states such as England continue to insist on the priority of national sovereignty over Brussels' attempts at full integration and union. Public debates about how much of its status the neutral will want to give up in exchange for membership in the Common Market, will neither serve its credibility nor its bargaining power in Brussels. As always, the final international evaluation depends on the credibility shaped by national determination.

No matter how one views these developments in Europe and in Austria, the changes are momentous and the options for future security policy tough and challenging.

NOTES

*   The author is grateful to AIC Vienna and Professor L. Bauer, WU, Vienna. Research for this article was supported by the Jubiläumsfonds of the Austrian National Bank. The paper was written under the auspices of the Center for International Studies, Princeton University.

1.   See Andrew Moravcsik, "Negotiating the Single European Act: National Interests and Conventional Statecraft in the European Community," *International Organization* 45 (1991)): 19-56; Paul Taylor, "The New Dynamics of EC Integration in the 1980s," in *The European Community and the Challenge of the Future* ed. Juliet Lodge (New York: St. Martin's Press, 1989), 3-26.

2. December 1991, the European Court of Justice blocked the EEA agreement by opposing the joint EFTA-EC court foreseen for the EEA. The seven EFTA members comprise Austria, Finland, Iceland, Liechtenstein, Norway, Sweden, and Switzerland; see Helen Wallace, "What Europe for which Europeans," and Wolfgang Danspeckgruber, "The European Economic Area, the Neutrals, and an Emerging Architecture," in *The Shape of the New Europe*, ed. Gregory Treverton (New York: Council on Foreign Relations, 1991), 15-34, 92-129.

3. Judy Dempsey and Laura Silber, "Yugoslavia's PM warns of total disintegration", *Financial Times*, 16 November 1990.

4. For the interpretation of the stability created by the Cold War, see John Mearsheimer, "Back to the Future: Stability in Europe After the Cold War," *International Security* 15 (1990): 1-56; Stephen van Evera, "Primed for Peace: Europe After the Cold War," *International Security* 15 (1990/91): 7-57; Stanley Hoffman, "Abschied von der Vergangenheit," *Europa Archiv* (1990): 595-606; See also Richard Ullman, *Securing Europe* (Princeton: Princeton University Press, 1991); Robert Pontillon, "Les nouvelles dimensions de la securite europeene," *Revue du Marche Commun et de l'Union Europeene* (March 1991): 171-5.

5. "The Paris Conference: The Thrill of Europe's Rebirth," *The Economist*, 24 November 1990, 50. Karl Otto Poehl, former president of the Deutsche Bundesbank, has warned about a new "currency divide" in Europe. The EEA will created the largest integrated market in the world and have "many characteristics of a currency union." He argues, "for most of the former Comecon countries it is hardly conceivable to fulfill the conditions to join this club," see Quentin Peel, "Poehl warns of Europe's 'currency divide'," *Financial Times*, 25 October 1991.

6. Richard Cooper, "Natural Resources and National Security", *Adelphi Papers*, No. 115 (London: The International Institute for Strategis Studies): 8; Boyce Greer, "European Economic Security", in *Securing Europe's Future,* ed. Stephen J. Flanagan and Fen O. Hampson (London: Croom & Helm); Peter Katzenstein, *Between Power and Plenty* (University of Wisconsin Press, 1978); Neil R. Richardson, *Foreign Policy and Economic Dependence* (New York, 1979); C.L. Schultze, "The Economic Content of National Security Policy", *Foreign Affairs* 51 (1973): 3; Arnold Wolfers, "National Security as an Ambiguous Symbol", in *Discord and Collaboration*, ed. Arnold Wolfers (Baltimore: The Johns Hopkins University Press, 1962).

7. Heinz Vetschera, "The Future Rold of Arms Control for European Security-From Arms Control to Force Control," in *Emerging Dimensions of European Security Polity*, ed. Wolfgang Danspeckgruber (Boulder-San Francisco-Oxford: Westview Press, 1991); 174.

8. Wolfgang Danspeckgruber, "Neutrality and Technology: The Implications of Technology on the Policy and Concept of Classical Neutrality in Europe," Ph.D. Dissertation in progress, The Graduate Institute of International Studies, Geneva.

9. "The poorhouse of this world may soon become dangerous to the rich West. Only if access to the resources continues to be guaranteed for the rich nations—if necessary by military—will they be able to help the poorer countries" see Hans-

Henning von Standard, cited by Hans Werner Scheidl, "Poverty as New Threat to Europe,"*Die Presse*, 4 December 1991, translated FBIS-WEU-91-235, 6 December 1991, p. 1 (Foreign Broadcast Information Service-Western Europe).

10. Uwe Nerlich, "Einige nichtmilitärische Bedingungen europäischer Sicherheit," *Europa Archiv* (Folge 19/1991): 547; also Jan Zielonka, "Europe's Security: A Great Confusion," *International Affairs* 67 (1991):127-137.

11. Edward Mortimer, "Scotland on the Danube River," *Financial Times*, 6 November 1991, p. 17.

12. According to Vaclav Havel, "a prolonged continuation of the Yugoslav conflict will bear much greater dangers for Europe than generally recognized, "*Washington Post*, 24 October 1991; James Gow, "Deconstructing Yugoslavia," *Survival* 33 (July/August 1991): 291-311; F. Stephen Larrabee, "Long Memories and Short Fuses," *International Security* 15 (Winter 1990/91): 58-91; Dusan Sidjanski, *Union ou désunion de l'Europe?: La Communauté européene à l'épreuve de la crise yougoslave et des mutations en Europe de l'Est* (Geneva: Edition IUEE, 1991).

13. Interestingly, this happens to be in the same areas, where some 40 years ago political observers recognized the communist domino effect in the other direction. Part of the problem can be found in the at least incorrect implementation of Woodrow Wilson's fourteen points.

14. The conflict between Croatia and Serbia in the Yugoslav civil war would enter a new stage if parties such as Bosnia-Herzegovina or Macedonia adhering to a religion different from Catholicism and orthodox believe would enter; this would make a future containment of the conflict much more difficult.

15. See the continuous conflict within and between the PLO and the Lebanese government which eventually led to Israeli intervention 1982, followed by an aborted international peace mission and now a Syrian controlled partition. I am grateful for discussions about this point to: Richard Falk, Abdlatif Y. Al-Hamad and Hannes Androsch.

16. Philip G. Roeder, "Soviet Federalism and Ethnic Mobilization," *World Politics* 43 (1991): 196-232; Stephan Kux, *Soviet Federalism—A Comparative Perspective*, I E W S S Occasional Papers, 18.

17. Daniel N. Nelson, "Europe's Unstable East," *Foreign Policy* (1990): 140-146; see also B. Guy Peters, *European Politics Reconsidered* (New York: Holmes and Meier, 1991); Special Issue, "The global context of democratization," *Alternatives: A Journal for social transformation and humane governance* 16 (Spring 1991): 119-274.

18. Thomas Nowotny, "Vom Aufstieg und Fall grosser Begriffe," *Europa Archiv* (Folge 2/1991): 41-49.

19. For instance, it is recognized in Estonia and Latvia, that ideally the harbor towns of Tallinn and Riga will become great gates for the St. Petersburg area, and serve as a gateway for the Russian and Belarus States.

20. Jiri Dienstbier, "Central Europe's Security," *Foreign Policy* (1991): 120.

21. It was also concluded that Austria would take over the presidency from Yugoslavia already on January 1, and that "the group adopts a uniform stand on the Yugoslav crisis as regards cooperation within the Hexagonale." See "International Affairs; Hexagonale Group meets in Venice 30 November," FBIS-WEU-91-231, 2 December 1991, pp. 1-2.

22. Projects include four highways, six railroad links between the member countries, an environmental data bank, and cooperation between news agencies and universities. Also the group submitted a joint resolution on the treatment of minorities at the CSCE conference 1990 in Copenhagen. See Bernhard von Platte, "Subregionalismus," *Europa Archiv* (Folge 19/1991): 558-566

23. François Heisbourg, "Population Movements in Post-Cold War Europe," *Survival* 33 (1991): 33-34.

24. Ian Davidson and Quentin Peel, "An Odd Couple Still in Tune," *Financial Times,* 14 November 1991.

25. John Lewis Gaddis, "Toward the Post-Cold War World," *Foreign Affairs* 70 (1991), 102-122.

26. This is the inverse argument of economic problems leading to political and eventual instability.

27. *Perspectives on Change in Europe: Implications for US-European Relations*, House of Representatives, Subcommittee on European Affairs, Washington, D.C., November 14, 1991.

28. This has surfaced for the first time during the Yugoslav conflict, when fights between Croatian and Serbian guest workers have spilled over into Germany and Switzerland.

29. For the theoretical argument, see Michael Doyle, *Empires* (Ithaca: Cornell University Press, 1988); Barry Buzan, "New Patterns of Global Security in the Twenty First Century," *International Affairs* 67 (1991): 431-451.

30. Kenneth Waltz, "The Emergent Structure of International Politics," lecture given at Princeton University, 15 November 1990.

31. The USS, Union of Sovereign States, may just create an area rotating around Russia, without the Ukraine and Belarus. Edward Mortimer, "An Empire in Tatters," *Financial Times*, 27 November 1991.

32. It should be emphasized, that the economic capabilities of a given country do not necessarily relate to its military-strategic weight. The GDP of the Soviet Union has been approximately one-third that of the United States, but the former has obtained nuclear second strike-capability, hence military power far exceeding its economic potential. See René Schwok, *U.S.-EC Relations in the Post-Cold War Era. Conflict or Partnership?* (Boulder, San Francisco, Oxford: Westview Press, 1991).

33. It seems to be much less costly to have a small tightly organized and well equipped presence in Europe—*a pied à terre*—than to be obliged to create such a force at once.

34. The amount of employment provided in Europe by Japanese companies via MITI today, have to be taken seriously. The pre-eminent question regards the Japano-German relationship, which will then influence the EC position to Tokyo. Japan should be ready to help but should not intervene without being asked to. Michael Borrus and John Zysman, "Industrial Strength and Regional Response: Japan's Impact on European Integration," in *The Shape of the New Europe*, ed. Treverton, 172-193.

35. Nansen Behar, "Regional Policy and World Crises: An East European View," *Journal of Peace Research* 27 (1990): 211-19; Andrew A. Michta, "East-Central Europe in Search of Security," *Sais Review* 11 (Winter/Spring 1991): 59-72; *Shifting into Neutral? Burden Sharing in the Western Alliance in the 1990s*, ed. Christopher Coker (New York: Pergamon Press, 1990).

36. David Marsh, "Europe's Honeymoon Starts to Sour," *Financial Times*, 21 December 1991, p. 7.

37. Germany holds one dramatic advantage over all other OECD states; it is the only member which has in its own territory both the expertise of most sophisticated Western technology and the necessary know-how Eastern European needs; also former GDR-CMEA trade relations may be exploited for building up new contracts between old customers and German firms.

38. See the diplomatic initiatives of the German government December 1991, regarding the recognition of Slovenia and Croatia and the related suggestion to the EC Commission, and the increase of the discount rate by the Deutsche Bundesbank.

39. The European Parliament will remain largely neutral as a political force, though its power has been strengthened. It will have the power to propose amendments to and veto some EC laws, but it will still be unable to initiate legislation.

40. Ian Davidson, "Differences Narrow Over Role for WEU," *Financial Times*, 22 February 1991, p. 4 In this context, Martin Bangemann, vice president of the EC Commission, has argued that "the European neutrals would be obliged to participate in a future EC-Army, and a related action, particularly if it is suggested by the UN." He contends that "the EPC will lead to a common defense policy and finally also to a European army," quoted in *Wiener Zeitung*, 15 February 1991.

41. "WEU proposes Hungary, CSFR, Poland Role," Budapest Kossuth Radio Network, 5 December 1991, transcribed in FBIS-WEU-91-235, p. 6; for instance one could be Hungarian participation in the new Satellite Control Center of the WEU in Spain which monitors implementation of disarmament agreements.
    German Foreign Minister Genscher announced that he will invite all East European foreign and defense ministers to establish a consultative council as well as create other cooperative measures. See "Genscher views WEU as EC Defense Element," *Frankfurter Allgemeine Zeitung*, 5 December 1991, p. 4, cited in FBIS-WEU-91-235, p. 4

42. Under the new institutional relationship, the NACC will hold annual meetings at ministerial level and bi-monthly meetings at ambassadorial level. The consultation will focus on security and related issues, such as defense planning, arms control, the conversion of defense production to civilian purposes and scientific and environmental cooperation. See Robert Mauthner, "Russian Republics Want to Join NATO Alliance," *Financial Times*, 21/22 December 1991.

43. Michael Doyle, "Liberalism in World Politics," *American Political Science Review* 80, (1986): 1151-1169; and idem, "Kant, Liberal Legacies and Foreign Affairs," *Philosophy and Public Affairs* 12, (1983): 205-235; also Raimund Graefe and Christian Tuschhoff, "Bringing Back Appeasement: The Case for Umbrella Solutions," in *Emerging Dimensions of European Security*, ed. Danspeckgruber, p.39.

44. Dieter Senghaas, "Friedliche Streitbeilegung und kollektive Sicherheit im neuen Europa," *Europa Archiv* (1991): 317; also Jack Snyder, "European Institutions," *International Security*, 16, (1991): 114-161. For an extensive debate of the European concert see Charles A. Kupchan and Clifford A. Kupchan, "Concerts, Collective Security, and the Future of Europe," *International Security*, 16, (1991): 114-161.

45. The Ukrainian SSR "proclaimed its intention to become in the future a constantly neutral state that does not take part in military blocs and adheres to the three non-nuclear principles." Declaration on the State Sovereignty of Ukraine adopted by the Ukrainian SSR Supreme Soviet on 16 July 1990, (Art. IX.) quoted in Alexander Dallin and Gail W. Lapidus, eds., *The Soviet System in Crisis* (Boulder-San Francisco-Oxford: Westview Press, 1991), 483.

46. For possible neutrality for Canada, see : Claude Bergeron, Charles-Philippe David, Michel Fortmann, William George, eds., *Les choix géopolitiques du Canada—l'enjeu de la neutralité* (Montreal, Quebec: Méridien, 1988)

47. For discussion of the wide ranging implications, such as giving up right to conduct offensive war, right for nuclear weapons, etc. see Wolfgang Danspeckgruber, "Neutrality and the emerging Europe," in *Emerging Dimensions of European Security Policy*, ed. Danspeckgruber, 265-289

48. Andreas Unterberger, "Vienna to be Observer at WEU?" *Die Presse*, 12 December 1991, p.4

49. Ibid.

50. Gustav Daeniker, "Mehr und Neues leisten mit weniger Truppen," *Neue Zürcher Zeitung*, 11 December 1991, p.27.

51. Defense Minister Fasslabend suggests the following additional Austrian contributions to a European security system: verification in arms control and disarmament, Peace Keeping supervision of peace agreements, control of international arms trade, international desaster relief operations, humanitarian help and assistance, assistance and support for cease fire agreements and other help for international peace and stability. See Werner Fasslabend, "Sicherheit im neuen Europa—Schwerpunkt Neutralität und Landesverteidigung," *West-Ost-Journal* 3/4 (1991).

52. Wolfgang Danspeckgruber, "The European Economic Area, the Neutrals, and an Emerging Architecture," 114

53. Curt Gasteyger, "The New Neutrals," *European Affairs* 4 (1989): 87-92;

54. In November 1991, the Sociological Study Association questioned more than 1,700 Austrians about minorities, foreigners, neutrality, and entry into the EC. Many think neutrality is very important: 57% were against changes in neutrality policy in order to make EC membership possible. See *Die Presse*, 9/10 November 1991. At the same time the State Secretary in the Foreign Ministry Thomas Klestil asked the EC Commission for speedy talks not mentioning neutrality at all.

55. The armed forces are to be reduced from 260,000 to 120,000, by getting more modern equipment (surface to air missiles, anti-tank missiles, helicopters) and allowing efficient border protection and rapid deployment.

Jewish Interests and the Austrian State Treaty

Thomas Albrich

Introduction

When in January 1947 the deputy foreign ministers of the Big Four met in London to begin discussing a treaty with Austria, they were confronted with demands, propositions and statements by all the major Jewish organizations. Based on the records of the American Jewish Committee (AJC), the World Jewish Congress (WJC), the American Jewish Joint Distribution Committee (JDC) and the American Jewish Conference,[1] this essay outlines the genesis of Jewish postwar planning with regard to Austria and describes and analyses the goals and strategies of Jewish organizations in the decisive stages of the treaty negotiations. [2]

Since more than 90 percent of all Austrian post-Anschluss refugees were Jewish, these Jewish organizations represented the interests of nearly all Austrians and former Austrians in exile. The majority of the 120,000 Austrian Jews, scattered all over the world, had come to the United States or Great Britain. Other places of refuge were Shanghai and Palestine. Yet only a minority was politically organized, not as Jews but as Socialists or even Monarchists and just a fraction can be regarded as Zionists or Jewish-Nationalists in their outlook what might be called Jewish postwar planning for Austria.[3]

Shortly after the United States had entered the war, the WJC began to organize the various scattered Jewish national emigre-groups in a Council on European Affairs. On 22 January 1942, two days after the "Wannsee-Conference", the Austrian Jewish Representative Committee (AJRC) was set up within the WJC. The most prominent members of the AJRC in 1942/43 were, among other leading figures of pre-*Anschluss*

Jewish life in Austria, its Chairman, Prof. Siegfried Altmann, former director of the *Wiener Blindeninstitut* and founder and director of the Austrian Institute in New York, Dr. Rudolf Glanz, historian and member of the Executive board of the Viennese Jewish Community, Dr. Siegfried Kantor, expert on international law and former president of the *Wiener Anwaltskammer*, organizer of the Jewish *Selbstwehr* in Austria, Dr. Oskar Karbach, author on Jewish social issues, former Secretary of the Jewish Association for the League of Nations (*Haruach*) and staff-member of the Institute of Jewish Affairs of the WJC between 1941 and 1945, and Ernst Stiassny, founding member of the *Bund jüdischer Frontkämpfer* in Austria, president in exile of the Zionist oriented *Ring der wehrhaften jüdischen Akademiker* and of the Jewish War Veterans and Chairman of the American Council of Jews from Austria.

Because of the Zionist outlook of the most active members of the Austrian-Jewish emigration, post-war planning was restricted more or less to material claims, restitution and indemnification of robbed Jewish property and to the reconstruction of Jewish community life. Taking part in the political shaping of post-war Austria therefore seemed to be not that important. The comittee held weekly meetings and later only met irregularly; it was supposed to speak and act on behalf of Austrian Jews who were "condemned to remain silent".[4] Without going into details about the internal struggle regarding the future of Austria among the various political groups of the Austrian emigration,[5] a very brief outline of the positions taken on two major issues by the WJC and the AJRC should be sufficient.

The Holocaust

The activities of the AJRC relating to the Holocaust were just as futile as those of any of the major American Jewish organizations. The AJRC was basically powerless and suffered from a lack of information. In addition, the group was obviously not prepared to champion Jewish causes that might not have been in line with the war aims of the Allies.[6] During spring of 1942 when the deportation of 65,000 Austrian Jews was under way and when 20,000 of them had already been murdered—the Committee was mired in discussions about whether relief to the suffering Jews of Europe would violate the Trading with the Enemy Act. Like the WJC, the AJRC concluded that neither relief nor rescue was possible during the war.[7]

When news of the Holocaust was officially confirmed by the State Department in November 1942,[8] the AJRC reacted with disbelief.

Discussions were more concerned with setting up an Austrian batallion within the U.S. Army[9] than with rescue efforts.[10] Records show little activity by Austrian Zionists during the winter of 1942-43; only in May 1943, after the Bermuda Conference, did the AJRC meet again to discuss the situation of Austrian Jews. By then, the majorty of the Austrian deportees had already been killed.[11] Nevertheless, the WJC and the AJRC set up two committees for postwar planning and relief for an estimated 75,000 Austrian Jews likely to return to Austria after the war, 49,000 of them expected to be survivors of various camps.[12] Less optimistic estimates by Austrian Zionists in Great Britain put the numbers in 1943 at 20,000 - 30,000 Austrian Jews surviving in continental Europe and returning home.[13] In reality, only about 4,000 Austrian Jews returned from the death-camps or out of hiding, about 65,000 Austrian Jews had been murdered.[14]

The first meeting of the American Jewish Conference in September 1943 marked, with a few exceptions, the end of all rescue plans and the beginning of Zionist postwar planning.[15] But at least some members of the AJRC would not tolerate this negative approach. Especially during the deportation of Hungarian Jews in the summer of 1944, individuals loudly protested against the appeasement policy of the WJC towards the International Committee of the Red Cross, which in the eyes of many European Jews failed to stand up to the Nazis and protect persecuted Jews.[16] Powerless and afraid of American anti-Semitism, most Austrian Jews in the United States, just like the American Jews, were convinced that nothing should be done to create the impression that the war against the Axis Powers was fought for the rescue of European Jews.[17]

Postwar Planning and the Future of Austria

From 1943 on, re-establishing a free and independent Austria became the goal of Jewish postwar planning. The Moscow Declaration of November 1943 was taken at face value as a statement of Allied political intentions,[18] and the main concern of the AJRC through the spring of 1944 was securing leadership among the Austrian-Jewish emigration both in the United States and in Great Britain.[19] Internal discussions questioned how active Jewish involvement in Austrian postwar planning should be. While Jews living in the United States stood a fair chance of gaining citizenship, Austrian Jews in Britain feared that participating actively in politics would increase the danger of repatriation at the end of the war.[20] Austrian Zionist groups in Britain stressed time and again that they did not regard themselves as Austrians any longer. In light of

Austria's past record, they would not trust the Austrians to become a democratic nation in the future.

> It cannot be overlooked that, after the occupation of Austria, the Austrian anti-Semites introduced persecutions against the Jews which were much more severe than all the previous measures of Germany and that the idea of the extermination of the Jewish people spread from Austria to Germany after the occupation.[21]

Nonetheless, Austria's role as "victim" of Nazi Germany was for pragmatic reasons accepted by all major Jewish organizations. In April 1944, the WJC issued the following statement:

> As the first victim of Nazi-aggression Austria was invaded in March, 1938. Pressure brought forth by a wave of ruthless terror, humiliation, and impover-ishment, resulted in an emigration of Austrian Jewry of such a size and rapidity that it still remains unparalleled even in the history of Nazi-persecution ... The Austrian Jewish Representative Committee of the World Jewish Congress, legitimate spokesman of Austrian Jewry, therefore regards it as its duty to devote a good deal of deliberation to post-war problems.[22]

All planning was based on a long memorandum laid down by Oskar Karbach, which was drafted and redrafted between November 1943 and May 1944. It included a number of proposals for the protection of a Jewish minority in Austria, including a Bill of Rights and some sort of international guarantee. Apart from that, the document raised two important issues: The first questioned the definition of Jewishness since survivors inside Austria would be Jews only according to the Nuremberg Laws. The second demanded that Jewish concentration camp survivors receive the same legal status and benefits as former soldiers of the *Wehrmacht*, should Austria enact special social legislation in favor of the latter.[23] At this early stage, postwar planning was more or less an internal Jewish affair and no representations on behalf of Austrian Jews were made to Allied Governments.

With the war coming closer to an end late in 1944, postwar planning became more concrete. In preparation for the War Emergency Confer-ence of the WJC in Atlantic City, the AJRC in October 1944 developed a program for the economic rehabilitation of Austrian Jews. An interest-ing feature of this program, in light of things to come, was the suggestion that all unclaimed Jewish property should be handed over to the Austrian state.

> All these properties shall, according to Austrian law, be transferred to the ownership of the Austrian state, but they should be used exclusively for relief and rehabilitation of Austrian Jews, including emigration and settlement in other countries, especially in Palestine.[24]

At the War Emergency Conference in November 1944, the WJC presented its program dealing with heirless property and demanding the inclusion of minority-right clauses in the impending peace treaties with Germany and her satellites. The WJC officially submitted these resolutions to the Allied powers, and leading members of Jewish organizations participated in various functions at the San Francisco Conference in the spring of 1945. [25] The stage was now set for what would become a long and only partially successful attempt to secure Jewish rights after the Holocaust. In the spring of 1945, the WJC and its Austrian group were convinced that Austria had not been looted but, on the contrary, had been economically developed by Germany since 1938. For this reason, they believed that sufficient means would be available for complete restitution and indemnification of stolen and expropriated Jewish property.[26]

Although the Jewish organizations had on various occasions acknowledged the Moscow Declaration, it is still significant that as early as 15 May, the WJC called the provisional Renner-Government "Austria's new democratic government,"[27] while it took the Western Allies months to arrive at the same decision.[28] This recognition was as important to future developments as Nahum Goldmann's assessment in early July, that the unity of European Jews had been endangered as the political, ideological and economic division of Europe had taken place. The division had created two parts: One was Western Europe, ending at the Elbe after Central Europe had ceased to exist, the other was Eastern Europe, under Soviet control. These two parts would have nothing in common in the near future.[29] With this analysis as the basis for future action, occupied Austria was bound to become a battlefield for Jewish organizations in what was soon perceived to be a fight against communism.

Consequently, the WJC, in collaboration with the AJRC, tried to oust the new communist dominated leadership of the Viennese Jewish community, which had been appointed by the Soviet occupation forces, and attempted to replace it with a Western-oriented leadership in order to gain influence in Austria. The first indicator of this strategy was the fact that no Austrian representative was invited to attend the first post-war conference of the WJC in London in August 1945.[30]

The main target of attack by the WJC was David Brill, newly appointed president of the Viennese Jewish community.[31] The WJC strategy worked on two levels: With an attempt to defame the Soviet appointed Jewish leadership in Vienna as criminal and crypto-fascist and with a debate on the question of "Who is a Jew?" in order to put an end to the dominant position of what Nazi terminology called *Geltungsjuden*.[32] Therefore, the WJC demanded the reconstitution of the Vienna Jewish community on the basis of the old law of 1890 as a purely Jewish body to exclude *Geltungsjuden* and democratic elections of a new board as soon as possible.[33] To cut a long story short, all attempts to discredit and remove the new Viennese Jewish leadership failed.[34] As was the case in other countries it became clear that the survivors themselves were taking control and that in the eyes of many European Jews the big American organizations had lost their moral claim to speak on behalf of European Jews.[35]

The central question in the conflict in Austria was who had the right to speak for Austrian Jews. In contrast to the situation in other countries the vast majority of Austrian Jews lived outside Austria. These emigres had a legitimate interest in selecting the representatives to the Austrian Government who would work toward restoring Jewish rights and property on the one hand, and who would control heirless property claimed by the Viennese Jewish community on the other hand.[36] By the end of 1945, only about 4,000 survivors, a remnant of the originally 180,000 Jews who had lived in Vienna prior to the *Anschluss*, had returned home. Sixty percent of them were over 45 years of age, 28 percent were over 60. Roughly one third of them wanted to stay in Vienna, one third planned to go to Palestine and one third wished to join their relatives in other countries.[37] This small remnant of the Austrian Jewish community became the first victims of the official Austrian interpretation of the Moscow Declaration: Since all Austrians were *victims* of National Socialism, there was no reason for a *privileged* treatment of Austrian Jews.[38] In fact, the remaining Austrian Jews thus suffered from "double victimization."

Until September 1945, when the U.S. Army at last moved into Vienna, the Jewish organizations were cut off from any first hand information of the situation in Austria. Even afterwards, the Department of State showed no special interest in Austrian Jews:

> The condition of the Jews in Austria has been fully reported by the representatives of the Joint Distribution Committee. The Central European Division has not kept a complete file on these reports. No specific reports on the condition of Jews have been made by the United States mission.[39]

With hardly any knowledge of the current situation inside Austria, making policies on behalf of Austrian Jews proved nigh impossible. Finally, in February 1946, the WJC decided to send a delegation to Vienna to gather on-the-spot first hand information. The records prove that the organizations, apart from the JDC, had hardly any idea of what was happening in Austria.[40]

The conflict between Austrian Jews in exile and the small Viennese

Jewish community continued to the disadvantage of Austrian Jews for years, since the Austrian Government sided with the Jewish leadership inside Austria and took advantage of Jewish disunity.[41] Apart from these fundamental disputes, within the Jewish community and vis-a-vis Austria, during the crucial negotiations with Austria regarding Jewish interests, Jewish organizations between 1946 and 1949 faced a difficult situation for the following reasons:

1. They had, from the beginning and in accordance with Allied policy, never disputed the Moscow Declaration, calling Austria the first victim of Nazi aggression. In contrast to Germany, Austria had a democratically elected government and had to be regarded as a liberated country. Jewish organizations had to accept the fiction of dealing with innocent victims and not with the perpetrators of Nazi war crimes. It was difficult to claim reparations from a "victim" and impossible to get Allied support for such claims. All the Jews could do was to appeal to Austrian goodwill and decency, hoping that Austria would not enrich herself with the property of Jewish victims of Nazi persecution.

2. For pragmatic reasons, Jewish organizations had to support Austria's claims to so called German assets in Austria. Although the Allies had agreed at the Potsdam Conference in July and August 1945 that Austria would not have to pay reparations, German property in Austria could be claimed by the occupying powers in their respective zones. At the end of the war, one fifth of Austrian industry could be regarded as German assets: 62 percent of all German foreign assets in Europe, with a total value of $1.5 billion were located in Austria.[42] The vague formulation of the Potsdam decision "opened the door for protracted wrangling over German assets that became a prominent feature of the negotiations for an Austrian treaty,"[43] in which the Jews had a vital interest.

The Austrian Government, Jewish Restitutions and German Assets

Restitution of Jewish property was the main objective of Jewish organizations in Austria prior to the State Treaty negotiations in London. The Austrian Government made it quite clear that there would be no restitution or indemnification without securing German assets for Austria. This goal could only be achieved by ignoring the *guilt clause* of the Moscow Declaration, which referred to Austria's responsibility for taking part in the war on the side of Nazi Germany. This clause was the basis of Soviet demands to seize German assets in Austria in accordance with the Potsdam Agreement. As a result, getting at least minimal Allied support for Jewish claims in the upcoming State Treaty negotiations proved to be a tough task. The complex network of interests gave the Austrian Government the chance to procrastinate.

In light of Allied treatment of Austria as a liberated country, the moral (but not the *legal*) culpability of Austria had to be established. This was done by a reinterpretation of the *guilt clause* of the Moscow Declaration. Still, set against Soviet claims to German assets in Austria, the new formula restricted the clause to Austrian participation in the Holocaust, but not to her participation in the war. Negotiations with the Austrian Government in 1946, either by correspondence or through delegations, show an amazing pragmatism on both sides. The WJC and the Austrian Government even formed what could be called "an alliance of the powerless" to secure the German assets. In early 1946 the WJC appealed to the Austrian Government to join the London Declaration of 5 January 1943, which had declared all transactions under Nazi pressure null and void. In this context, Austria's role as a "victim of Nazi aggression" was again stressed:

> Austria having been prevented by reason of the illegal occupation by Germany from joining the declaration of 5 January 43, it would appear to be desirable that the Government of liberated Austria should align its policy on restitution of property with that of the liberating and allied states.
>
> The Austrian Government should therefore as soon as possible make an official statement announcing its adherence to the Declaration, since such a statement would be welcomed throughout the democratic world as a further indication of the just intentions of the Government of liberated Austria and their [sic] determination to guide the Austrian state upon the principles of fundamental human rights recognized as one of the essential elements of membership of the United Nations into which Austria, in due course, will wish to enter."[44]

For different reasons, the Austrians had the same idea, since the London Declaration of 1943 was seen primarily as a means to strengthen the Austrian position vis-a-vis the Potsdam decision on German assets in Austria. In February 1946, the Austrians discussed this problem twice and Foreign Minister Karl Gruber hinted that the Austrian Government was advised to agree with the demands of the Jews ("*eine gewisse Seite*", in Gruber's loaded diction) to make progress on the question of German assets.[45] In May 1946, the WJC even presented Austria with legal interpretations regarding German assets, telling the Austrians that the WJC was "considering whether reason should be brought forward on behalf of Congress which would support not only Jewish claims but simultaneously the request of the Austrian Government."[46]

One of the key issues was the problem of heirless property. The first restitution laws were discussed in the spring of 1946, closely monitored by the Jewish organizations and the Austrian Jewish community.[47] It was apparent that the Austrian Government was conscious of the wishes of the U.S. Government and the political dangers lurking for Austria in case of public protests from the emigres now living in the United States.[48] Public protests had already been voiced by the Viennese Jewish Community at the beginning of June, stating that a Jewish representative should participate in each step of the restitution process. Both the Austrian Government and the U.S. Military Government deemed such representation unnecessary: They emphasized "that restitution was not primarily a Jewish matter." American officers insisted "that they were ignoring considerations of race and creed in their attitude and added that the Jews should not have special recognition." Special privileges would result in hatred of the Jews "and therefore it is important not to draw too much attention to the Jews as Jews".[49]

The legal implementation of an actual policy of property restitution in Austria was delayed until October 1946. Early in November, as a result of embittered protests by Austrian Jews, the draft of the third restitution bill was called back for further study. In the months before the first treaty negotiations, the Jewish organizations voiced sharp criticism of the Austrian restitution legislation.[50] The third restitution law was presented to the Allied Council on 14 March, 1947 and as a result of Allied disunity automatically became a law after 31 days.[51] The motives of Austrian restitution legislation were interpreted by the AJC as follows:

> It is legitimate to say that the aforementioned initial steps would not have been undertaken by the government if they were not recognized as a necessary device for preventing the Soviet Union from claiming Austrian property once held by the Germans under the title of reparations.[52]

The main reason for this assessment could be found in what the organizations regarded as the generally negative Austrian attitude towards Jews and Jewish Displaced Persons (DPs) in particular. During 1946, the protection of Jewish DPs in Austria, who faced growing anti-Semitism, became the second field of interest for the Jewish organizations. In many respects, the Jewish DPs provided an ideal scapegoat for the starving Austrian population. In the eyes of the general populace, they enjoyed certain "special privileges," such as better rations and exemption from the duty to work—indeed, they were foreigners and Jews to boot! As the target of traditional anti-Semitic stereotypes, a reservoir of bias that had survived Nazi fascism virtually intact, the Jews became the negative showcase example *par excellence*.[53]

In the spring and summer of 1946, this development was carefully followed, especially by certain segments of the American press such as the *New York Times* and *Der Aufbau*. The Austrian State Department left the government in no doubt about the possible consequences of increased anti-Semitism. Foreign Minister Karl Gruber warned in an internal discussion that, as a result of this agitation, Austria might end up forfeiting the support of the great powers, which could have unpredictable consequences.[54] Especially during the Council of Foreign Ministers in Paris in 1946, where the subject of Austria was briefly discussed,[55] the Austrian Government could not afford to risk such a prospect. This message was driven home to the Austrians not only by official contacts and influential U.S. papers, but also in a series of talks with the delegates of the WJC, who visited Austria during the critical phase in the summer of 1946, when 100,000 newly arriving Polish Jews caused considerable problems.[56]

The Paris Conference and the peace treaties with the satellite countries served as test cases for Jewish influence on Allied policy. All joint efforts by Jewish organizations in Paris were completely unsuccessful. In the hope of achieving at least a bare minimum of Jewish demands, the about fifty propositions regarding Jewish interests in the treaties with Italy, Rumania and Hungary initially contained in various statements were reduced to two fields, namely *human rights* and *restitution*. Probably as a face-saving device in their final assessment, the AJC still asserted that they regarded the outcome to be a great success:

> The Roumanian and Hungarian Governments in particular now realize that the united Jewish organizations of the world have enough strength to bring about the inclusion of provisions in the peace treaties which guarantee the rights of Jews and they will hesitate to infringe upon those rights, knowing we are vigilant.[57]

This turned out to be too optimistic, but it became clear that the provisions contained in these treaties would serve as precedent for the treaties with Germany and Austria.[58] For obvious reasons, the Jewish organizations concentrated most of their planning and preparation on a possible German Peace Treaty. They acknowledged that the treaty under consideration with Austria was not a peace treaty in the proper sense of the word "because Austria was never at war with the allies." The whole purpose for an Austrian treaty was "to confirm the independence of Austria and to secure the re-establishment of the democratic government in Austria." Therefore, the Austrian treaty was given lower priority than even the satellite treaties. First preliminary preparations, like inquiring about the demands of the Viennese community for inclusion in the treaty, were only started in October 1946.[59] The WJC analyzed the Viennese proposals in mid-November. Significantly, they neither included demands on behalf of the great number of Austrian Jews living abroad, who "apparently do not concern the remaining Austrian Jewry," nor mentioned the matter of regaining Jewish property. Regarding the minority provisions demanded, the experts in the WJC were "under the impression that the present spokesmen of the Austrian Jews do not know their own constitution,"[60] since these provisions were already part of the Austrian constitution.

The first *Draft Resolution on the Settlement with Germany and Austria* of the European Council of the WJC was dated 14 November 1946. It covered four major fields: The legal position of German (Austrian) Jews, the special status of Jewish DPs, restitution and claims, and reparations. As far as Austria was concerned, the last point seemed quite astonishing. Despite the nature of the treaty with Austria, it should contain special provisions for reparations to the Jewish people, in a form which may best serve its interests, available for Jewish reconstruction, as partial satisfaction of the claims of the victims to their murderers.[61]

Austrian Treaty Negotiations and Jewish Claims in London and Moscow in 1947

In anticipation of Jewish demands and presumed influence, the Austrian Government prepared for the upcoming 1947 treaty negotiations of the Foreign Ministers and their Deputies in London and Moscow on different levels. Apart from working out a memorandum to be presented to the Deputies of the Foreign Ministers, the Austrian press and leading politicians engaged in a very intensive campaign of international image polishing. Press reports on Austrian anti-Semitism had accused the Austrian people of being vengeful, and of harboring a considerable number of Nazi elements. The press even claimed that Jewish DPs would have to fear for their lives once the Allies had left Austria. In the light of such reports, the government was well aware of the danger an open expression of anti-Semitism could pose for Austria. Thus, Chancellor Leopold Figl, in an interview with an American journalist, "vehemently rejected the notion that Austria was still an anti-Semitic country."[62] One can sense behind these efforts the Austrian government's fears of the presumed or actual influence of a Jewish lobby on U.S. policy-making. In the eyes of the Austrians, the Jewish DPs served only as tools of the Jewish organizations to achieve advantages in the upcoming negotiations on reparations and the restitution of Jewish property.[63]

The Jewish organizations began preparations for the negotiations in London quite late. On 17 December 1946 the WJC decided "to start working immediately on the preparation of a Statement of Views of the WJC on the German treaty and of draft provisions for the Austrian Treaty."[64] These initial deliberations[65] formed more or less the basis for all Jewish demands raised in London, where extensive lobbying by the Jewish organizations started in January 1947. When Maurice Perlzweig, Head of the Foreign Affairs Department of the WJC, met with Patrick Dean, Head of the German Department of the Foreign Office, the Austrian Treaty was not even mentioned and Dean stated that it would be unlikely for the Deputies to deal with Jewish demands.[66] Nevertheless, by mid-January various organizations, in a last minute effort, were trying to coordinate their proposals. This lack of cooperation among Jewish organizations would prove costly. The WJC and the British Board of Deputies agreed on a short, three page memorandum consisting of a preamble and ten articles,[67] but there was major disagreement between the two organizations as far as the planned Jewish Rehabilitation Fund was concerned. The WJC refused to accept the clauses of the satellite treaties which would hand over the control to the Jewish community in Austria.[68] The WJC and the American Jewish Conference spent the rest of the month trying to reach an agreement. The result was a document twice as long, but half as clear as the original. According to Perlzweig, he was sure that the Allies were "not going to fight another battle on points on which they have already achieved agreement in order to enable the Conference to write what it calls 'history'."[69]

The Deputies of the Foreign Ministers began their meetings in London on 16 January 1947 and worked until 25 February 1947 on the preparation of treaty drafts.[70] Between 14 and 20 February, all major Jewish organizations presented their own statements, each with different demands; they even differed in their language and their assessment of Austria's legal status in the war. They all demanded the inclusion in the Austrian Treaty draft of a basic clause regarding Jewish properties. Austria should be compelled to restore to victims of Nazi oppression the properties of which they were deprived after 11 March 1938; if full restitution would be impossible, adequate compensation should be paid. In addition, they demanded a clause commanding the Austrian Government to hand over unclaimed or heirless properties of the victims to a Jewish rehabilitation fund. Since the majority of Austrian Jews lived outside Austria, unclaimed and heirless properties should be mainly dedicated to these Austrian refugees who would not return to Austria.

This fund should be administered by representatives of Jewish organizations, especially Jewish refugee organizations outside Austria, together with the Jewish community in Austria, to support Austrian victims of Nazi-oppression wherever they lived. This last demand met with strong Austrian and Allied opposition. It differed from the clauses in the peace treaties with Hungary and Rumania, which designated heirless property to be handed over to the Jewish communities in those countries.

A second objective was to secure the legal status of Jewish DPs in Austria, who constituted the large majority of the Jewish population left in that country. A third provision dealt with the legal status of Austrian Jews, such as minority clauses or safeguarding the rights of Austrian Jews living abroad. All Jewish draft clauses were peppered with statements about Austria's role in the mushrooming anti-Semitism before 1938, Austrian influence on shaping anti-Jewish ideas in Germany as well as the vast record of the participation of Austrians in the Nazi movement and the persecution of the Jews.[71]

The Austrian delegation had also submitted a memorandum on their position. On 30 January, Chancellor Figl had the opportunity to present the Austrian case;[72] On the same day, Foreign Minister Gruber presented the Austrian position on the issues of German assets and Yugoslav territorial claims in Carinthia.[73] As far as Jewish interests were concerned, Gruber noted in his summary of the London talks that the Jewish organizations started a "full-scale offensive" with all four delegations, increasing the compensations provided for in Article 44. The tone of the memorandum of the WJC was in Gruber's mind "particularly vindictive (*"gehässig"*) and tried to burden Austria with responsibility for participating in the war."[74]

Gruber objected strongly to the British draft on article 44, which was based on the satellite treaties and proposed two-thirds compensation to U.N. nationals for the war damage. Gruber argued with Oliver Harvey, Deputy Under-Secretary of State in the Foreign Office, that two-thirds compensation for 60,000 mostly Jewish ex-Austrians, who had assumed British and American nationality, might arouse "afresh the embers of anti-Semitism in Austria." It would also be "unfair that these Austrians who had escaped should receive better terms than those who had remained and been placed in concentration camps."[75] Gruber shrewdly applied the specter of Austrian anti-Semitism—much like Interior Minister Oskar Helmer with regard to Jewish DPs—very intentionally, only with the British, whom the Austrians regarded to be anti-Semitic themselves.[76] In the long run, Gruber achieved his principal goal—to have Austrian Jews treated as Austrians, and to have U.N. nationals (mostly former Austrian Jews) treated the same way. In the end, the Austrian Treaty contained no special compensation clauses for Jews, as none of the satellite treaties did either.

High Commissioner General Mark Clark, who acted as the American Deputy in the London negotiations, supported the Austrian position, rejected the Jewish demands outright and was furious about the style of the Jewish presentations. The British disguised their rejection of Jewish demands in diplomatic clothing.[77] They refused any discriminatory treatment, not even in the positive sense, for Jewish victims of Nazi persecution. The British argued that demands for special international guarantees regarding Jews would restrict Austrian sovereignty and therefore be against the spirit of the proposed treaty, whereas reparations or indemnification would hamper Austria's economic recovery. It became quite clear that there were no intentions on the side of the Allies to go beyond the clauses contained in the satellite treaties. Dean concluded, "that the provisions of these clauses in a restored and vigorous Austria will provide the best guarantee for the protection of the Jewish population."[78]

The Allies in fact agreed on provisions similar to those in the satellite treaties. Not even the most important question for the Jewish organizations was solved according to their interests: heirless property should be used for the benefit of all victims of Nazi persecution and not exclusively for Jewish victims. Despite all protests, the recipients of heirless property and the confiscated properties of the Jewish community were to be the Jewish communities in Austria and not the Jewish organizations. The American delegation even pointed out to Jewish representatives that it was not conceivable that the word Jew would appear in the Austrian or German Treaty, just as it did not appear in any of the satellite treaties.[79] In London, the Foreign Ministers' Deputies had agreed on the Austrian Treaty in the course of 29 meetings fully or in part on thirty articles of the Austrian treaty draft, covering about one half of the final treaty.[80] The draft was to be completed at the Council of Foreign Ministers' meeting which began in Moscow on 10 March 1947. Jewish interventions in London had failed not only because the organizations did not speak as one and voiced demands overly ambitious, but more fundamentally because of a general misjudgment of Allied interests.

The London draft treaty was a big disappointment to the Jewish organizations. They had no more success in influencing on the outcome of the subsequent CFM deliberations in Moscow. No Jewish representatives were invited to attend and the Jewish organizations were completely cut off from any information regarding these negotiations. The conference began at a time of a general hardening of East-West relations. The Truman Doctrine was announced two days after the conference had started, and in the context of the gradual formation of a Soviet satellite system in Eastern Europe, the United States was no longer inclined to compromise with the Soviet Union on the early conclusion of an Austrian Treaty. As far as the German assets were concerned, the Americans regarded the Soviet insistence on their terms as part of a larger scheme to gain economic influence in Austria and ultimately to make Austria a Soviet satellite.[81] The Austrians, in turn, blamed the inflexible attitude of the United States on this issue for the failure to achieve a settlement.[82]

Nevertheless, the conference agreed that Austria should be freed from reparation payments. While not a single Jewish demand was met, the Soviets accepted a crucial component of the Austrian position, as put forward by the American delegation: Compensation for losses to victims of racial persecution should only be paid to the same extent as may be given to Austrians generally for war damages.[83] Since the Austrian Government had no intentions to reimburse its own nationals for war damages, the issue seemed to be settled for the Austrian Government. Austria, without any doubt, benefitted for the first time from the clash of interests between the West and the Soviet Union, while Jewish interests were the first to be sacrificed in the now openly-emerging Cold War. How negligible the influence of the Jewish organizations was at the time is seen in the fact that this lobby learned about the course of the negotiations only afterwards, through the press. The Jewish organizations were "very much troubled at the newspaper reports of what happened in Moscow with respect to the Austrian treaty."[84]

Jewish Claims and Austrian Treaty Negotiations 1947-49

After the uncoordinated and largely unsuccessful interventions in London and the disappointing outcome of the Moscow Conference, all major Jewish organizations agreed on preparing a joint document on the German and Austrian treaties to be presented to the Allies. In the summer of 1947 the Austrian Treaty Commission in Vienna discussed the remaining articles without any positive results,[85] and the working committee, set up by eleven Jewish organizations in May 1947, also turned out to be a waste of time. By the autumn of 1947, the Allies cordially acknowledged Jewish planning but it left no further traces in the Austrian State Treaty.[86] When the joint document was handed over to the Allies, the State Treaty negotiations had already proceeded to a point where further interventions by the Jewish organizations seemed useless.[87]

This memorandum was in some ways a symbol of total resignation, a desperate attempt to achieve at least minimal results. It even went as far as dropping any explicit *guilt clause* in the preamble of the Austrian State Treaty. Instead, Austria's responsibility was reflected in the clauses dealing with human rights, with the legal nondiscrimination of Jews, with retaining Jewish DPs under Allied jurisdiction and with restitution of aryanized Jewish properties. Austria's status as a "victim of Nazi aggression" was again, at least implicitly, recognized.[88]

The treaty negotiations of 1947 marked the end of the first phase of Jewish efforts, focusing on restitution, on human rights and on the protection of Jewish DPs in Austria. By now, the Allies had agreed upon most articles in the proposed treaty covering Jewish interests. Until February 1949 Jewish organizations tried with little success to achieve minor changes in articles that were not yet definitely agreed upon by the Four Powers. The second goal at this stage was getting a solution on the problem of heirless Jewish property in Austria. During the Foreign Ministers' Deputies' meeting in London from 20 February to 6 May 1948, due to the events in Czechoslovakia, the timing was not propitious for successful negotiations between East and West.[89] With the beginning of restricted of access to Berlin, the fear of a blockade of Vienna also increased.[90] Discussion on the Yugoslav issue at last offered an opportunity to the Americans to break up negotiations and adjourn *sine die*. [91]

In late 1948, with the prospect of treaty negotiations resuming in 1949, the Jewish organizations became active on different levels. In October 1948 Jacob Blaustein, president of the AJC, saw Ludwig Kleinwächter, the Austrian Minister in Washington. Kleinwächter promised sympathetic consideration of the problem of heirless property, and a long series of fruitless efforts to reach an understanding began.[92] In Vienna, representatives of the Viennese Jewish community, of the JDC and the WJC were met by Chancellor Figl and Finance Minister Krauland on 8 November. They presented what they called the "minimum demands" of Austrian Jews. On the following day—coincidentally, the tenth anniversary of the 1938 November Pogrom—these Jewish demands were turned down by the Austrian Cabinet meeting.[93]

At a protest meeting of the Viennese Jewish community on 18 November 1948, the Jewish leadership informed the public of the dire situation of the Austrian Jews three and a half years after the liberation of Austria. In a protest resolution sent to Figl, a number of demands were filed: The passing of further restitution laws, immediate creation of a restitution fund financed by heirless property in accordance with the third restitution law, immediate financial help to overcome unbearable material needs, extension for claims under the third restitution law, speeding up of the restitution procedure, appointment of the Jewish community as public commissioner for all heirless property in Austria, participation of the Jewish community in reviewing draft laws on restitution, monthly allotment of housing/apartments to the Jewish community for returning survivors, dissolution of the *"Verband der Rückstellungsbetroffenen"* — the organization of the aryanizers—(!), and energetic efforts to fight anti-Semitism in Austria.[94]

In identical letters to the Deputy Foreign Ministers, who began a new round of treaty negotiations in London on 9 February 1949, the Jewish organizations again presented their memo *Comments and Proposals Respecting the Treaty with Austria*, dated September 1947. They submitted additional requests to protect human rights and fundamental freedom effectively and to place heirless and unclaimed Jewish property in Austria under the administration of a Jewish Rehabilitation Fund. They then made a last appeal, "for the sake of justice, not to deviate from the principle according to which the property, legal rights and interests of victims of racial or religious persecution shall be restored, together with their accessories, or if restitution is impossible, that fair compensation shall be made therefore."[95]

This letter arrived the day after the appropriate Article in the Treaty had been agreed upon.[96] The negotiations were suspended in mid-April 1949 and ended, after their resumption on 25 April, without results on 10 May 1949. Before the final decision was taken on the famous Article 44, dealing with "Property, Rights and Interests of Minority Groups in Austria," Jewish representatives made final attempts to get some minor changes in the wording. Reference to compensation in Article 44 seemed too vague, and it did not specifically indicate that the appropriate agency to take over heirless or unclaimed property should be a Jewish organization. Regarding compensation, Michael Cullis, the Austrian desk officer in the Foreign Office, in response to this intervention, made quite clear, that it had been decided at a high level that Austria should be regarded as a 'liberated' country and not responsible for the actions of the German Government in Austria since the Anschluss. In these circumstances it would be difficult to impose on the Austrian Government the obligation to compensate Jews beyond the measure of compensation allowed to U.N. nationals and it had already been agreed that U.N. nationals would not obtain more compensation than Austrian nationals.[97]

After long debates at the CFM in Paris in May, Austria was put on the agenda, and on 19 June 1949, substantial agreement was reached due to Soviet concessions to the Yugoslav demands. As far as Jewish interests were involved, Article 44 was finally and definitely agreed upon on 22 July.[98] On the last day of the CFM meeting, the Deputies were instructed to resume their sessions in order to reach agreement on the treaty as a whole by 1 September 1949. At the CFM in New York in the fall of 1949, the key problem remained the question of German assets. Nevertheless, agreement on article 35 dealing with German assets, was reached in the wording of the Soviet draft. By now, 48 out of 53 articles were agreed on and the signing of the Austrain treaty appeared to be a matter of only days. But in the course of this autumn, with the foundation of the two Germanies, and the Communist victory in China—the formation of the blocs and growing tensions between East and West became increasingly apparent. In this situation, the Soviets engaged in dilatory tactics, tabling new claims as a result. The treaty negotiations dragged on without any further progress.[99]

Conclusion: Preview of Austrian-Jewish Negotiations 1950 - 55

With the end of the 1949 treaty negotiations, the second phase of Jewish efforts came to an end. At this stage, it was clear to all concerned that the language of the treaty did not provide for the principle of indemnification.

> The representatives of the four agencies agreed that the only step open to them is to urge the enactment of such legislation, both in Austria and through representatives in Washington.[100]

1950 was a watershed year for a number of reasons. The Korean War put the Austrian treaty negotiations on hold from mid-1950 until 1953,[101] while the Jewish organizations and the U.S. Government referred to the treaty draft as a *fait accompli*.[102] Between 1950 and 1953 the U. S. Government pressured the Austrians in what was termed the *Austro-Jewish War of Succession*, namely the fight for heirless Jewish property in Austria.[103] Extensive lobbying, especially on part of the AJC and its Chairman, Jacob Blaustein, in a number of meetings with President Truman and the State Department hardened the U.S. attitude towards Austria in this question. Austrian amnesty laws were vetoed in the Allied Council due to interventions of the AJC and other organizations,[104] and amendments of restitution laws were prevented. The Austrians felt the pressure even more in 1953 when the new Eisenhower Administration cut back the U.S. economic aid to Austria. The Austrians reacted to these cuts by stating that there no longer would be any need to be overly too compromising with Jewish organizations just to please American public opinion.[105] Austria's position had been strengthened by Israel's renunciation of any reparations from Austria in 1952. Therefore, Austria could negotiate from a position of strength when it came to dealing with the "Committee for Jewish Claims on Austria" in 1953.[106]

This committee was to set up to deal with Austrian-Jewish problems with a two-fold objective: First, to obtain from Austria funds for the relief of Jewish victims of Nazi persecution who were in need, and secondly to improve Austrian legislation for the benefit of Jewish victims of Nazi persecution. Austria rejected any Jewish demand under the term "reparation", since "only he can make reparation who was guilty of the damage done [...] At the time when persecutory measures were initiated against political opponents of National Socialism, partly for racial, national, religious or philosophical reasons, Austria was no longer free to act."[107]

The Austrian Government emphasized that not even in the draft State Treaty any reparation was demanded from Austria, but that Austria had always recognized that everything had to be done in order to compensate the victims. This compensation, however, would find its limits in the economic capacity of the country. Austria did not want to enrich herself with the property of the victims of Nazi persecution who died heirless and therefore indicated its readiness to make these assets available to political persecutees.

Total material losses of Austrian Jews were estimated by the Jewish organizations at the beginning of 1953 at 1.25 billion dollars. Recovery under Austrian restitution laws was secured only to the extent of approximately 250-280 million dollars, meaning that at least 720 million dollars worth of property and several hundred million dollars worth of non-property damages remained unrecovered:

> Now we realize that at this late stage nothing can be done to improve the restitution legislation. Fortunately, even the most fanatically restitution-minded Austrian Jew realize this fact, which indicates that our demands must be confined to the area of indemnification for non-property damages. While it is very difficult to estimate the value of these damages, it is more than likely that for over 90,000 people they would amount, on the basis of the Hague agreement, to at least 250-300 million.[108]

The experts believed that Austria was not likely to be able and willing to spend more than five percent of the annual social budget on the settlement with the Jews, which would be 6.6 million dollars per annum to be paid over a period of ten to twelve years. In addition, the organizations would claim heirless property estimated at some 200 million Austrian Schillings to be paid in ten or twelve annual rates. The maximum value of all claims was estimated at 75 million dollars.[109]

The Committee for Jewish Claims on Austria started off with a demand of 80 million dollars and finally settled for 22 million to be paid to former Austrian Jewish citizens now living abroad. In addition, heirless property was to be traced and should be turned over to the Austrian Jewish community. A detailed study of these very delicate and complicated Austrian-Jewish behind-the-scene contacts has so far not been carried out. Nevertheless, preliminary studies indicate a strong linkage with the German-Jewish negotiations for *Wiedergutmachung* in 1951/52.[110]

These Austro-Jewish negotiations remained up to the final settlement in July 1955 a factor in the U.S. Government's attitude towards Austria.[111] The State Department made it sufficiently clear that a satisfactory settlement between the Jewish organizations and the Austrian Government would influence U.S. ratification of the State Treaty.[112]

The Austrian State Treaty, signed on 15 May 1955, eventually contained two provisions of importance to the victims of Nazism: Article 26, (the former Article 44), was most important. It imposed on Austria the obligation, insofar as it had not already been done, to return all property and to restore all rights and interests which were subject to forced transfer or measures of confiscation on account of the racial origin or religion of the owner. Where return or restoration was impossible, compensation was to be paid to the same extent as may be given to Austrians generally in respect of war damages. Since Austria enacted no general war damage law, this provision remained a dead letter. A similar provision was contained in Article 25, (the original Article 42), which related to property, rights and interests of national of the United Nations. Article 26 (2) provided for the assignment of heirless and unclaimed properties for relief and rehabilitation of victims of persecution.[113]

But this was not the end of the story: Immediately after the 1955 signing of the State Treaty, new arguments started regarding the interpretation of the language of Article 26. Austria refused to accept additional obligations pursuant to the provisions of the State Treaty; nevertheless it continued negotiations with the Western powers. At the same time, follow-up negotiations between the "Committee for Jewish Claims on Austria" and the Austrian Government regarding the implementation of the settlement began and dragged on until the early sixties.

Despite all criticism, the provisions of the State Treaty and the settlement between Austria and the Committee for Jewish Claims on Austria compare, at first sight, favorable with the terms of the agreement between the Federal Republic and the Conference on Jewish Material Claims Against Germany.[114] Since Austria was officially regarded by all interested parties as a "liberated" country, and consequently, the State of Israel refrained from demanding reparations, one can only compare the roughly 120 million dollars the Claims Conference received from the Federal Republic until 1964 for the benefit of the victims of Nazism[115] to the 22 million dollars of the Austrian settlement with the Committee on Jewish Claims, earmarked for the same purpose. In this respect, Austria seemed to have paid a fair share in relation to the size and economic strength of the Federal Republic.

However, the difference remains that Austria, in contrast to Germany, felt no moral obligation for *Wiedergutmachung*. The Moscow Declaration, the Allies' "gift of a clean bill of national health", enabled the Austrians until 1986 "to concentrate on national reconciliation rather then large-scale retribution for questionable wartime activities."[116]

NOTES

1. The records of the WJC are kept at the American Jewish Archives (AJA), Cincinnati Ohio; records of the AJC are at YIVO, the Institute for Jewish Research, in New York, the records of the JDC are at the JDC archives in New York and the records of the AJCf. are in the Central Zionist Archives (CZA) in Jerusalem.

2. For the Austrian treaty negotiations, see Gerald Stourzh, *Geschichte des Staatsvertrages 1945 - 1955: Österreichs Weg zur Neutralität*, 3rd ed. (Graz-Vienna-Cologne: Styria, 1985); Günter Bischof, "Between Responsibility and Rehabilitation: Austria in International Politics, 1940 - 1950," Ph.D. diss., Harvard University, 1989; for a brief summary, see Kurt Steiner, "Negotiations for an Austrian State Treaty," in *U.S.-Soviet Security Cooperation: Achievements, Failures, Lessons,* ed. Alexander L. George, Philip J. Farley *et al.* (New York-Oxford: Oxford University Press, 1988), 46-82.

3. Thomas Albrich, "Österreichs jüdisch-nationale und zionistische Emigration: Holocaust und Nachkriegsplanung 1942-1945," *Zeitgeschichte* 18 (August 1991): 183-197.

4. Meeting AJRC, 22 January 1942, WJC, H 43/Austria J.C.R. Minutes 1942-46, AJA.

5. For details on the Austrian political emigration, see Helene Maimann, *Politik im Wartesaal: Österreichische Exilpolitik in Großbritannien 1938 bis 1945* (Vienna-Cologne-Graz: Böhlau, 1975); Franz Goldner, *Die österreichische Emigration 1938-1945* (Vienna-Munich: Herold, 1972); Manfred Marschalek *Untergrund und Exil: Österreichs Sozialisten zwischen 1934 und 1945* (Vienna, 1989).

6. For details on the American-Jewish reaction to the Holocaust, see David S. Wyman, *The Abandonment of the Jews: America and the Holocaust, 1941-1945*, (New York: Pantheon Books, 1984).

7. Meeting AJRC, 29 March 1942, WJC, H 43/Austria J.C.R. Minutes 1942-46, AJA.

8. David S. Wyman, "The American Jewish Leadership and the Holocaust," in *Jewish Leadership during the Nazi Era: Patterns of Behavior in the Free World*, ed. Randolph L. Braham (New York, 1985), 4.

9. Meeting AJRC, 25 November 1942, WJC, H/43 Austria J.C.R. Minutes 1942-46, AJA.

10. Meeting AJRC, 21 October 1942, WJC, H 43/Austria J.C.R. Minutes 1942-46, AJA.

11. Jonny Moser "Österreich," in *Dimension des Völkermords*, ed. Wolfgang Benz (Munich: Oldenbourg, 1991), 67-93.

12. Summary of Prof. Altmann's report on the Austrian immigration in the United States, 1 June 1943, WJC, H 43/Austria J.C.R. Minutes 1942-46, AJA.

13. Notes on lecture given by Dr. Eugen Felix at The City Literary Institute on 22 June 1943, Henriques Collection, Wiener Library, London.

14. Herbert Rosenkranz, *Vertreibung und Selbstbehauptung: Die Juden in Österreich 1938 - 1945* (Vienna-Munich: Herold, 1978).

15. American Jewish Conference, *Program for Postwar Jewish Reconstruction* (New York, 1945), 3-4.

16. Siegfried Kantor to Leon Kubowitzki, 9 August 1944 and 17 August 1944, WJC, H 43/AJRC Misc. 1942-44, AJA.

17. One of the numerous examples is a letter by Gottwald Schwarz to the AJRC, 11 November 1943, WJC, H 43/AJRC Hitachthut Oley Austria/Palestine, AJA.

18. Robert H. Keyserlingk, *Austria in World War II: An Anglo-American Dilemma* (Kingston and Montreal: McGill-Queen's University Press, 1988), 190-191; Bischof, "Between Responsibility and Rehabilitation," 25-42.

19. Meeting of the Committee on Post-War Problems of the AJRC, 15 November 1943, AJA, WJC, H 43/Austria J.R.C. Minutes 1942-46, AJA.

20. Meeting AJRC, 4 January 1944, , WJC, H 43/Austria - Free Movements 1942-45, AJA.

21. Memorandum Franz Rudolf Bienenfeld, January 1944, WJC, H 43/Austria-Free Movements 1942-45, AJA.

22. WJC press release, 10 April 1944, WJC, H 46/Austria, AJA.

23. Oskar Karbach, Draft Memorandum on particular post-war problems of the Jews in Austria, 3 November 1943, WJC, H 43/Austria 1943, AJA.

24. Meeting AJRC, 12 October 1944, WJC, H 43/AJRC Committee 1943-44, AJA.

25. WJC Activities, October 1945-December 1946, WJC, A 5/Activity Report 1946, AJA.

26. Schirn to Office Committee of the WJC, 23 February 1945, WJC, A 74/5, AJA.

27. WJC, Office Committee, 15 May 1945, WJC, A 74/2, AJA.

28. For this decision, see Manfried Rauchensteiner, *Die Zwei. Die Große Koalition in Österreich 1945-1966* (Vienna: Österreichischer Bundesverlag, 1987)

29. WJC, Administrative Committee, 2 July 1945, WJC, A 80/16, AJA.

30. European Conference of the WJC, London, 19-23 August 1945, WJC, A 92/1, AJA.

31. Moser, *Die Katastrophe der Juden in Österreich, 132.*

32. Karbach to Office Comittee, 13 September 1945, WJC A 75/2, AJA.

33. Meeting AJRC, 20 October 1945, WJC, H 43/AJRC Committee 1943-1944; Oscar Kerbech to Leon Kubowitzki, 3 October 1945, WJC #43/Austria J R.C. Minutes 1942-1946, AJA.

34. Helga Embacher, "'Lassen Sie uns für uns selber sprechen!' Der World Jewish Congress (WJC) und die Israelitische Kultusgemeinde (IKG) im Kalten Krieg," *Zeitgeschichte* 18 (August 1991): 198-208.

35. Siegfried Kantor to Leon Kubowitzki, 9 August 1944, WJC, H 43/AJRC Misc. 1942-44, AJA; this attitude became quite clear at the European Conference of the WJC, London, 19-23 August 1945, WJC, A 92/1, AJA.

36. Wolkowicz to AJRC, 11 October 1945, WJC, H 43/AJCR Misc 1942-1944, AJA.

37. Richard Crossman, *Palestine Mission. A Personal Record* (London, 1946), 101.

38. PALCOR, Bulletin, 20 February 1946.

39. Francis Williamson, Memorandum on the Jews in Austria, 5 January 1946, Box 1, Lot 54 D 331, Record Group [RG] 59, National Archives [NA] Washington, D.C.

40. Minutes of a joint meeting of the Executive Committee WJC and the Austrian Advisory Committee, 6 February 1946, WJC, H 43/AJCR Committee 1943-1944, AJA; Nehemiah Robinson to Office Committee, WJC, 6 February 1946, WJC, H 43/Austria 1946, AJA.

41. Saul Kagan to Jerome Jacobson, 19 August 1952, GEN-10, Restitution and
    Indemnification (Austria) General 1952, RG 347, AJC.

42. Rauchensteiner, *Die Zwei*, 84.

43. Steiner, "State Treaty," 48.

44. Alex Easterman to Leopold Figl, 28 February 1946, WJC, H 43/Austria 1946,
    AJA.

45. Robert Knight ed., *"Ich bin dafür, die Sache in die Länge zu ziehen" : Wortprotokolle
    der österreichischen Bundesregierung von 1945 über die Entschädigung der
    Juden* (Frankfurt/M: Athenäum, 1988), 132.

46. Alex Easterman to Hans Schmitt, 16 May 1946, WJC, H 43/Austria 1946, AJA.

47. Correspondence with the Austrian Government and Allied representatives and
    internal discussions are contained in WJC, H 43/Austria 1946, AJA.

48. Knight, *Wortprotokolle*,123-134.

49. Albion Ross, *New York Times*, 7 June 1946.

50. Herbert Elias to Karl Gruber, 25 November 1946, Zl. 919-K/46, Box 5 Kabinet des
    Ministers [KdM], Bundesministerium für Auswärtige Angelegenheiten [BMfAA],
    Archiv der Republik [AdR], Vienna; Nehemiah Robinson to Karl Gruber, 20
    November 1946, Zl. 919-K/46, Box 5; Franz Rudolf Bienenfeld to Adolf Schärf,
    20 December 1946, 100033 K/47, Box 5, both KdM, BMfAA, AdR.

51. Knight, *Wortprotokolle*, 147-158.

52. Restitution of Property, the American Jewish Committee, Committee on Peace
    Problems, Third Session, January 23-24, 1947. GEN-10, Box 276. Restitution and
    Indemnification Property 47.

53. For the attitude of the Austrian population towards Jewish DPs, see Thomas
    Albrich, *Exodus durch Österreich: Die jüdischen Flüchtlinge und Displaced
    Persons 1945-1948* (Innsbruck Haymon, 1987), 180-193.

54. Thomas Albrich, "Asylland wider Willen," in *Die bevormundete Nation*, ed
    Günter Bischof and Josef Leidenfrost (Innsbruck: Haymon, 1988), 232-233.

55. Steiner, "State Treaty," 49.

56. Ernest Stiassny, Report on the Mission to Austria (June-September 1946), 2
    December 1946, WJC, H 43/Austria J.R.C. 1946-47, AJA.

57. American Jewish Committee, The Decisions of the Council of Foreign Ministers,
    3 December 1946, RG 347, AJC YIVO. GEN-10, Box 310, Paris Peace Conference
    1946, RG 347, AJC, YIVO.

58. Franz Rudolf Bienenfeld to Alex Easterman, 23 October 1946, WJC, H 43/Peace Treaty 1946-49, AJA.

59. Bernhard Braver to WJC, 23 October 1946, AJA, WJC, H 43/Peace Treaty 1946-49, AJA.

60. Oscar Karbach to Leon Kubowitzky, 13 November 1946, WJC, H 43/Austria 1946, AJA.

61. Draft Resolution on the Settlement with Germany and Austria to be submitted for Discussion and Eventual Approval by the European Council of the WJC, Paris, 14 November 1946, WJC, C 121/3, AJA.

62. Knight, *Wortprotokolle*, 156-159.

63. Albrich, *Exodus*, 196-197.

64. Minutes of Meeting WJC, 17 December 1946, WJC, A 76/2, AJA.

65. Oskar Karbach to Jacob Robinson, 23 Dezember 1946, WJC, H 43/Peace Treaty 1946-49, AJA.

66. Maurice Perlzweig to Office Committee WJC, 2 January 1947, WJC, C 121/2, AJA.

67. Memorandum on Jewish Proposals of Clauses for Inclusion in the Treaty with Austria, 16 January 1947, WJC, H 43/Peace Treaty 1946-49, AJA.

68. Franz Rudolf Bienenfeld to Leon Kubowitzki and Maurice Perlzweig, 17 January 1947, WJC, H 43/Peace Treaty 1946-49, AJA.

69. Perlzweig to Office Committee WJC, 6 February 1947, AJA, WJC, H 43/Austria 1946-47.

70. Stourzh, *Staatsvertrag*, 14-16, Bischof, "Between Responsibility and Rehabilitation," 562-588.

71. For details of the proposals, see A.G. Brotman to Foreign Office, 14 February 1947, WJC, H 45/Austria 1947, AJA; Stephen Wise, Nahum Goldmann, Alex Easterman to the Secretary General of the CMF and to the four Deputies, 14 February 1947, WJC, H 45/Austria 1947, AJA; The American Jewish Conference, Proposals for inclusion in the Treaty with Austria, 18 February 1947, WJC, H 43/Peace Treaty 1946-49, AJA; The Peace Treaty with Austria, Recommendations of the American Jewish Committee (with cover letter to George C. Marshall), 20 February 1947. William Frankel, the London Representative of the American Jewish Committee, forwarded the Memorandum to Clark on 20 February, see Folder 7, Box 41, Clark Papers, The Citadel, Charleston, South Carolina.

72. Statement and Memorandum (nos. 11 to 23 and 26-StV/47) of the Austrian Delegation, London January-February, 1947.

73. Stourzh, *Staatsvertrag*, 32-34; Knight, *Wortprotokolle*, 165-170.

74. Österreichischer Staatsvertrag. Bericht des Bundesministers für die Auswärtigen Angelegenheiten über das Londoner Beratungsergebnis, 3 March 1947, Zl. 147.600-6VR/47, Gruber Papers, Institute of Contemporary History, University of Innsbruck.

75. Memorandum of conversation by Oliver Harvey, 11 February 1947, FO 371/ 63955/C 2941, Public Record Office [PRO], London.

76. Albrich, *Exodus*, 67-72.

77. For the British attitude, see Robert Knight, British Policy Towards Occupied Austria, 1945-1950, Ph.D diss., London University (LSE), 1985, 101-105.

78. Patrick Dean to Stephen Wise, 21 February 1947, WJC, H 43/Peace Treaty 1946-49, AJA.

79. Abraham S. Hyman to Rabbi Philip S. Bernstein, 3 March 1947, C7/320/1, CZS.

80. Steiner, "State Treaty," 49.

81. Ibid., 50.

82. Eva-Marie Csaky, *Der Weg zur Freiheit und Neutralität: Dokumentation zur österreichischen Außenpolitik 1945-1955* (Vienna: Selbstverlag der österreichischen Gesellschaft für Außenpolitik und internationale Beziehungen, 1980), 140-149.

83. A comparison of the draft at the end of the Moscow conference with the final treaty is to be found in Stourzh, *Staatsvertrag*, 241-301; the Moscow negotiations are covered in detail in Bischof, "Between Responsibility and Rehabilitation," 588-604.

84. Bernard Bernstein to David Ginsburg, 7 May 1947, C7/267/2, CZA.

85. Steiner, "State Treaty," 50; Stourzh, *Staatsvertrag*, 48; Manfried Rauchensteiner, Der *Sonderfall: Die Besatzungszeit in Österreich 1945 bis 1955* (Graz-Vienna-Cologne: Styria, 1979), 217-218.

86. John D. Hickerson, Director, Office of European Affairs, to Morris Halperin, 27 November 1947, GEN-10, Box 312, Peace Treaties Germany and Austria, US Government 1946-1947, RG 347, AJC, YIVO.

87. David Bernstein to John Slawson, 10 November 1947, GEN-10, Box 310, Paris Peace Conference 1946, RG 347, AJC, YIVO.

88. Comments and Proposals Respecting the Treaty with Austria. Submitted to the Council of Foreign Ministers by Agudas Israel World Organization, World Jewish Congress, Alliance Israelite Universelle, American Jewish Committee, American Jewish Conference, Anglo-Jewish Association, Board of Deputies of British Jews, Conseil Representatif des Juifs de France, Council of Jews from Germany,

Federation of Jews from Austria, South African Jewish Board of Deputies, 10 September 1947, C 7/348, CZA.

89. Steiner, "State Treaty," 51-52.

90. Günter Bischof, "Prag liegt westlich von Wien," in *Die bevormundete Nation*, ed. Bischof and Leidenfrost, 315-345.

91. Stourzh, *Staatsvertrag,* 52-54; Steiner, "State Treaty," 52-53.

92. Memorandum Saul Kagan, 4 December 1951. GEN-10, Box 276, Restitution and Indemnification (Austria) General 50-54, RG 347, AJC, YIVO.

93. Leitung der Israelitischen Kultusgemeinde Wien to Chancellor Leopold Figl, 29 November 1948, 100647-K/48, Box 10, KdM, BMfAA, AdR.

94. Israelitische Kultusgemeinde Vienna, Resolution of November 18, 1948, sent to Chancellor Leopold Figl, November 29, 1948, 100647-K/48, Box 10 KdM, BMfAA, AdR; for more background material regarding Cabinet discussions, see Knight, *Wortprotokolle*, 194-200.

95. Paris Cooperating Organizations to the Deputy Foreign Minister of the U.S.S.R., February 22, 1949. YIVO, FAD-1, Box 6, Restitution Austria 48-51, RG 347, AJC, YIVO.

96. William Frankel to Foreign Affairs Department (AJC), February 24, 1949, FAD-1, Box 6, Restitution Austria 48-51, RG 349, AJC, YIVO.

97. Not of Meeting between Cullis (Foreign Office), Barnet Janner (Board of Deputies of British Jews) and R.H. Landman (Anglo-Jewish Association), May 20, 1949. FAD-1, Box 6, Restitution Austria 48-51, RG 347, AJC, YIVO.

98. Draft Treaty for the Re-Establishment of an Independent and Democratic Austria, Department of State, September 6, 1949.

99. Steiner, "State Treaty," 53.

100. Notes on Meeting no. 49-11 of the Four Organizations, October 13, 1949, FAD-1, Box 4, Austria 46-49, RG 347, AJC, YIVO.

101. Steiner, "State Treaty," 55-57.

102. Seymour Rubin to Eugene Hevesi, 7 December 1951. GEN-10, box 276, Restitution and Indemnification (Austria) General 50-54, RG 347, AJC, YIVO.

103. Saul Kagan to Jerome Jacobson, 28 November 1951. GEN-10, box 276, Restitution and Indemnification (Austria) General 50-54, RG 347, AJC, YIVO.

104. Zachariah Shuster to Leo Margolin, 1 August 1952. GEN-10, box 276, Restitution and Indemnification (Austria) General 1952 RG 347, AJC, YIVO.

105. Außenministerium to Max Löwenthal-Chlumecky, 13 June 1953, Box 1034, Kreisky Papers, Kreisky Archives, Vienna.

106. Michael Wolffsohn, "Das deutsch-israelische Wiedergutmachungsabkommen von 1952 im internationalen Zusammenhang," *Vierteljahrshefte für Zeitgeschichte*, 36 (1988): 691-731, especially 721.

107. Claims Against Austria, AJC memo, January 6, 1953. YIVO, RG 347, AJC, GEN-10, box 277. Restitution and Indemnification (Claims Austria) 52-57.

108. Ibid.

109. Ibid.

110. A study by the author on the "Committee for Jewish Claims on Austria" is to be published in 1993; for an account by a negotiator, see Gustav Jellinek, "Die Geschichte der Österreichischen Wiedergutmachung," in *The Jews of Austria,* ed. Josef Fraenkel (London: Vallentine, Mitchel & Co, 1967), 365-426; a first study, mainly based on printed material is Dietmar Walch, *Die jüdischen Bemühungen um die materiellen Wiedergutmachungen* durch die Republik Österreich (Vienna: Geyer, 1971).

111. Dulles to U.S. Embassy, Vienna, 14 October 1953. 663.001/10-1453, RG 59, NA; Memorandum of Conversation, The Secretary's Meeting with the Austrian Chancellor, 22 November 1954, *Foreign Relations of the United States, 1952-1954*, vol. VII (Part 2) (Washinton, D.C.: Government Printing Office, 1986), 1983.

112. On various occasions from May to July 1955, Ambassador Karl Gruber was informed on the questions raised in the Senate during the ratification process, for an example, see Department of State, Memorandum of Conversation, 3 June 1955, 611.63/6-355, RG 59, NA.

113. For the provisions of the State Treaty, see Stourzh, *Staatsvertrag*, 241-301.

114. For the German-Jewish negotiations see Nana Sagi, *German Reparations* (Jerusalem, 1980).

115. Ronald W. Zweig, *German Reparations and the Jewish World. A History of the Claims Conference* (Boulder-London: Westview Press, 1987), 27.

116. Keyserlingk, *Austria in World War II*, 190-191.

Austria's Approach To European Integration - A Review Essay

Sieglinde Gstöhl

The relations between the European Community (EC) and the non-member countries in Europe have always been a stepchild of political science literature. Integration theories have focused almost exclusively on the EC, leaving no room for the "small brother", the European Free Trade Association (EFTA), and the rapprochement between the two organizations. The "1992 relaunch" will rectify this shortcoming but only slowly. This essay highlights two contributions worth mentioning which deal primarily with Austria's approach to European integration.[1]

Austria's Solo Run to Brussels

The first book is Heinrich Schneider's *Alleingang nach Brüssel*,[2] a remarkable analysis of the debate that led to Austria's full EC membership. Schneider describes briefly the historical context of Austria's approach to European integration: the end of the multi-nation state after the First World War, the birth of the idea of a united Europe, and the creation of the Second Republic. The political circumstances after the Second World War brought Austria a "concordance democracy" with strong parties and a "social partnership" with influential interest groups. Austria became a founding member of the European Free Trade Association since joining the EC was considered incompatible with the status of permanent neutrality. From the beginning, however, Austria was seeking closer economic association with the Community. When British aspirations of EC membership and the association hopes of the neutrals failed in the early 1960s, Austria continued its efforts alone. For several reasons, this first *Alleingang* did not succeed and has finally been buried with the second failure of EC enlargement in 1967. Five years later, Austria concluded a free trade agreement for industrial goods with the Community, in parallel with the other EFTA countries.

Schneider is quite right that the historical setting is key to understanding Austria's *Europapolitik*, a fact that is not always taken for granted in political science. A second crucial factor often neglected in foreign policy analysis is the interplay with domestic politics. The author examines the particular role of the two big political parties. The coalition of the Socialist Party (SPÖ) and the People's Party (ÖVP) began, in cooperation with the influential interest groups, the *dirigiste* reconstruction of the Austrian economy with massive nationalizations. In the early 1970s, the *Austro-Keynesianism* aiming at full employment and a hard currency led to disparities in the economic structure. Some branches of the economy were exposed to increased international competition whereas other sectors were protected.

While Austria's first solo run toward the European Community lacked broad political consensus the decision to apply for full membership in July 1989 represented an overwhelming majority. In the second part of his book, Schneider analyzes the economic and political background of this new approach. The basis for the Parliament's approval was the Austrian Cabinet's decision specifying that the application for membership should be pursued subject to the following conditions:
- the maintenance of permanent neutrality,
- the functioning of the principles of Austrian federalism,
- the protection of the Austrian social security system against the internal market's competition,
- the defence of high environmental standards,
- the maintenance of agriculture and forestry covering the whole territory, and
- a solution to the problems of the transit traffic.

In the following chapters, Schneider evaluates why the applicant must set conditions for membership. He points out that the EC debate reflects peculiarities of Austria's political system and culture, and he develops the following hypotheses:

First, Austria fears considerable economic disadvantages as a result of exclusion from the internal market, whereas the prospect of participation creates specific economic policy expectations. Joining the Community should help prevent significant discrimination and should promote the necessary structural reforms needed to fight *Austrosclerosis*. The protected sectors in Austria's neo-corporatist, dual economy need greater adjustment since they have not been forced to increase productivity but have passed rising costs on to consumers. Participation in the internal market serves as a strategy to overcome this dualism against the resistance of *vested interests.*

Second, the government's estimations of its negotiating position rest on the belief that Austria is not a petitioner but a partner with something to offer.

Third, the Austrian approach is characterized by a specific assessment of the system and the policies of the European Community—an approach that diverges from the views of Brussels and the member states. From the point of view of Vienna, the EC is primarily an economic community without a relevant political dimension and one that has misunderstood Austrian neutrality. For the Austrian government, neutrality means primarily a renunciation of military alliances, and it is believed that Austria's membership would be a clear advantage for the EC in terms of wider European challenges. Vienna conceives economic integration as "negative" integration in the sense of eliminating barriers to economic transactions and political integration as mainly an intergovernmental cooperation. Schneider argues rightly that the political reality and *finalité politique* of the EC is underestimated not only by the politicians but also by many scholars in Austria.

Fourth, the Austrian proponents of accession consider neutrality to be a smaller obstacle than do the Commission and some member states. Schneider tries to explain with several options why Austria now declares its neutrality to be compatible with EC membership. He suggests that the policy of neutrality has to be distinguished from the law of neutrality. In an appendix the author devotes some additional critical remarks to this question.

Fifth, Austria's EC policy is shaped by conceptions of the general situation in Europe, conceptions which do not fully correspond to those in the Community. Vienna seems to count on developments in Europe to tone down the problems of neutrality versus integration by favouring a reinterpretation of neutrality as a positive contribution to peace in Europe.

In the third part of the book, the author touches upon East-West relations. The future of Europe is full of uncertainties, and the evolution in the East will have a particular impact on the Austrian membership application. Schneider sheds some light on the positions toward EC membership of the two big parties, the social partners, the representatives of the Länder, and the smaller opposition parties. He concludes that

Austria's integration policy finds itself in a multi-dimensional area of conflict where it has to reconcile not only legal obligations with economic imperatives but also the requirements of internationalization and modernization with quality of life. In addition, politicians have to perceive more accurately the determinant factors of the political interaction in the European Community and the conditions of participating in it.

As a basic finding, the book shows that the Austrian expectations and perceptions that led to the *letter to Brussels*[3] are partly colliding with those of the Community and its member states. Although the author claims not to plead for or against the Austrian policy, his study implies on the one hand a criticism of the somewhat biased, *austrocentric policy* of the government. This criticism becomes particularly evident in his discussion of neutrality. On the other hand, Schneider makes more comprehensible those attitudes and patterns of behavior that tend to lack understanding outside Austria. It would have been interesting to investigate in more detail how the European Community or the EFTA countries perceive the Austrian policy.

With a *global approach* Vienna aimed at the conclusion of a whole package of bilateral agreements with the Community, reaching a quasi-membership that leaves aside the *political dimension* and smoothes the way for the other EFTA countries. The author argues that this way turned out to be impracticable for two reasons. First, the EC wanted to grant full participation in the internal market only to full members. Second, Austria realized that no satisfactory solution could be found in a common approach with the other EFTA countries. Although the Austrian politicians might have jumped to this conclusion when applying for full membership, one cannot but recall that in January 1989—half a year before Vienna filed its application—Jacques Delors, the President of the EC Commission, launched the initiative to create a real European Economic Area (EEA) with a more structured partnership and common organs in which the EFTA countries would *speak with one voice*. In a prompt reaction, the EFTA countries welcomed this idea. The notion of a European economic space had already been established by the joint EC-EFTA ministerial meeting in Luxembourg 1984, promoting selective cooperation beyond the bilateral free trade agreements. With Delors's new concept, however, the EEA would extend the internal market to the EFTA countries with the main exceptions of the Common Commercial Policy, Common Agricultural Policy (CAP) and the European Political Cooperation (EPC).

Apart from the book's structural weakness, its major flaw lies in its treatment of the EEA as a *non-issue*. Schneider mentions the European Economic Area only once in a footnote and even then in the old sense of the Luxembourg follow-up. He overlooks the qualitative change this notion has undergone as a result of Delors's January 1989 speech and two years of intensive negotiations. At first sight, it seemed to solve both the dilemmas of EFTA and the Community: the EFTA countries would be able to avoid economic marginalization (by taking part in the internal market) as well as political satellization (by having a say in the decision-making process) whereas the EC could settle the *deepening versus enlargement* debate by preventing further membership applications (in particular from neutral EFTA countries and later, also from the former Communist countries of Central and Eastern Europe). The Commission, however, had gradually lowered its offer on the institutional level: by reducing the EFTA countries' participation in the decision-making process, the Commission obliged them to *speak with one voice* and to opt out collectively as well as to accept a supranational judicial mechanism and enforcement of competition rules. In addition, the end of the Cold War seemed to have weakened the need for a policy of neutrality. Thus, the EFTA countries that supported the EEA concept the most, such as Switzerland, have become the most reticent, and the states that were the most skeptical, like Austria, have become the most favorable. For Switzerland, Finland and Norway, the EEA has lost its real value as a permanent solution since there is no true co-decision; for Austria and Sweden, however, it has become an excellent means of preparing for and anticipating full membership which the community will not negotiate before 1993.

Although the outcome of the EEA exercise was different from the original intention and Austria was right in the end, the European Economic Area seems too important to be omitted in a study on Austria's integration policy. This applies all the more since the development of the EEA negotiations and the "revolution" in Eastern Europe could not have been foreseen at the time Vienna decided to apply for full EC membership. Apart from this omission, Schneider's analysis of the Austrian approach to European integration is comprehensive and all the more commendable as he treats its political and economic as well as its legal aspects.

Neutrals into the EC?

The second publication to be mentioned is the more specific study *Neutrale in die EG?* by Paul Luif,[4] published in 1988, two years before

Schneider's book. The author explores the political aspects of Austria's revived debate on integration. His exploration enriches the debate since Austrian literature thus far has concentrated mainly on economic issues and international law.

Part A constitutes a general introduction explaining theoretical approaches to integration and describing the historical development of West European integration. Here, Luif discusses extensively the organizational structures and decision-making processes both of the European Community and EFTA. Although very informative, such a lengthy introduction would not really be expected in a study on the neutrals and the EC. It is worth mentioning, however, that Luif explicitly points out the political dimension of the Community in his chapter on the EPC and does not fall into the "cognitive dissonance" trap denounced by Schneider.

Part B offers a comparative analysis of the integration policies of three neutral EFTA countries: Austria, Sweden and Switzerland. Luif focuses on Austria and mentions the Swedish and Swiss policies only where they differ from the Austrian. He excludes Finland from the study because of language problems and because of Finland's special relationship with the Soviet Union. A first chapter describes the integration efforts of the three countries, which were all founding members of EFTA, before the conclusion of the bilateral free trade agreements with the EC. When Great Britain applied for membership in the Common Market in 1961, the neutrals tried to coordinate their actions and asked the Community to take up association negotiations with them. They were willing to harmonize their customs duties toward third countries, to negotiate participation in the CAP and to discuss free movement of persons, services and capital. For this far-reaching cooperation, the neutrals required the following minimal reservations. First, the three EFTA countries would retain their treaty-making power to conclude agreements with third countries in their own names. Second, in addition to war materials, certain vital supplies should be safeguarded in wartime, partly through the maintenance of domestic agriculture. Third, in cases of war and international crises, the neutrals might have to introduce controls on trade, refrain from taking part in embargoes or even suspend parts or the whole of the association agreements.

When the British application was rejected in 1963, Sweden and Switzerland withdrew their requests, and Austria started its first *Alleingang*. Like Schneider, Luif describes the positions of the political parties and the interest groups. He also summarizes the scientific debate that took place at the time in Austria over economics and international law. He criticizes the economists for not having made it clear enough to the politicians that the predicted consequences of exclusion from EC integration were encumbered with uncertainties. In the 1960s the majority of Austrian international lawyers agreed that EC membership would not be compatible with permanent neutrality, whereas an association would be. The same attitude prevailed in the two other neutral states. In spite of Austria's failure, Sweden tried to resume negotiations with the EC in connection with the second application of the United Kingdom. De Gaulle's repeated veto, however, precluded any talks. The Swiss policy was more cautious than the Austrian or Swedish policy, not only for reasons of neutrality but also because of its federal system and direct democracy. In spite of their different policies on the domestic and international level, the three neutral EFTA countries finally concluded in 1972 practically identical free trade agreements with the Community.

Luif next describes the contents, organizational implementation and economic impact of the bilateral free trade agreements in Austria, Sweden and Switzerland. He analyzes and compares their relations to the EC, going beyond the association agreements, in particular in the fields of agriculture and research. In a shorter section, the author discusses the EC position toward the neutrals. He shows the change of the Community's originally negative attitude in the sixties as well as the different degrees of interest in EFTA association of its member states. In the first decade after the signing of the free trade agreements, the EC was still cautious with EFTA, stressing the bilateral nature of the treaties and interpreting its rules in a restrictive way. The more flexible attitude at the beginning of the eighties led in April 1984 to a meeting of ministers of all EC and EFTA countries in Luxembourg where they agreed to work toward *a dynamic European economic space.*

In the following chapter, the author tackles the policies of the neutrals in response to the new dynamics of the EC in the mid-1980s. He outlines the government policies in the three countries as well as the positions of the parties and the interest groups until 1988 (year of publication). In contrast to Schneider's study, Luif's approach allows us to compare the domestic constellations of the neutrals. They all reacted relatively quickly with study groups on the possible implications of the internal market. While in Austria a movement to join the EC with a neutrality reservation took shape, Sweden and Switzerland still excluded the membership option.

The swing of opinion that took place among many international lawyers in Austria was impressive. Luif attributes this swift to the trend toward greater interdependence in international economic relations and to the novel interpretation of safeguard clauses in the Rome Treaty. The attitude of the Soviet Union towards Austrian EC membership was ambiguous but rather negative. Luif argues that the contradictory statements stemmed from Moscow's uncertainty about European integration. On the one hand, Moscow acknowledged that neutral EC members could serve as *Trojan horses* disturbing the Community's closer integration, in particular toward a common foreign and security policy. On the other hand, the Soviet government suspected that the inclusion of the neutrals in the Western block would weaken the military situation in the East. After the *1989 velvet revolution* in Central and Eastern Europe and the Russian *August revolution* in 1991 that led to the disintegration of the Soviet Union, Moscow definitively gave up any opposition.

Luif's analysis of the Swedish integration policy helps to explain the surprise caused by the unexpected turn-around of September 1990 when the Social-Democratic Party announced that Sweden's (self-imposed) permanent neutrality and EC membership were from now on compatible. In July 1991, two years after Austria's application, the Swedish government applied for full membership without any reservation. The end of the Cold War and the increasing economic difficulties in Sweden as well as the disappointing course of the EEA negotiations might have contributed to this decision. Both its system of direct democracy and its neutrality seem to be obstacles to integration for Switzerland, the de facto most integrated EFTA country. The Swiss government has been waiting for the final shape of the EEA Agreement and has declared EC membership as its ultimate goal of integration, however, so far leaving the date of application open.

In his summary of the neutrals' recent integration policies, the author develops an interesting chart of their possible objectives and strategies. He distinguishes four objectives (the maintenance of the status quo, a selective rapprochement, a global rapprochement, and membership) as well as four strategies to achieve the objectives (autonomous unilateral adaptation to the EC, bilateral, bilateral-coordinated, or multilateral action). This table usefully demonstrates the neutrals' changing approaches to integration in the 1980s. The "extremes" of status quo and autonomous adaptation being excluded, the neutral countries started out from selective (Sweden, Switzerland) and global (Austria) rapprochement with a bilateral(-coordinated) strategy. The Luxembourg follow-up fits into the field *bilateral-coordinated and multilateral selective rapprochement* whereas the EEA belongs to the *multilateral global rap-*

prochement. Austria and Sweden moved to the bilateral strategy of membership, followed by Finland, while the Swiss policy line is still unclear. In contrast to Schneider, Luif mentions the Luxembourg process, the precursor of the EEA. He demands a coordination of the positions of the EFTA countries and a strengthening of the EFTA Secretariat. These elements have been taken up in the EEA process.

In his concluding remarks, Luif summarizes the political integration problems of the neutral states. First, the common commercial policy, which the Council may decide by majority, creates problems when embargoes are imposed. Second, participation in the European Political Cooperation may be difficult, although each member state may exercise its veto. Third, the negative attitude of the Soviet Union might put an end to the *bridging function* of a neutral EC member. (Since the book's publication, however, this problem has taken care of itself). Fourth, doubts about the duties of neutrality cannot permanently be excluded. In this respect, Luif suggests a common reinterpretation of the minimal reservations the neutrals had established in 1961 although he doubts that Austria, Sweden, Switzerland and probably Finland could agree on new principles. He correctly points out that the future development of the European Community itself and of the East-West relations will be crucial for the membership question of the neutrals. He describes different scenarios and concludes that the least likely one was the dissolution of the blocks leading to close East-West cooperation and the creation of a European federal state.

Today, just three years later, this potentiality does not seem that far-fetched. Even if the EC's Intergovernmental Conference on Political Union in December 1991 will not yet create the United States of Europe, the Community has to decide whether future foreign policy cooperation continues to include, as foreseen in the Single European Act, only political and economic aspects of security or also military ones. The membership applications of the neutral EFTA countries force such a decision and thereby shape not only their own but also the Community's fate.

Conclusion

Both books enhance our understanding of Austria's integration policy by illuminating its historical and domestic context. This task is particularly important for a neutral country that is a candidate for full membership in the European Community. Schneider's study helps to correct misperceptions on both sides. We can hope that Schneider will carry his research on to cover the European Economic Area and the implications for Austria of the developments in Eastern Europe and the Soviet Union.

Paul Luif's analysis investigates a problem that up to now has been discussed inadequately. Although at the time of writing he could not possibly have foreseen the events that would change the face of Europe one year later, his book opens up a debate on the role of neutrality in a continent that is challenged simultaneously by integration in the West and disintegration in the East. On the one hand, all the neutral EFTA countries today are re-evaluating their neutrality vis-a-vis their relations with the European Community. On the other hand, the European Community itself has to decide how to deal with neutral countries in view of "an ever closer union" which does not exclude cooperation on military security any more. In spite of some shortcomings, both books are pointing the way ahead.

NOTES

1. For literature covering all the EFTA countries see for instance Finn Laursen, ed., *EFTA and the EC: implications of 1992* (Maastricht: European Institute of Public Administration, 1990; Professional Papers); Kari Möttölä and Heikki Patomäki, eds., *Facing the change in Europe: EFTA countries' integration strategies* (Helsinki: The Finnish Institute of International Affairs, 1989); Peter Robson, ed., *The European Community, EFTA and the new Europe: changing dimensions of economic integration in Europe*, special issue of the *Journal of Common Market Studies*, 28 (1990); and Helen Wallace, ed., *The wider Western Europe: Reshaping the EC/EFTA relationship* (London: Pinter Publishers for the Royal Institute of International Affairs, 1991). Concerning Liechtenstein, the seventh full member of EFTA since 1991, see Thomas Bruha "Liechtenstein im europäischen Integrationsprozess" in *Liechtenstein: Kleinheit und Interdependenz*, ed. Peter Geiger and Arno Waschkuhn (Vaduz: Verlag der Liechtensteinischen Akademischen Gesellschaft; Liechtenstein Politische Schriften, 14), 181-219.

2. Heinrich Schneider, *Alleingang nach Brüssel. Österreichs EG-Politik* (Bonn: Europa Union Verlag, 1990; Europäische Schriften des Instituts für Europäische Politik, 66).

3. The *letter to Brussels* is a often used metaphor in Austria for its formal application for full membership in the European Community.

4. Paul Luif, *Neutrale in die EG? Die westeuropäische Integration und die neutralen Staaten* (Vienna: Wilhelm Braumüller, 1988; Informationen zur Weltpolitik, 11).

Gordon J. Horwitz, *In the Shadow of Death: Living Outside the Gates of Mauthausen* (New York: The Free Press, 1990).

Evan Burr Bukey, University of Arkansas

This book should have a major impact in the debate about Austria's confrontation with its Nazi past. In eight absorbing chapters the author brilliantly reconstructs the world outside the gates of Mauthausen, its subcamps at Redl-Zipf and Melk, and the euthanasia center at Castle Hartheim. Using archival evidence, postwar testimony, and fifteen personal interviews conducted in 1982-84, Horwitz shows how local men and women directly observed SS beatings, witnessed shootings, and, at the end of World War II, participated personally in murder. Several vivid accounts show how eagerly locals assisted the Nazis. In February 1945, for example, the SS had little trouble recruiting farmers and foresters to help chase down and kill some 495 Soviet officers who had staged a spectacular escape from Mauthausen. In what was called the "Mühlviertel rabbit hunt" civilians behaved with frenzied brutality, shooting at the poor beings kneeling before them, observing "with satisfaction their last shudders" (pp. 131-32). Even more horrifying was the popular response to the tens of thousands of Jews who were marched in April 1945 from the Hungarian border to Mauthausen and Gunskirchen. Though some bystanders handed out bread or potatoes, others spontaneously beat or shot helpless inmates, including women and children. In one particularly nauseating episode, an SS-*Blockführer* was assisted by his girlfriend, who chortled, "Bubi, you have already made boom-boom so often, now let girly make boom-boom for once" (p. 156).

No one completing this book can have any doubt that Austrians living near Mauthausen or its many subcamps were aware of what was happening behind the barbed wire. Nevertheless, the evidence does not show conclusively that the local populace was as indifferent or morally obtuse as Horowitz's moving prose suggests. In Upper Austria alone there were more concentration camps than in any other *Reichsgau* of greater Germany. The author himself stresses as mitigating factors fear and intimidation under which common people lived and, in fact, provides examples of individuals who helped starving inmates or even sheltered escapees from the SS or Gestapo.

What emerges with great clarity from these pages is the leading role of the Austrian NSDAP in executing and, in some cases, perpetrating the outrages of the Mauthausen system. Nearly all the physicians, officers, and personnel employed at Castle Hartheim, for example, were "local party members, many of whom had personal connections to leading figures from Upper Austria and who could be assumed to be dependable" (pp. 64-65). Given the well-known dominance of native-born Nazis in the Ostmark, at least outside Vienna, it is surprising that Horwitz does not provide more information about them, especially since they and their families, comprising perhaps twenty five percent of the population, were the ones who carried out their Führer's orders and after 1945 had the most to hide. Information about Austrian party members available at the Berlin Document Center could have provided a more differentiated picture of the social world adjacent to local concentration camps. Unfortunately, the author has not bothered to consult that material or, for that matter, to review the transcript of the U.S. Army's postwar Mauthausen trial, readily available at the National Records Center in Suitland, Maryland.

On the whole, Horwitz's study offers frightening snapshots and penetrating glimpses of the behavior of witnesses to the Holocaust in Austria. It is exceptionally effective in showing how inhuman cruelty and mass murder "altered the physical and moral landscape of the country" (p. 98). It also makes a strong case for popular complicity, but despite an evocative and gripping style, its overall portrait of society remains imcomplete and blurred.

Peter A. Ulram, *Hegemonie und Erosion: Politische Kultur und politischer Wandel in Österreich* (Vienna-Cologne-Graz: Böhlau, 1990).

Kurt K. Tweraser, University of Arkansas

During the 1970s the Second Austrian Republic labored away in a calculable and predictable style, thanks to the country's astonishing prosperity. Some celebrated this quiet, uneventful and dependable stability as the Austrian way, but it dampened scholarly interest in Austrian politics. Beginning in the mid-1980s however, turmoil, corruption, electoral volatility, environmentalism, feminism, *Vergangenheitsbewältigung* or the lack thereof, and other good stuff made the study of Austrian politics fun again.

While journalistic treatments of the rumblings in the apparently solid political system only scratched the surface, Austrian scholars began to dig deeper in analyzing the changing structure of the party system and the increasing adventurousness of the Austrian voter. Three years ago, Anton Pelinka and Fritz Plasser provided us with a landmark compendium of the Austrian party system (*Das österreichische Parteiensystem,* Vienna, 1988). In the same vein of excellence, Peter Ulram adds significantly to our knowledge about Austrian politics in his *Habilitationsschrift*, submitted to the faculty of the University of Vienna in the fall of 1988. Ulram's objectives are twofold: (1) to describe and analyze the change in the political culture of Austria, and (2) to demonstrate the impact of these changes on the political system, especially the political parties.

In the introduction, the author lays out the main themes of his book. He differentiates among three developmental phases of the Austrian political culture: (1) the *"versäulte Konkordanzdemokratie"* of the first two post-World War II decades, (2) the political culture of the social-liberal consensus of the 1970s (*"begrenzte Konkurrenz und Beteiligungsdemokratie"*), and (3) a transitional phase in the 1980s which he names the political culture of malaise (*"politische Kultur des Unbehagens"*). His thesis is that phases of political stability and political party hegemony are followed by phases of pronounced change and erosion.

In the second chapter, Ulram summarizes and explores arguments from the literature about political change in Western Europe and the United States, with emphasis on political secularization, changes in the social structure, and the impact of the mass media. These arguments point to the waning of traditional cleavages and to the concomitant erosion of the structural and cultural bases of the party systems. The author places emphasis on the changes in the social and political agenda, showing new "post-materialist" issues vying for attention with old materialist ones.

In the third chapter, Ulram surveys—not uncritically—the conceptual problems of political culture theories with more than a whiff of Gabriel Almond, Lucian Pye, and Sidney Verba present. Indeed, the schema of their thinking is evident throughout the book. Echoing them, Ulram defines political culture as subjective orientations toward political objects at three levels: (1) the systemic culture, referring to the political system and its rules of the game; (2) the process culture, referring to political decision-making; and (3) the policy culture (*"Politikfeldkultur"* p. 24) referring to the specific outputs and policy performance of the political system.

Next, a brief chapter on the traditional Austrian political culture moves over familiar ground, describing it as a consociational system with encapsulated subcultures or *"Lager"* along the old cleavages of class and religion, but mitigated by elite accommodation.

Almost half the book is devoted to a wide ranging discussion of change in Austria from the late 1960s to the late 1980s. In more than 180 tables, charts and graphs, the author provides an exhaustive wealth of empirical findings elaborating the structural and process elements of the political system. At the heart of the chapter is the impact of changes in the social structure and the weakening of the religious-secular cleavage on a well established party system. The signs of electoral de-alignment are everywhere, indicating the uncoupling of the social structure and electoral behavior. The core constituencies of the two major parties, the ÖVP and the SPÖ, are dwindling, a new middle class is rising, and partisan loyalties are waning. The floating voter and the late decider are becoming ever more influential for election outcomes. Emerging alternatives of political action and organization are eroding the very function of political parties. Leader images, especially of chancellor and chancellor candidates, play a telling role.

The evolution of the political agenda points to another de-alignment phenomenon. In the 1970s, material issues such as job security and social security were dominant; in the 1980s, environmental problems have become high-ranking issues. Ulram is properly cautious, however, on the value change from materialism to Inglehart's concept of "postmaterialism." While acknowledging the increased salience of "quality-of-life" themes, especially among the young and educated, he warns of the instability of phenomena labeled "post-materialist trends." (p.87)

Waste of tax resources, characterized by numerous scandals and gigantic cost-overruns and crisis in the nationalized industries caused by the political "sleaze" factor have contributed to a deep pessimism about the future especially among the young and the better educated. Austrians are afflicted with a low sense of political efficacy; the average person has little or no control over public policy. The rise of protest voting, an increased willingness to vote for smaller parties, marks a growing weariness directed against the two major parties (*"Parteiverdrossenheit"*). Interestingly enough, though, the social partnership, that proven Austrian method of conflict regulation, is still highly appreciated by the citizens (p. 207).

For the reader who might be daunted by the overwhelming amount of quantitative evidence, Ulram provides in later chapters a synopsis of the three developmental phases of Austrian political culture: the historical compromise of the two great camps, the social-liberal consensus, and the transitional political culture of malaise. He organizes his argument around the themes of hegemony and erosion but does not quite succeed in differentiating the phases with sufficient precision. Still, these chapters are masterful in their compression of broad, complex subjects and arguments into coherent, pointed accounts.

During the first two phases, a high degree of correspondence existed between political culture and the political system, with culture and system being interdependent and mutually reinforcing (p.291). The political system of the historic compromise—a shared hegemony of the two major parties—was based on the political culture of the *"versäulte Konkordanzdemokratie"*. The political and socioeconomic elites succeeded through innovative strategies in weakening hostile forces and strenghening liberal democratic elements. They thereby established their hegemony on corresponding mentalities. The social-liberal consensus was characterized by the erosion of "Lager mentality", a weakening of party affiliation and identification, dominance of material orientations and a comprehensive acceptance of social partnership. But the power structures of the Socialists, the dominant, had a weaker cultural foundation than the ÖVP-SPÖ hegemony of the great compromise. Finally, the political culture of malaise is characterized by political secularization, weak party identification, strong voter mobility, high political alienation, unconventional forms of political participation, enlargement of the political agenda to include "life quality" issues, reduced satisfaction with governmental performance, yet still high acceptance of social partnership (pp.293-294).

After mapping the changes that have taken place in Austrian politics, Ulram extrapolates from these changes possible scenarios of the future. The first alternative developmental pattern he sketches out (but to which he assigns low probability of realization), he describes as a *formation of hegemony* through structural groups and issues, and a reconciliation of economy and ecology. A second and more likely scenario he calls with a touch of regret, *normalization through adjustment*. This scenario incorporates West European perspective, which would demand fewer innovative efforts. It would be an adjustment more or less forcibly dictated by economic and cultural-political developments. The great parties would display a declining ability to attract and integrate voters, thereby creating space for new smaller parties that would position themselves along new cultural cleavages. The de-alignment of the old parties and the rise of a new axis of politics, based on the polarization between "left" and "right" post-materialist values and traditional cultural values would result in the "end of Austrian exceptionality" (p.296).

For good measure, Ulram develops a rather pessimistic third scenario: *erosion through exhaustion* (the "Italian Perspective"), which would be the result of systemic sclerosis and tendencies toward anomie reinforcing each other. While Italian society, through centuries-long experiences with inefficient and corrupt institutions and an unresponsive political class, managed to develop admirable survival skills, Ulram doubts whether Austrian society could develop these "Italian" qualities in due time.

In a short epilogue, Ulram ponders the results of the provincial elections on 12 March 1989 in Carinthia, Salzburg, and Tirol, the *dies irae*, that led to trenchant changes in the political landscape. Changed participatory orientations away from the party state, increased non-

voting, new issue conflicts, reduced confidence in governmental effi-
ciency, *Parteienverdrossenheit*, general distrust of the political class,
and a growing protest potential all corroborate Ulram's "end of exceptionality" thesis. Yet his pessimism is guarded. These changes have not
led to hostility against the central institutions of democracy and social
partnership; credible systemic alternatives are simply not apparent
(p.311).

The elections to the *Nationalrat* in October 1990 only confirmed the
end of stability in political culture and voting behavior. The very fact that
the attractiveness or unattractiveness of political leaders had such an
impact on the election only testifies to the restlessness of the times. But,
it may well be that high levels of system performance, accumulated
during the good old days of *"Windstille,"* have created sufficient support
for the political system to survive a whole season of anger. Policy and
process may totter, but the system holds.

Ulram's study enriches our understanding of Austrian political culture
and political parties from the Kreisky era to the present. It should also put
an end to Austria's continued designation as a consociational political
system.

Austria can no longer be treated as a nation apart, but must be
recognized as one integrated into the larger subset of post-industrial
democracies. If there is one defect in the book, it is Ulram's attempt to
include almost everything. He pays a price in style and clarity; the reader
sometimes feels he is plodding through a dense forest of data. This is a
small criticism for a study that furnishes further proof of the maturity and
sophistication of Austrian political science, which has convincingly
overcome its reputation as a latecomer to the profession.

Michael P. Steinberg, *The Meaning of the Salzburg Festival* (Ithaca and London: Cornell University Press, 1990).

William M. Johnston, University of Massachusetts

One might expect that the translator of Hermann Broch's *Hugo von Hofmannsthal and His Time [1952]* (Chicago, 1984) would interpret the Salzburg Festival in the footsteps of Broch. Indeed there are significant parallels between that book and this one. Both Broch and Steinberg use Hofmannsthal as a peg on which to hang the largest issues of Austrian historiography; both excel as dialecticians; both show a taste for paradox as a way of exposing ambivalence; and both show radical originality. Yet it would be misleading to view Steinberg as a disciple, much less an epigone of Broch. Consistently, the American criticizes the Austrian for having reified categories, for having perpetuated some of the impasses that stymied Hofmannsthal, and for having underestimated the latter's cultural *engagement* during the 1920's. The *Meaning of the Salzburg Festival* is as much a corrective as an extension of Broch's argument.

A clue to Steinberg's methodology comes in a review essay he wrote for Volume 22 (1991) of *The Austrian History Yearbook*. There he distinguishes "modernisms" that perpetuate "post-enlightenment models of coherence and order" from a sense of "modernity" that offers new models. Such models emerge by exploring "the fleeting, the transient, and the contingent" (the phrase is Baudelaire's) through a "dialogical contact with culture" (pp.152-153). Steinberg cites Walter Benjamin as the only figure who carried out Baudelaire's summons to complete "the analytical passage from the nineteenth to the twentieth century" (p.153). One would scarcely infer such homage to Benjamin from the "Conclusion" of *The Meaning of the Salzburg Festival*, which balances in an evenhanded way Benjamin and Hofmannsthal as interpreters of the baroque. More substantially, Steinberg takes from Baudelaire and Benjamin a resolve to reinterpret all categories as embodying "the fleeting, the transient, and the contingent." He dissolves frozen categories by discerning ambivalence where his predecessors postulated stability and coherence. The revolutionary thrust of this book lies in its commitment to exposing ambivalence behind every attempt at coherence.

In this endeavor Steinberg's key categories are those of "theatricality" and "totality," categories that he adapts from Broch: "By totality I mean a dialectic of power, identity, and coherence that united nation, monarch, and God" (p.7). Theatricality "refers to the claim not merely that this political cosmology could and should be represented through action and images...but that it comes to exist through representation [i.e. theatrical performance]." Thus showmanship becomes definitive for all Austrian culture, which is seen as striving to impose coherence on the content and manner of performance, whether on stage or in social intercourse. The drive to all-embracing coherence implies a claim to have included everything worth considering; totalizers feel no need to heed dissent. Or rather as Theodor Adorno put it: ...whereas drama acknowledges conflict to be irresolvable, theatricality purports to resolve problems "according to a predetermined set of ethical principles" (p.38). Operating on the assumption that Austrian society and culture abound in irresolvable problems, Steinberg argues that theatricality transposed these problems into tableaux whose apparent coherence concealed ambivalence. Having saluted Freud as one of the few Austrians who could stare irresolvable problems in the face (p.182), Steinberg is no less determined than Freud to expose what others have ignored or covered up.

With unflagging originality Steinberg reappraises virtually every category that has mattered to Austrian cultural historians since 1970. His method is to show that concepts like "Jewishness," "Catholic culture," "nationalism," "rationality," and "liberalism" disclose affinities with their opposites that make a mockery of intellectual historians' codified vocabualry. Social historians' categories fare no better when Steinberg shows that processes like advocacy of the Anschluss, conversion to or from Catholicism, or resisting anti-Semitism mobilized contradictory principles in different protagonists. The categories upon which previous scholars of Austria have relied turn in this book into something "fleeting, transient, and contingent." So too do all Austrian efforts to define a national identity.

The grandest revision of all concerns a proposal to interpret "the entire

process of the late-nineteenth century development of the Ringstrasse" as
consummating the triumph not of bourgeois liberalism (as in Schorske
and McGrath) but of "a neobaroque ideological agenda" (p.7). Thereby
the bourgeoisie appropriated a past style that identified a Catholic
monarchy with itself. It is tempting to erect upon this foundation an
Alternative Agenda for rethinking Austrian cultural history. We get a
foretaste of such a research program in a passage where Steinberg
compares opera in Second Empire Paris with that in late nineteenth-
century Vienna (pp.8-17). In the wake of Walter Benjamin, Steinberg
shows how partisans of neobaroque under Napoleon III could accept the
commercialization enshrined in department stores, while supporters of
neobaroque in the Hofburg, the Hofoper, and the Burgtheater could not.
Courtly Vienna comes to look like an anti-commercial version of Paris
of the 1860's, one where Second Empire values (shorn of commercial-
ism) lingered not merely until 1870, but until 1918.

As this contrast between Paris and Vienna shows, *The Meaning of the
Salzburg Festival* applies Steinberg's talent for rethinking fundamentals
to many topics beyond what the title suggests. Central to every chapter
is of course Hugo von Hofmannsthal's evolution from lyric poet (up to
1903) to expounder of the "language crisis" (1903-1914) to exponent of
neobaroque ideology. No less pervasive is an analysis of the repertoire,
backers, and reception of the Salzburg Festival. More broadly still,
chapter three proposes a category of "nationalist cosmopolitanism"
which connects German enlightenment conceptions of cosmopolitanism
(Goethe, Moeser, Kant) with Austria's subsequent quest for a national
identity that would embrace cosmopolitanism. Against this backdrop,
chapter four expounds with subtlety various advocates of Austrian
identity under the First Republic, rightly insisting that all Austro-German
proposals for cosmopolitan culture presupposed the supremacy of German over Slavic participants. Today's observers may well ask: How
much has Carinthia changed in this regard?

It would be folly to criticize a book of this scope for omissions, for
what we have here is less a monograph than a proposal to rethink all of
Austrian intellectual and cultural history since 1683. Steinberg's Alternative Agenda involves seeing Vienna's modernists (e.g., Schnitzler,
Loos, Schoenberg, Freud, Wittgenstein) as a small minority who after
1890 protested against the neobaroque ideology that animated their
contemporaries. New work waits to be done appraising exponents of the
neobaroque ideology: Richard von Kralik before 1914, Walter Brecht
and Anton Wildgans in the 1920's, Ernst Karl Winter in the 1930's,

Friedrich Heer in the 1950's. If, as Steinberg suggests, the Salzburg Festival of the 1920's represented neo-neobaroque, a book like Reinhold Schneider's *Winter in Wien* (1958) might be dubbed neo-neo-neobaroque.

Besides stimulating a revision from the ground up of periodization, critique of ideology, and the mapping of allegiances in Austrian cultural history, Steinberg's exposition of theatricality and ideology stimulates questions that no one has yet asked. A monograph should investigate what Rudolf Steiner (1861-1925) owed to the neobaroque ideology of Vienna (where he studied in the 1880's). In what ways does the theatricality of his maturity derive from what he absorbed in Vienna during his youth? A larger question involves the role of neobaroque ideology in Prague after 1890. If we adopt Adorno's distinction between theatricality and drama, it would appear that Prague intellectuals like Franz Kafka, Max Brod, and Christian von Ehrenfels not only acknowledged the irresolvability of conflict but project such conflict onto the cosmos. The apparent reason would be their experience of the feud between Czechs and Germans, a rift which no amount of theatricality could disguise. There could be no equivalent of the Salzburg Festival for German-speakers in Bohemia.

Scholars of the Second Republic of Austria will want to inquire in what ways the ideology of neo-neobaroque lives on in today's cultural politics, at both the national and regional levels. The very concept of *Proporz* in public life might seem to evoke the notion of a "harmonizing theatricality." When equal numbers of the two political parties join the civil service at every level, aesthetic symmetry is being substituted for deep-seated cooperation. Some of Austria's present sense of self-sufficiency might be traced to a quest for all-inclusive totality like that which animated the early Salzburg Festival. But let those who wish to pursue such Alternative Agendas be warned: they will be hard-pressed to match Steinberg's dialectical skill, range of comparison, or sense of nuance. It remains to be seen whether this pathbreaking book can elicit worthy successors.

Melanie A. Sully, *A Contemporary History of Austria* (London - New York: Routledge, 1990).

Andrei S. Markovits, Department of Political Science,
Boston University and Center for European Studies,
Harvard University

Rarely in recent history has Europe undergone a more momentous change than we see occurring at the present. As daily events completely rearrange the postwar order, none of the conventions, axes or formerly inviolate premises pertain any longer. Not even the "island of the blessed"—better known as Austria—is exempt from these profound, revolutionary developments. Indeed, one of this *island's* most insulating characteristics—its neutrality—which had so successfully shielded this Alpine republic from the hard-ball politics of the East-West rivalry and had bestowed upon Austria a legitimating identity in the process, has become all but moot in this new European (perhaps even world) order.

Although Melanie Sully's fine study does not address this particular aspect of Austria's changed reality to my satisfaction, she nevertheless presents a learned and insightful analysis of modern Austrian politics in a period of transition. One should expect no less of this young British political scientist whose publications on Austrian affairs—most notably those related to social democracy—have established her as perhaps the foremost analyst of contemporary Austria currently writing in English.

Sully's argument is simple but persuasive: the days of Austrian "exceptionalism" are waning, if not totally disappearing. The formerly all-powerful political parties, whose camp-like subsocieties could only co-exist via a finely-honed system of consociational elite management have lost much of their sway in the course of the 1980's. As a result, Austrian politics is a lot less predictable but all the more exciting. If, for understandable historical reasons, the second Austrian Republic's trademark had been an overemphasis on stability, continuity and consent— what Anton Pelinka has aptly termed "government for the people"—the 1980's have seen a sea change. What seems to be emerging might be called a politics of irreverence or—to paraphrase Pelinka once again— "government by the people". In short, if institutionalization of conflict management received pride of place in postwar Austrian politics until the 1980's, the balance seems to have shifted toward increased popular participation and a more spontaneously active "civil society."

Sully leaves little doubt in this reviewer's mind that she not only welcomes these developments as more exciting for social scientists but also—and of greater importance—as more democratic for the Austrian people. While the author analyzes this process of secularization and demystification with aplomb, I would have liked her to label its essence the "Europeanization" instead of the "Americanization" of Austrian politics since the latter concept only refers ot the personalization of party politics in the wake of a media-dominated polity. Yet, there is clearly much more afoot in Austria than the ubiquitous tendency towards Madison-Avenue-style-sound-bite campaigning, and it is occurring in the context of a revolutionary transformation of European politics in which Austria is an obvious participant. I would have also preferred to see a bit more reasoning about why and how these formerly *frozen* political camps began thawing when they did. Interesting in this context would have been a more detailed sociological discussion of the major changes in Austrian society, ranging from shifts in the labor market to alterations in the education system, from the increased usage of credit cards to the emergence of a VCR culture. All told, Austria's "modernization" throughout the 1980's rendered the country more West European than at any previous time in its history.

Sully should be commended for having written a textbook for connoisseurs. Instead of following the usual convention of writing a chapter on political parties, another on interest groups, and a third on institutions, Sully has successfully presented typical textbook material in a thematically appealing fashion. Thus, for example, in a chapter entitled "Socialism in Transition," Sully explains the organizational framework and ideological currents of the SPÖ in the context of the concrete events shaping "*Kreiskyism*" and the post-Kreisky era.

Calling on Sully's earlier work in this area, the chapter on Austrian social democracy is the finest in the book. Also of note is Sully's discussion of the dire straits in which the ÖVP has found itself for the past two decades. She euphemistically labels the situation a "conservative dilemma" instead of the disaster which it has been. Her chapter on the FPÖ correctly concentrates on the rise of Jörg Haider, or, to be more precise, on the phenomenon of "Haiderism" which she—again correctly—sees as part of the larger de-institutionalization of the postwar republic's consociationalism. As a result, Sully excludes any explanations that would analyze the emergence of the FPÖ in Austrian politics as the revival of a hitherto latent political right.

I am a good deal less sanguine about such an analysis for three reasons: First, the two need not exclude each other. In other words "Haiderism" could be a consequence of both a shift to the right *and* a major dismantling of the old red-black pact. Second, precisely because Austrian politics has become much more European, Haiderism has to be seen—at least in part—as an expression of the Europe-wide xenophobia and intolerance that has spawned crypto-fascist parties and movements in virtually every country of the continent. Lastly, the self-examination Austria has undertaken since the Waldheim debacle may not yield the results Sully optimistically assumes. Sully devotes two chapters to Austria's belated efforts to come to terms with its past, and she argues that one of the fortuitous side effects of the Waldheim debacle was Austria's first concerted examination of its recent history. This self-examination may indeed delegitimate aspects of the right commonly associated with the old FPÖ, or it may not.

The book could have used a thoughtful, analytic conclusion. As it currently stands, the last chapter offers a plethora of seemingly disparate scandals. Not only are these scandals qualitatively different, but Sully's—correct—assumption that they collectively bespeak the seamier side of the currently disintegrating *"Modell Österreich"* needs greater theoretical elaboration and analytic explanation. In spite of these shortcomings, Sully should be congratulated for having presented us with a learned and lucid study of a fascinating European country in transition.

Friedrich Stadler, ed., *Vertriebene Vernunft: Emigration und Exil österreichischer Wissenschaft*, 2 vols. (Vienna-Munich: Jugend und Volk, 1987 - 1988).

Robert Knight, Loughborough University

These two massive volumes raise methodological, historical and ethical problems that begin with the title and increase thereafter. *"Vertriebene,"* of course, in post-war German and Austrian usage are those ethnic Germans driven out of their homes in Eastern Europe and the former *"Reich"* at and after the end of the Second World War. By contrast, those Jews forced out seven years earlier from Austria (or from Germany after 1933) are invariably termed *"Emigranten,"* which, whether deliberately or not, veils the compulsion involved. We could read this title, therefore, as a praiseworthy attempt to reclaim the perspective of those affected even if otherwise "emigrant" is still the preferred term.

Yet before the Anschluss this point is not clear-cut. Professional motives mingled with political. And even when the compulsion was brutally evident later academic success tended to make it seem less significant than the expanded opportunities it created. The plight of individuals caught between academic interest and a murderous dictatorship is a dominant theme in these two volumes.

The sheer detail (and occasional repetitiousness) in these volumes will probably leave many readers feeling slightly dazed. But this problem is inherent in the project of publishing the proceedings of such a large conference. The editor, who lucidly describes the methodological and definitional difficulties of research into exile, can hardly be blamed either for this weight of detail or for the fact that many of the contributors paid less attention to these problems than he did. Nevertheless one cannot help feeling that out of these two fat books there are several (slimmer) books struggling to get out.

The first book might cover the transfer of knowledge and cultural interaction that arises when intellectuals find themselves in a new milieu. Seen in these terms, the exodus that followed the Anschluss was only a special case of a general phenomenon that had started well before. Josef Schumpeter and Ludwig Wittgenstein are merely the two most prominent examples. In many cases we do not gain much by knowing that this interchange resulted from Nazi racial policies rather than from professional advancement. What may make the interchange more interesting is examining where, as after 1938, whole "schools" resettle. Notable examples here are the Wiener Kreis, the Freudian psychoanalysts or the psychologists surrounding Alfred Adler. But even here it is difficult to detect a pattern. The greater affinity of the Wiener Kreis with American pragmatism may explain why this group exerted more influence than, say, the Frankfurt school. Alternatively, the economic liberalism of von Mises and his followers was initially favored by American conservative opponents of the New Deal. In other cases the impact was more immediate. In offering scientific consumer research to American industry, Paul Lazarfeld's empirical social research, as vividly described by Paul Neurath, filled a market gap in every sense of the term. However, as Anton Amman's account of the correspondence between Alfred Schütz and Talcott Parsons suggests, mutual incomprehension might be as likely as mutual enrichment. The attempt to conceptualize or even quantify this interchange (including an impenetrable one by Karl Müller in Volume II) much less assess a particularly Austrian component are fraught with difficulty. The most interesting contributions here (including those by Christian Fleck on sociology, Claus-Dieter Krohn on economists and Mitchel Ash on psychology) suggest that further investigations of disciplines will prove more fruitful than a search for the grand synthesis.

A second book could comprise the refugee experience. Here it is naive to imagine that intellectuals experienced the Anschluss differently from the rest of Austria's Jewish population. Johannes Reichmayer even argues (unconvincingly) that Viennese pschoanalysts were *worse* prepared than they should have been because the political dimension was excluded from their analytical method. Nor was the intellectuals' way of coping with the trauma that resulted, graphically described in many eyewitness accounts, qualitatively different from that of other refugees. (Bruno Bettelheim's account of his concentration camp experience is the exception which proves the rule.) Although many academics were able to utilize a range of formal and informal contacts that non-academics did not have, we must beware, as Oliver Rathkolb points out, of taking the glittering, self-selecting few as being representative. Generalizations about the refugees' state of mind are even more hazardous. It might appear plausible that secular, assimilated Jews-some of whom could speak foreign languages-would cope better with exile than less assimilated compatriots. Yet there is plenty of evidence of the reverse. Above all exile meant the loss of their *"gesamten wissenschaftlichen Diskussionszusammenhang"* (Achim Eschbach and Gabi Willenberg on the pschychologist Karl Bühler).

A third book would set the refugee experience in a variety of national contexts. The contributions here are of variable quality. In the case of Shanghai, for example, as Francois Kreissler rightly points out, the importance of the wider context was a European penetration, compared to which the Austrian "ghetto" was insignificant indeed. Others— including Herbert Steiner's cursory account of Great Britain—are less perceptive on the 'host' countries. It seems doubtful whether the distinction between Jewish refugees from Austria and those from Germany (or the *"Sudentenland"*) is particularly helpful in this context (see for example, Werner Mosse (ed.), *Second Choice: Two Generations of German-speaking Jews in the United Kingdom*, Tübingen 1991; Marion Berghahn, *German-Jewish Refugees in England. The Ambiguities of Assimilation*, London 1984). The evidence here suggests that while few countries lived up to the best of their traditions, even an approximation to them produce a different world from the one the refugees had left behind.

A fourth concern is the light which the expulsions of these refugees throws on Austrian society, particularly in regard to anti-Semitism. Günter Fellner (history) and Michael Hubenstorf (medicine) trace this anti-Semitism back to well before the First World War. The second continuity after 1945 raises the crucial question of why those expelled were not asked back. After the mass of evidence presented here, it will be difficult for anyone to seriously deny that the chief reason was anti-Semitism. Here Zeisel cites Adolf Schärf's revealing comment (related by Bruno Kreisky) that he only preferred an "Arian" candidate for a job if he was at least as good as the Jewish candidate! Incidentally, if the interest is in Austrian society, the often-heard argument that many Jews would not have wished to return anyway having successfully established themselves in their country of refuge is irrelevant.

The other side of this coin is the myth-making of some of those who did return. Bruno Kreisky for example, spins an unlikely yarn of how as a young socialist in Sweden, together with his British Labour Party friends, he blocked a British plan to redraw the Carinthian border! Several of the other contributions are at pains to stress their Austrian patriotism. One result is an overestimate of the numerical and political (as opposed to the psychological and pastoral) importance of the Free Austria Movement. The loss of those expelled, often described as a "blood-letting" (*"Aderlass"*), undoubtedly led to an impoverishment of Austrian intellectual and cultural life after the war, though this should not lead to the adoption of utilitarian profit-loss criteria. Although it is unfortunate that some of these—and other—issues tend to be buried under the mass of empirical data, these two volumes are both important scholarly milestones and signposts to future research.

Survey of Austrian Politics 1990/91

Rainer Nick and Sieghard Viertler

The National Council Elections of October 7, 1990

For quite some time, the Austrian electoral landscape has been undergoing a profound and lasting reorganization. The character of the continuing changes was impressively documented by the 1990 National Council Elections. There is further erosion of party loyalties, a process which started in the early seventies and reached a first climax with the National Council Elections of 23 November 1986. The Austrian party system is changing from a two-and-one-half party system (two big parties and a third, significantly smaller power) to a loose multi-party system.

At the beginning of the campaign for the 1990 National Council Elections (*Nationalratswahl*), two big parties (SPÖ and ÖVP) of approximately equal strength were confronting each other, both able to count on approximately 40 percent of the voters. They were opposed by the FPÖ (Austrian Freedom Party) and the Green Alternative List as opposition parties, which entered the race on a basis of about 15 percent, counted together. The election results of 7 October brought about a significant change in this strategic, competitive relationship among the Austrian parties.

The course of the electoral campaign designed by the Social-Democratic Party of Austria (SPÖ) had been clear a long time before the intensive electoral campaign proper started. The SPÖ was forced to realize the great difference in popularity between the party itself and the personality of Chancellor Franz Vranitzky. As a consequence, a modification of the "Kreisky—who else?" slogan of the 1970s presented itself as the most natural choice. (In each of the demoscopic surveys conducted between June and September 1990, 38 to 40 percent of all voters indicated their willingness to vote for the SPÖ election Sunday. Vranitzky, by comparison, achieved 59 to 65 percent of the straw vote for the future chancellor.) The extraordinarily high acceptance of Vranitzky and sufficient sympathy for him in large sections of all occupational groups—including the traditional bourgeois camp—caused the SPÖ to conduct an electoral campaign focused exclusively on the personality of Chancellor Vranitzky. Finally, this culminated in the slogan "Vranitzky has to remain chancellor!" Throughout the whole electoral campaign (which had been decisively cut short by the early elections in the fall and the fact that the summertime is not suitable for electoral campaigns), the importance of the Socialist Party was placed second behind Chancellor Vranitzky.

The strategy of the SPÖ consisted in redefining the National Council Elections as a plebiscite for the chancellor, something they tried to force upon the other campaigning parties (above all the Austrian People's Party). During the final stage of the electoral campaign, the SPÖ tried to conduct a campaign for preference votes in favor of Vranitzky. Those who gave their preference votes to Vranitzky could do so without checking off the Social-Democratic Party of Austria on the ballot sheet. Thus, the SPÖ campaign strategists tried to reduce the psychological barrier of "being forced to *buy* the Social-Democratic Party of Austria together with Vranitzky" by means of product differentiation.

This campaign for preference votes was supported by a committee "for the re-election of Chancellor Vranitzky," founded by distinguished persons of diverse social origins. Many members of this non-partisan committee could not have been mobilized to the same extent in favor of the SPÖ. The legal basis of this massive campaign for preference votes was the fact that Vranitzky was the top candidate in each of the nine constituencies (and therefore in all states).

In the early phase of the election campaign, the Austrian People's Party (ÖVP) tried to present an alternative to the absolute personalization of the campaign. The ÖVP criticized the SPÖ for not being able to offer something better than a mere populist star cult focused on its chairman. This "star cult" was supposed to be countered by a team (Josef Riegler together with Marielies Flemming, Wolfgang Schüssel, Erhard Busek, Alois Mock and others). At the same time, the ÖVP tried to assume programmatic leadership by emphasizing their program of an "ecologically sound social market economy." A few weeks before the elections, however, the leaders of the Austrian People's Party radically altered their campaign strategy and tried to advance Riegler's claim to leadership as

Federal Chancellor. Doing so, they accepted the challenge of the SPÖ to a man to man show-down, thus providing the dramatic impact necessary for the success of the long-prepared plans of the Social-Democratic Party of Austria.

The Austrian Freedom Party (FPÖ) officially entered the race with Norbert Gugerbauer, the chairman of the FPÖ party group in Parliament, as its top candidate. Yet from the very beginning, the election campaign was cut out for the three-person-team Jörg Haider, Norbert Gugerbauer and Heide Schmidt. They presented themselves as "the party controlling the undifferentiated power group of the SPÖ and the ÖVP" (election slogan: "The Incorruptibles") and defined themselves in strong contrast to both of them. During the final stage of the electoral campaign, Haider, too, took part in the conflict of personalization around the "best man for the position of the federal chancellor," presenting himself (due to a lack of charisma on the part of Josef Riegler) as the true and only middle-class opposition candidate against Vranitzky.

Four years after their unification in 1986, the Austrian Greens once again entered the race with separate lists of candidates. The Green Alternative List (GAL) as well as the more conservatively oriented Austria's United Greens avoided personalization and tried to focus the public on their ecological program. The GAL presented a team of four top candidates, which, however, remained unknown to a great part of the population.

Several key issues emerged in the course of the campaign for the 1990 National Council Elections. Scandals involving socialist politicians dominated media reports for weeks (the *Rechberger scandal* stood for party functionaries with multiple functions leading to income higher than the chancellor's; the *Volkshilfeskandal* was the mishandling of donations by an organization close to the SPÖ; moreover, the former socialist chancellor Fred Sinowatz was convicted by a court of law for false testimony). However, when election day drew nearer, special attention was focused on the outcome of the elections (horse-race-journalism) as well as on possible coalition variations. The last days before the elections were marked by the latest opinion polls, by the issue of "top-candidates," and the SPÖ model of preference votes. Thus, the election campaign itself became an issue.

The elections brought about results which have had a lasting effect on the competitive relationship between the Austrian parties:

* At present, the new distribution of seats is: Social-Democratic Party of Austria 80 (80 in the 1986 elections), Austrian's People's Party 60 (77),

Austrian Freedom Party 33 (18), GAL 10 (8).

* The Social-Democratic Party of Austria almost succeeded in maintaining its 1986 share of voters and only lost 0.3 percent. Considering its rather bad starting position (involvement in many scandals, above all the *Rechberger case*, and the *Volkshilfeskandal*), many people were surprised by this result. Especially the campaign for preference votes turned out to be an extremely successful and clever political move. More than half a million Austrians gave their preference votes to Vranitzky. This result alone would have been enough for eighteen seats in the National Council.

* The Austrian People's Party lost 9.1 percent and therefore its position as one of the two large parties in Austria. The election result reduced the ÖVP to a size of just under 33 percent, the worst result for the Austrian People's Party in the Second Republic. Moreover, the difference between the SPÖ the ÖVP increased from 88,000 to more than half a million votes.

* The Austrian Freedom Party established itself as a small middle-sized party, reaching 16.6 percent and thus adding 6.9 percent to the result they had achieved in the National Council Elections of 23 November 1986.

* Because the candidacy of the VGÖ, the second Green group mentioned above, the other opposition party in Parliament was unable to improve its share of 4.8 percent. Almost one third of the Green voters preferred to give their votes not to the GAL but to the VGÖ, their conservative competitor, which succeeded in reaching two percent of the votes in all constituencies. This was, however, not enough for the VGÖ to enter parliament.

* Voting turnout declined to 86.1 percent. Thus, the extraordinarily high degree of voting discipline, characteristic of Austria up to now, is also decreasing. Nevertheless, voting turnout in Austria still exceeds the international average.

The 1990 National Council Elections therefore marked another climax in eroding party ties, decreasing voting discipline, increasing potential of mobile voters, fluctuation of voters, and increasing numbers of late-deciders. The elections were characterized by issue- and personality-oriented voting. Although the changes in the Austrian party system may seem to have reached a climax, They do not, however, constitute an exception with regard to the international situation. Therefore, the Austrian party system does not represent a "special case". On the contrary: it becomes more "normal" in terms of a Western European average.

The New Formation of Government

The prolongation of the Grand Coalition was confirmed when the SPÖ and ÖVP signed the coalition agreement on 17 December 1990. In the course of the negotiations neither of the governing parties pursued any intention of presenting a large-scale and visionary program. Instead, both sides termed the revival a "coalition of common sense." During the final stage of the relatively short negotiations (two months), both coalition partners stood under time pressure: the ÖVP because more and more people within the party advised against a revival of the Grand Coalition, preferring an opposition role on the one hand or cooperation with the FPÖ on the other. The SPÖ finally came to the conclusion that—under the given circumstances—no improvement of position was possible, something that at the outset had seemed logical considering the significant surplus of seats compared with the ÖVP. Excessive claims would probably have driven the ÖVP away from the conference table. Moreover, the SPÖ had—from the point that Vranitzky became the top candidate onwards—renounced the possibility of any kind of coalition with the FPÖ under Jörg Haider's leadership, and therefore suffered from strategically rather restricted coalition possibilities (either a coalition with the ÖVP or a minority government).

In view of Austria's favorable economic situation between 1987 and 1990, the new agreement concentrated on topics different from the ones the coalition agreement of 1986 had emphasized with the slogan of "restoring Austria to economic stability." Social welfare, health, as well as science and research were—above all—issues dealt with in greater detail than the last time. Focus was also put on issues such as the reorganization of the chamber system, which had become a central topic in the election campaign, the reformation of democracy and election laws, as well as additional measures for returning state-owned enterprises to private ownership.

In public, personnel questions were much more extensively discussed than issues. The new federal government consisted of eight ministers appointed by the SPÖ which promoted the former Under-Secretary Johanna Dohnal to the post of Minister for the Coordination of Women's Affairs in the Office of the Federal Chancellor. As before, seven ministers were supplied by the ÖVP, which might be regarded a success for the party, if one takes into account its historic electoral defeat. After serious conflicts about his assignment, the former President of the Chamber of Notaries Public, Michalek, finally was appointed Minister of Justice. Before that, the former director of the Austrian Broadcasting Corporation (ORF), Oberhammer, had been designated as "independent" Minister of Justice. Obviously, this solution proved to be unacceptable for broad sections of the Austrian People's Party. These were the other personnel changes:

* The sales manager Werner Fasslabend replaced Robert Lichal as Minister of Defence. Lichal became Second President of the National Council.
* Josef Hesoun, the former chairman of the Trade Union for Construction and Woodworkers, replaced Walter Geppert as Minister for Social Affairs. His appointment caused severe criticism and was met by the opposition with a motion of no-confidence in the very first session of the National Council.
* The previous Minister for Education and the Arts, Hilde Hawlicek, was replaced by Chancellor Vranitzky's former secretary, Rudolf Scholten.
* Peter Jankowitsch was made Under-Secretary of State for internal coordination of Austria's future membership in the European Community. This way, the Social-Democratic Party of Austria tried to strengthen its position in foreign policy.
* Because the SPÖ had given in on the Oberhammer case, it was necessary for the ÖVP to find someone else for the position of Under-Secretary of State for residential building construction in the Ministry of Economics. The ÖVP had wanted their former General Secretary Helmut Kukacka to fill the post, who now was—in a final rotation of jobs—replaced by Maria Fekter, who also comes from Upper Austria.
* Another new appointment was that of the previous secretary of the Social-Democratic Party of Vienna, Peter Kostelka, as Under-Secretary of State for civil servants.
* In March 1991 another change in government took place: the Minister for Environmental Questions, Flemming, resigned because of her participation in her husband's film business, something she had not reported to the Committee for Incompatibility Questions. As a surprise for many, Ruth Feldgrill Zankel, former member of the municipal council of Graz, was appointed new Minister for Environmental Questions.
* In October 1991, Vice-Chancellor Riegler and Under-Secretary of State Stummvoll of the Austrian People's Party left the Federal Government. The position of Vice Chancellor was taken over by the Minister of Science and Research, Erhard Busek; Riegler's responsibilities as Minister of Federal Affairs were assumed by Weiss (Vorarlberg). In the government, Stummvoll was replaced by his predecessor Johannes Ditz, while he himself became general secretary of the Federal Chamber of Trade.

The Increasing Criticism of the
Austrian System of Chambers

The second important ballot of 1990 concerned the Chamber of Trade Elections on 22 and 23 April. For the first time Chamber of Trade

Elections took place in all states (except Vorarlberg) within two successive periods (1985 and 1990).

Compared to 1985, the political preconditions of the elections had changed decisively. Because of the federal coalition of SPÖ and FPÖ effective in 1985, the Austrian Business League (the ÖVP party suborganization for economic issues) was able to offer an opposition program for all those who were dissatisfied with the economic and governmental measures taken by the ruling coalition. In 1990 the Austrian People's Party itself was part of the government and therefore had to present itself as a loyal supporter of governmental economic policy. Thus, it was no longer the ÖVP that could count on protest voters. As a consequence, the Chamber of Commerce Elections of 22 and 23 April 1990 showed clear losses for the Austrian Business League (*Wirtschaftsbund* of the ÖVP) and an increase of votes for the FPÖ and party independent candidates.

In addition, the traditional Austrian system of chambers is being confronted with increasing criticism. The chambers as such are put into question; their machinery is felt to be inefficient. The ability on the part of the chambers to advance the interests of their members has been criticized, as compulsory membership has been. The Austrian Freedom Party, above all, has again and again pleaded for abolishing "compulsory membership."

The Chamber of Agriculture, because of its specific and clearly defined clientele, hardly needs to be worried about its traditional form. The Chamber of Labor, on the other hand, increasingly feels the need to legitimize its function and, above all, compulsory membership. This can primarily be attributed to scandals over the privileges of some of the leading functionaries of the Chamber of Labor. The position of the Chamber of Trade is equally critical. As a consequence of its necessary function to balance the interests of the various economic groups internally, the Chamber of Trade has frequently been unable to advocate more than the lowest common denominator. Its bureaucratic structures have often been criticized by its own members; the Chamber has been confronted with internal tensions, a loss of importance of the previously dominating ÖVP Austrian Business League and, moreover, with new, small, but mobile lobbies which in part compete with the Chamber.

Finally, the Chamber of Trade Elections of 1990 have to be analyzed in terms of the changing leadership at the top, that is to say the Austrian Business League. The president for many years, Rudolf Sallinger, was succeeded by Leopold Maderthaner, another member of the Austrian

Business League. Thus, after Anton Benya's retirement as President of the Austrian Trade Union Federation, the two most prominent figures of the Austrian system of social partnership in the last 20 years had left the political stage.

The Reform of the Austrian People's Party (ÖVP)

The Austrian People's Party reacted to its historic defeat in the National Council Elections of 7 October 1990 by to reorganize the party. Chairman Josef Riegler charged the Management Center St. Gallen (Switzerland), led by the management consultant Fredmund Malik, with the presentation of plans.

Malik is regarded as a specialist in organizational structures, but up to that point he had not had much experience with political parties. As a consequence, he mainly was working on the development of a new organizational structure for the ÖVP. The ÖVP's position regarding central issues, its profile of competence which had been lost in central political spheres, its presentation of personalities, its image in the media--all were decisive reasons for the party's election defeat on 7 October 1990. Those aspects were only integrated to a small extent in the reform which was proposed by the Swiss Management Center. Therefore, from the very beginning, Malik's team was exposed to severe criticism from within the party (and from political scientists). The corporate structure of the ÖVP, still a de facto dominating organizational aspect (Austrian League of Workers and Employees, Austrian Peasants League, Austrian Business League), is seen as a decisive obstacle to a reorientation of the Austrian People's Party in the direction of a modern party organisation able to focus on maximizing the number of votes.

The former general secretary of the Austrian People's Party, Helmut Kukacka, was replaced by the banking manager Raimund Solonar shortly after the elections. Josef Riegler himself first planned to make his position as head of the party contingent on the success of the reform work. However, on 23 May 1991—half a year after the beginning of the reform of the ÖVP—he declared he would not run again for the position of Chairman of the Austrian People's Party at the party convention on 28 June 1991. As a consequence, Raimund Solonar stated that he would resign from his post as well. Solonar had always made his own fate dependent on that of Josef Riegler; in addition, his work had mostly been judged rather negatively by the media. Thus, the result of the party convention in June was not only to be the adoption of reform measures, but also a new team at the top of the Austrian People's Party.

Thus, the race for succession to the chairmanship had started. As a surprise to many, the personnel consultant and former IBM-manager Bernhard Görg offered himself as candidate. He was officially supported by the Austrian League of Workers and Employees (ÖAAB), above all by Lichal, the Second President of the National Council, by Mock, the Minister for Foreign Affairs, by Siegfried Ludwig, the Governor of Lower Austria (representing the conservative wing of the ÖVP), and by the Young Austrian People's Party. Erhard Busek (representative of the more liberal wing of the ÖVP), who had been regarded as the logical successor of Josef Riegler, initially withdrew his candidacy after this surprising coup, and only after extensive negotiations finally declared his willingness to run for chairman after all. Thus, the party convention in June did not only become the arena for a personal competition between Busek and Görg, but also for the fundamental decision between two different recruiting models: "political newcomers" versus the traditional system of party elites.

Under the effect of the civil war in Yugoslavia, the party convention in June was reduced to a minimum. The speeches of the two candidates were delivered: Görg, on the one hand, stressed the atmosphere of reform and political renewal, while Busek, on the other hand, pointed out that "in times like this experience was essential"—especially in view of the difficult situation in Europe. Erhard Busek emerged from the subsequent vote as new chairman of the Austrian People's Party and Josef Riegler's successor. He had reached 56.4 percent of the delegates' votes.

Erhard Busek, the new chairman of the ÖVP, has been active in politics since 1964. Busek was trained as a lawyer and started his political career as secretary of the ÖVP parliamentary party group. In 1968 he changed over to the central office of the Austrian Business League, became its deputy general secretary in 1969, and was general secretary of the Austrian Business League from 1972 to 1975. At that time he was appointed general secretary of the Austrian People's Party, which he remained for one year. Between 1975 and 1978 Busek was a representative in the National Council, then member of the Vienna City Council, and in 1983 he became deputy chairman of the Austrian People's Party. From 1976 to 1989 he was Chairman of the People's Party in Vienna.

Along with Busek's appointment as Chairman of the Austrian People's Party a new team was integrated into the management of the party. The number of his deputies was reduced to two—a visible result of the party reform. The president of the Chamber of Trade of Salzburg, Helga Rabel-Stadler, and the deputy governor of Lower Austria, Erwin Pre, were appointed to these posts. In addition, the Austrian People's Party engaged two general secretaries: Ferdinand Maier, former representative in the Vienna State Diet, and Ingrid Korosec, functionary of the Lower Austrian Trade Union Association.

Haider's Fall as Governor of Carinthia

After the state elections in Carinthia on 12 March 1989, Jörg Haider was the first representative of the FPÖ in the history of the Austrian Republic to become Governor of a state (*Bundesland*). In 1991 this test case of a coalition between the FPÖ the ÖVP in Carinthia came to an end, an attempt which the FPÖ regarded as a model for the whole of Austria and as a step in the direction of a middle-class coalition on the federal level.

The reason for Haider's fall was one of his statements about the Carinthian employment policy in a debate on June 13, 1991. When, during that debate of the State Diet, Governor Haider was accused of planning actions similar to those known from the Third Reich, he countered by pointing out that "the Third Reich at least had a proper employment policy." This statement caused some sensation, not only in Austria. For instance, Haider had to justify himself for this statement before the executive committee of the Liberals' International in London. The chairman of the Liberals' International, the German Otto Graf Lambsdorff, maintained that Haider's remarks were "absolutely unacceptable and to be strongly disapproved of." Because of this statement and other positions (for instance the FPÖ policy for foreigners), some of the members of the Liberals' International intended to have the FPÖ expelled from this organization. Finally, the following compromise was agreed upon: the Austrian Freedom Party remains a member of the Liberals' International but until 1992 loses its right to vote in their committees.

The Austrian Federal Government, too, dealt with the case of Haider, and in an official declaration called upon him to resign from his position as Governor of Carinthia—something that had not happened before to a governor of a state in the Second Republic. The SPÖ Carinthia presented a motion of no-confidence against Jörg Haider and made an offer to the smallest party in the State Diet of Carinthia, the ÖVP, to elect the ÖVP chairman Christoph Zernatto without any conditions. On 21 June Jörg Haider was voted out as Governor of Carinthia by a motion of no-confidence of the SPÖ Carinthia together with the votes of the ÖVP. On 25 June Christoph Zernatto (ÖVP) was elected Governor of Carinthia with the votes of the Social-Democratic Party and the People's Party, while Jörg Haider was elected Second Deputy Governor with the votes of the Austrian Freedom Party of Carinthia. This way, Christoph Zernatto was the first ÖVP politician to become Governor of Carinthia in the Second Republic. The posts in the State Government were newly assigned.

Carinthia at the moment shows the quite unusual situation that each chairman of the three parties represented in the State Diet of Carinthia was Governor at one point within the last three years.

After having been voted out of the governor's office Jörg Haider made his political future depend on the results of the elections in Styria and Upper Austria. He aimed at doubling the election results in Styria and Upper Austria—a result that he thought good enough to retain the chairmanship of the Austrian Freedom Party. In both of these states the FPÖ started out from a proportion of votes not only doubled, but tripled in the National Council Elections of 1990. Haider reached his own aim without any difficulties notwithstanding his loss of the governorship of the Austrian Freedom Party. He finally emerged—after initial criticism, even by his own people—strengthened within his party.

State Elections 1991

In 1991, four important state elections took place, each of them confirming most impressively the increasing de-concentration of the Austrian party system. The two national coalition parties—the Social-Democratic Party of Austria and the Austrian People's Party—lost heavily, whereas the Austrian Freedom Party gained substantial votes. The latter could boast its greatest success in Vienna, where it became—as in Carinthia—the second largest party after the SPÖ and in front of the ÖVP.

The State Elections in Burgenland

The series of state elections was opened by those in Burgenland on 23 June 1991. The elections took place prematurely because the chairman of the SPÖ state party organization and Governor of Burgenland, Hans Sipötz was suspected of giving wrong evidence during the so-called "Sinowatz trial." Moreover, he was reproached (even from within the SPÖ) for having used informers when vacancies of subordinate posts had to be filled. By calling early elections, the SPÖ Burgenland intended to regain the 18 mandates (out of 36). This would have given them once more the advantage of an absolute majority in the state government. The final stage of the election campaign was affected by Haider's fall as

Governor of Carinthia. The chairman of the FPÖ Burgenland and its leading candidate, Rauter, repeatedly defended Jörg Haider's statements ("proper employment policy in the Third Reich") and therefore was severely criticized.

The state elections brought some gains for the Social-Democratic Party of Austria (48.2 percent compared to 47.3 percent before the elections) as well as for the Austrian Freedom Party. They also brought losses for the Austrian People's Party. Compared to the results of the National Council Elections, however, both the SPÖ the FPÖ lost. The SPÖ once again received seventeen of thirty-six mandates; the ÖVP lost one mandate and now holds fifteen seats, and the FPÖ as able to win one mandate and now holds four seats. The Greens did not succeed in entering the State Diet of the Burgenland, receiving no more than 3.3 percent. Thus, the state elections, moved up from fall 1992 to June 1991, hardly changed the political landscape of the Burgenland.

The question of who should be governor was again raised after the elections. Even before they had taken place, the ÖVP and the FPÖ had declared their unwillingness to re-elect Hans Sipötz because of the incidents mentioned above. Since the SPÖ was not able to appoint the governor unilaterally (because of the lack of an absolute majority) it presented a compromise by suggesting Karl Stix, a former member of the state government, as governor. Stix, a locksmith by trade, was accepted by the ÖVP and elected as the new Governor of Burgenland on 18 July 1991.

The State Elections in Styria

There were two crucial questions that marked the starting point for the elections in Styria. First of all, to which degree would the Styrian ÖVP succeed in separating itself from the general downward movement of the Austrian People's Party, and secondly, Haider attain results good enough to compensate for his defeat when he was voted out of office as Governor of Carinthia. Accordingly, both parties focused on totally different campaign strategies. While the FPÖ and its chairman Haider stressed the federal aspects of these local elections, the Styrian ÖVP tried, above all, to take advantage of Josef Krainer's image as a long-term governor of Styria. The Styrian People's Party conducted a campaign for preference votes in favor of Krainer similar to the one in favor of Vranitzky during the National Council Elections. At the same time, they avoided, if possible, any reference to the federal ÖVP organization. The Greens, represented in the Styrian State Diet since 1986, were unable to agree on a common candidate. The Social-Democratic Party of Austria tried to appear as a reformed party by downplaying their personnel scandals (above all the "Rechberger case") and presenting their new top candidate, Schachner-Blazizek.

The election day, Sunday, 22 September 1991, ended with a debacle for the Austrian People's Party in Styria. Due to losses of almost 8 percent (44.2 percent compared to 51.75 percent in 1986) it clearly lost its absolute majority in the State Diet, reaching only twenty-six of fifty-six mandates. The SPÖ lost nearly 3 percent of the votes (especially in its strongholds), reached a total of 34.9 percent lost one mandate, and now hold twenty-one seats. The Greens did not get enough votes to enter the State Diet of Styria. The big winner of the elections was the Austrian Freedom Party. It was able to more than triple its votes (from 4.6 percent in 1986 to 15.4 percent) and now holds nine seats in the State Diet. In the future, it will also appoint one member of the state government, which is based on a system of proportional representation. After thirty years of absolute majority, the Styrian People's Party is now forced to share its power. Even though the ÖVP succeeded in getting better results than in the 1990 National Council Elections, and although the FPÖ was not as successful in Styria as in the National Council Elections, the election outcome in Styria was interpreted as a further step in the decline of the Austrian People's Party on one hand and as a come-back of the FPÖ chairman Haider on the other.

The State Elections in Upper Austria

The starting point in Upper Austria was very similar to the one in Styria. Here, too, it was to be seen in how far the political changes in Austria since the last state elections in 1985 would manifest themselves. Similar to Styria, the Austrian People's Party had to defend its absolute majority of 52.1 percent; here as well, the Austrian Freedom Party tried to stress aspects of federal policy in an election campaign cut out for its Chairman Haider; in Upper Austria, too, the SPÖ fought against struc- tural changes in its strongholds and against signs of inefficiency regard- ing its functionaries, and here, too, the Greens were not able to agree on a common candidate. Another parallel to the situation in Styria was the ÖVP campaign, designed especially for the long-term Governor Josef Ratzenböck.

Just as in Styria, the election day, Sunday 6 October 1991, in Upper Austria ended with defeats of both of the big parties and another spectacular success for the FPÖ. Once again, the Greens failed to enter the State Diet. While the ÖVP lost somewhat less than in Styria, namely 6.9 percent (45.2 percent compared to 52.1 percent in 1985), the losses of the SPÖ were more evident, namely 6.6 percent (31.4 percent compared to 38 percent). The Austrian Freedom Party increased their votes from 5.0 percent to 17.7 percent and reached eleven instead of three seats six years ago. The two big parties lost four mandates each and now hold twenty-six (ÖVP) and nineteen (SPÖ) seats in the Upper Austrian State Diet. In contrast to the Governor of Styria, Krainer—who had offered his resignation (which had not been accepted by his party)—the Governor of Upper Austria, Ratzenböck, insisted on keeping his position and tried to restrain FPÖ claims (for a second member in the government) in the course of the government formation.

As a consequence of the electoral defeat of the two coalition parties in Styria and Upper Austria and the tremendous success of Haider's FPÖ, the climate in the Federal Government seemed to be burdened. Confusion had come up within the FPÖ regarding Haider's course after his defeat as Governor of Carinthia—this was no longer a question. The Greens realized the necessity to change the style of their election campaign, at least with regard to the municipal elections in Vienna, if they wanted to win again.

The Municipal Elections in Vienna

The municipal elections in Vienna on 10 November formed the climax of the series of state elections in 1991. The elections were held several months early and were preceded by the big event that had become before the elections in the Austrian capital, Vienna's refusal (by referendum) to organize a World Exposition together with Budapest. The political and strategic starting position of the parties was characterized by the following situation: the SPÖ was able to present Mayor Helmut Zilk, its very popular top candidate, a politician well known all over Austria. In contrast, the ÖVP Vienna, weakened by years of intraparty struggle, nominated Dr. Heinrich Wille, a lawyer, only recently appointed Chairman of the ÖVP Vienna and lacking political experience. In Styria and Upper Austria comparative data regarding the state elections stemmed from the pre-Haider era of the FPÖ. In Vienna, on the other hand, the last municipal elections had taken place in 1987, after Haider's appointment as Chairman of the FPÖ. At that point the Freedom Party had already reached the best results since 1949 (9.7 percent), mainly at the cost of the ÖVP.

After Haider's personal success in Styria and Upper Austria it was clear that the election campaign in the capital, too, would count on Jörg Haider's strong support, in spite of the local character of the elections. After the bad results in the National Council Elections and the preceding state elections the Greens totally changed their personnel strategy and clearly presented one of their most popular politicians, Peter Pilz, as top candidate.

The election campaign in Vienna became increasingly dominated by an issue brought forward by the FPÖ: the so-called "problem with foreigners." The position of the FPÖ presented in strong terms by its chairman Haider, consisted—in the final analysis—in nothing but the simplistic formula "stop foreigners." The housing problems of the Viennese population as well as the high proportion of foreign children in Viennese schools were pointed out vividly to fuel this demand. Issues touched upon by the other parties, such as environmental and traffic problems, more and more faded away in the course of the election campaign. Indeed the ÖVP and SPÖ tried to jump on the bandwagon of issues steered by the FPÖ and by doing so violated basic principles of modern election campaigning. Equally problematic was the way the top candidates treated each other during a television debate. Their behavior violated principles of modern election campaigning and painted a negative image of the leading Viennese politicians.

The election in Vienna resulted in heavy losses, not only of the ÖVP—as predicted by many—but also of the SPÖ. The municipal elections (state elections) in Vienna on 10 November 1991 brought the worst results for the two coalition parties since 1945. This ballot was a special disaster for the ÖVP in Vienna. Votes for this party came only from an extremely reduced number of traditional ÖVP voters. The ÖVP was clearly left behind by the FPÖ which—just as in Carinthia—replaced the ÖVP as the second strongest political force in Vienna. The SPÖ achieved 47.7 percent (minus 7.2 percent) the ÖVP reached a mere 18.1 percent (minus 10.3 percent), the FPÖ 22.6 percent (plus 12.9 percent), and the Greens received 9.1 percent (plus 4.7 percent) of all votes.

Since in Vienna the method of calculating the allocation of seats favors the party with the largest number of votes, the SPÖ was, however, able to achieve its predominant election objective, namely to reach the absolute majority of seats and thus be able independently to form the government: the SPÖ received fifty-two, the FPÖ 23, the ÖVP eighteen and the Greens seven seats. More detailed analyses have shown that the FPÖ was not only able to draw votes from the ÖVP supporters, but that they were also able to profit heavily from votes from traditionally social-democratic voters, the workers that is to say. In addition, the election results in Vienna (just as in Styria and Upper Austria before) have confirmed the obvious success of the neo-populist line of Jörg Haider, the chairman of the FPÖ The extremely favorable results achieved in Vienna by the Greens and their chairman Peter Pilz might lead to a strategic turn within the Green movement. The first election success after several years of moderate performance can be attributed to an electoral campaign conducted in a professional manner and to signals of an opening in terms of personnel and issues directed at ecologically interested, yet less fundamentally inclined citizens.

Waldheim's Renunciation of His Candidacy and the Candidates for the 1992 Presidential Elections

The debate about the 1992 presidential elections started in 1990 and led Kurt Waldheim, the Federal President, to declare that in the summer of 1991 he would announce his decision about a possible renewed candidacy for the presidential office. Already at the preliminary stage of decision-making even leading personalities in the Austrian People's Party, who had supported Waldheim's candidacy in 1986, indicated that they would not be happy if Waldheim entered the presidential race once more. As consequence, on 21 June 1991, Kurt Waldheim announced that he would not seek re-election, because he "wanted to spare Austria further polarization." Most commentators saw Waldheim's renunciation as a responsible decision in the interest of Austria. Thus, Kurt Waldheim became the first Federal President in office who did not try to run for president a second time.

As soon as Waldheim had renounced his candidacy, an increasing number of people began to question whether both governmental parties could nominate a common candidate, one not committed by party politics. The wish to stabilize the political climate after the Waldheim affair (in 1986) and to avoid the drain on party funds, numerous candidates would cause arguments in favor of a common candidate. The search for a candidate for the presidential office, constantly commented on by the media, became increasingly grotesque. As a consequence a debate about the office of the Federal President started, re-examining the direct election of the Austrian Federal President, his constitutional position, and the fact that his importance (underlined by his direct election by the people) does not correspond with the real political significance of the Federal President of Austria. Finally, the parties announced that they would present a decision about the number of candidates for the office of the Federal President of Austria after the municipal elections in Vienna. Since the two governmental parties were not able to agree on a common candidate, in mid-November of 1991 the SPÖ, ÖVP and FPÖ presented their own candidates: Rudolf Streicher, the Minister for Traffic, (next to Chancellor Vranitzky the second most popular SPÖ politician), Thomas Klestil, the Secretary-General in the Foreign Ministry and former ambassador to the United States as candidate of the ÖVP and Heide Schmidt, the Third President of the National Council, for the FPÖ. Initially the Greens did not seem to nominate their own candidate but then they presented the seventy-eight-year-old writer Robert Jungk as a surprise candidate without any real chances of success. It was remarkable that right after the nomination all candidates clearly expressed their appreciation of their opponents.

Austria and Europe

The question of Austria's role in a future Europe is increasingly assuming central significance. The creation of a European-wide domestic market by the EC in 1993 and the new political structures in Central and Eastern Europe form the framework within which Austria has to position itself. With regard to this question, the Federal Government as well as an overwhelming majority of the National Council—the official political forces in Austria, that is to say—have been aiming at full membership for Austria in the European Community. This is clearly documented by Austria's official application for membership. Other smaller and neutral nations (especially Sweden but also Switzerland) also seem to define this strategy as the only feasible alternative.

The so-called "EC-notification" ("Avis") thus far the most important reaction to Austria's application for membership in the EC, was made public on 1 August 1991. For the most part, this extensive test report by the EC commission paints an excellent picture of Austria. It praises social and economic stability as well as the dynamics of economic development. It comments positively on Austria's hard currency policy—for a long time linked to the Deutsche Mark—as well as the legal system, which conforms to European standards. Overall the "EC-notification" affirms that Austria shows an extremely high degree of economic integration in and interdependence with the EC, one that is hardly reached by comparable countries. The report also mentions, however, the core problems connected with Austria's integration into the EC: the question of political neutrality, which could be an obstacle to Europe's further political integration, the method of subsidizing the structurally weak Austrian agriculture, and the traffic problems connected with the transit traffic through the Alps.

In addition to the positive "EC-notification" there are numerous other positive signals coming from the European Community regarding Austria's entry into the EC. As a consequence, *Austria will rather have to overcome internal than external obstacles* to its entry into the EC. Numerous opinion polls indicate that it is not at all certain that a majority of all Austrians will vote for an EC-membership in the course of the necessary forthcoming plebiscite.

SELECT BIBLIOGRAPHY

Andreas Khol, Kurt Ofner, and Alfred Stirneman, eds., *Österreichisches Jahrbuch für Politik 1990* (Vienna: Verlag für Geschichte und Politik, 1991).

Andreas Khol, Kurt Ofner, and Alfred Stirneman, eds., *Österreichischer Jahrbuch für Politik 1989* (Vienna, Verlag für Geschichte und Politik, 1990).

Rainer Nick and Anton Pelinka, *Politische Landeskunde der Republik Österreich* (Berlin: Colloquium Verlag, 1989).

Der Standard

Die Presse

Profil

Österreich Bericht

List of Authors

Thomas Albrich is an assistant professor of history in the Institute of Contemporary History at the University of Innsbruck.

Felix Butschek is the Deputy Chairman of the Austrian Institute of Economic Research and lectures at the Economics University, Vienna.

Wolfgang Danspeckgruber, a native of Austria, is a lecturer at the Department of Politics at Princeton University; he also directs the Liechtenstein Colloqium on European and International Affairs.

Sieglinde Gstöhl, a native of Liechtenstein, is a PhD student at the Graduate Institute of International Studies in Geneva, Switzerland and a fellow at the Center for International Affairs, Harvard University.

Paul Luif is a research fellow at the Austrian Institute for International Affairs in Laxenburg (Lower Austria) and lectures at the University of Vienna.

Charles S. Maier is the Krupp Foundation Professor of European Studies at Harvard University, and Senior Fellow at Harvard's Center for European Studies.

Rainer Nick is an assistant professor of Political Science at the University of Innsbruck.

Manfred Prisching is an associate professor of Sociology at the University of Graz.

Oliver Rathkolb is a research fellow in the Ludwig Boltzmann Institute for History and Science at the Institute of Contemporary History at the University of Vienna and the scientific director of the Bruno Kreisky Archives in Vienna.

Sieghard Viertler is a political consultant in Innsbruck.